UNOFFICIAL DIPLOMATS

Prepared and Published with the Support of the
Academy for Educational Development and
the Charles F. Kettering Foundation

UNOFFICIAL DIPLOMATS

MAUREEN R. BERMAN
AND
JOSEPH E. JOHNSON

EDITORS

New York   Columbia University Press   1977

Library of Congress Cataloging in Publication Data
Main entry under title:
Unofficial diplomats.
Includes bibliographical references and index.
1. Diplomats.   2. International relations.
3. World politics—1945—   I. Berman, Maureen R.,
1948—   II. Johnson, Joseph Esrey, 1906—
JX1699.U56   327   77-9376
ISBN 0-231-04396-1
ISBN 0-231-04397-X pbk.

Columbia University Press
New York and Guildford, Surrey

Printed in the United States of America

289235

FOREWORD

DISTINCTLY UNOFFICIAL EXPLORATIONS have often had an effect on the course of international negotiations. Sometimes they have paved the way; sometimes they have smoothed out a sticky point. On occasion, they may have complicated matters. Yet they have been inadequately studied and reported.

All of this became highly evident in the course of the Communications Institute's continuing studies of the arts and skills of official negotiating. There was no significant book available on the field of unofficial diplomacy. There was no broad report on the work done at the Pugwash or Dartmouth Conferences, on the efforts of the Quakers or International Committee of the Red Cross, on the demi-diplomacy of many individuals, and on various related activities.

At a conference organized by the Institute at Bellagio, Italy, in 1973, there developed a consensus that the role of non-officials in international peacemaking had been far too neglected, and that a major book on the subject should be developed. This volume is the result.

The editors and the Institute staff decided that the major part of the book should be prepared by those individuals most familiar with the various unofficial undertakings—so long as they responded adequately to difficult questions put to them by the editors. It was felt that this would yield a more authoritative, useful volume than would any presentation filtered through the mind—and prejudices—of a single author. Essential coherence could be achieved through directions given to the writers and through extensive introductory and concluding chapters, written by the editors themselves. I believe this has been achieved.

Some call the practitioners in this field unofficial go-betweens; some call them diplomats without portfolio; a few have simply called them meddlers. We have chosen the term unofficial diplomats. The editors are the first to acknowledge that they could not dream of covering all such unofficial approaches. However, they have winnowed out a representative selection that they believe provides an overview of how private individuals have contributed, or tried to contribute, to the resolution of specific conflicts and to the general improvement of the ways nations conduct their business.

Acknowledgments

We gratefully acknowledge the assistance of a number of individuals who made important contributions to this project. We thank first the authors who contributed to this volume, most of whom took time out from very busy schedules to do so. Participants in the Bellagio meeting (and at an earlier conference organized by the Academy in Greenwich, Connecticut) helped to define the void this volume would fill. Support for the project came from the Charles F. Kettering Foundation and the Rockefeller Foundation. Phillips Ruopp of the Kettering Foundation was particularly helpful in defining the task. Mrs. O. Frederick Nolde, Mrs. Leo Szilard, Professor Roger Fisher of Harvard University, and Professor Chadwick Alger of the Ohio State University provided helpful background material. Robert Barnett of the Asia Society and Professor Bernard Feld of M.I.T. read parts of the manuscript. Barbara Rotenberg, a graduate student at Columbia University, served ably as research assistant. The Oral History Project of Columbia University, and particularly the director, Professor Louis Starr, and the associate director, Mrs. Elizabeth Mason, have given invaluable assistance in transcribing and then storing the proceedings of Bellagio and many other projects. Finally, special gratitude is owed to the Schweppe Research and Education Fund for its continued support which has made publication of this volume possible.

Edward W. Barrett

Communications Institute
Academy for Educational Development
New York, N.Y.
February 1977

CONTENTS

UNOFFICIAL DIPLOMATS

ONE

THE GROWING ROLE
OF UNOFFICIAL DIPLOMACY

MAUREEN R. BERMAN and JOSEPH E. JOHNSON

I N A SIGNED ARTICLE that appeared on the front page of the *New York Times* of January 19, 1959, former President Harry S. Truman strongly denounced the recent crop of what he labeled "diplomatic tourists"—those individuals who had traveled to Moscow and those who had entertained visiting Soviet Deputy Premier Anastas I. Mikoyan "with solicitous attention and social glamour resulting in pressure on the White House."

To Truman it was clear that at a time when the West was trying to find out how to deal with the East, "diplomacy by press interview, special audiences or fishing expeditions could only compound an already complicated situation." Noting the considerable difference between negotiations by governments and probing by private individuals for some kind of deal, Truman cautioned that citizens with no official responsibilities who engage in diplomatic activities should first understand that only the President makes foreign policy; he cannot delegate or share this responsibility, nor can others assume it. Moreover,

> . . . until the President of the United States decides what our foreign policy is and says what it is and stays with it, any statements or declarations made by diplomatic tourists serve no useful purpose in our relations with the Communist world. . . .
>
> I would caution some of our well-meaning, self-appointed, self-assumed peace-makers to be careful lest they forget, in their ardor, that the President makes foreign policy, and they may inadvertently lend themselves to the propaganda purposes of our adversaries. . . .

While critical of diplomatic activities of private citizens, Truman had high praise for the expanding network of exchanges of various groups between the two countries and also expressed pleasure that top Soviet officials had accorded interviews to so many U.S. businessmen, writers, journalists, and political leaders visiting the Soviet Union. "Any new information that came out of those interviews was certainly a net gain," Truman wrote, but he added the following cautionary words: "I do feel that in some interviews those who are not journalists have lent themselves unwittingly to maneuvers of the Kremlin to appeal to our people over the heads of government."

Although the political climate has greatly changed since the cold war years in which Truman wrote, we have quoted extensively from his article because many of the arguments advanced by professional diplomats—and highly placed responsible statesmen like himself—in opposition to the "meddling" of outsiders in what they consider government business remain in use today.

At best, Truman felt, the intervention by nonprofessionals might complicate a difficult situation; at worst, amateur excursions into diplomacy would benefit our adversaries. To the office of the Presidency falls the responsibility for the conduct of foreign policy, and statements by "diplomatic tourists" not only serve no useful purpose; they might, in Truman's opinion, play into the hands of other governments.

Truman's self-protective argument against the intervention of individuals holding no governmental responsibility in foreign affairs was nothing new. Governments, including that of the United States, dislike meddling; as early as 1799, in fact, Congress, at President John Adams' behest, passed a law that made it illegal for any United States citizen without authorization to "directly or indirectly commence or carry on any correspondence or intercourse with any foreign government or any officer or agent thereof, with intent to influence the measures or conduct of any foreign government or of any officer or agent thereof, in relation to any disputes or controversies with the United States. . . ." [1]

[1] U.S. Code, Title 18, Ch. 45, sec. 953, known as the Logan Act. For more on the Logan Act, see pages 31–33.

In 1798, the year before the law was enacted and after diplomatic relations with France had been severed by the United States, Dr. George Logan, a Philadelphia Quaker and eminent Jeffersonian, traveled to France on a mission of peace carrying a letter of introduction from Jefferson. Logan had interviews with Talleyrand and members of the Directory (who had refused to receive the members of President Adams' official mission) and returned to the United States with word of the French desire to renew relations. The Federalists were infuriated with the good doctor, and they passed the law that has taken Logan's name.

Professional resistance to the meddling of outsiders, although not initiated by President Truman, was given an air of urgency by him. What emerges clearly from Truman's article, although it is unexpressed, is his awareness that by the second half of the twentieth century the circumstances in which international diplomacy is carried on have considerably changed. Advances in communication and transportation have made it easier for private citizens acting alone or attached to nongovernmental organizations to become involved in the conduct of interstate relations. Although throughout history private individuals like Dr. Logan have made uninvited—or sometimes invited—excursions into diplomacy, private citizens can now to a degree never before true inform themselves on the foreign policies of their own and other governments, visit and entertain the leaders of foreign governments, suggest new policy positions or probe for changes in policy during those meetings, bring back feelers for policy changes, and then publicize the results of those meetings to large numbers of people through the news media.

Also altering the conduct of international diplomacy is the increased capacity of governments to inform not only their own population but citizens of other countries on foreign and domestic policies. At the same time government foreign policy and actions in many countries are more accessible to public scrutiny and criticism.

Another change is that it is perhaps less true than ever before that politics stops at water's edge. Once a line separating national and international systems was widely accepted, but in the 1970s recognition has grown that the imaginary boundary is becoming increasingly fuzzy. Now it is quite clear that there is an interrelationship between domestic political processes and what goes on abroad, and indeed it is often impossible to separate what goes on at home from what goes on abroad.

One other change is that increasingly private citizens attempt to influence not only their own government's policies, but also those of foreign governments.[2]

Recognizing that these developments were bound to affect the centuries-old practice of having relations carried on only by designated envoys of governments, Truman thought it important to warn of the dangers inherent in the conduct of interstate relations by other than accredited diplomats through other than official diplomatic channels. This is not to say that professional diplomats no longer are responsible for the conduct of most interstate relations; they are. Nor is this meant to imply that the majority of interstate business is no longer conducted through normal diplomatic channels; it is. Yet beginning after World War II and burgeoning in the international system of the 1970s, an increasing proportion of internation interactions bypasses, complements, or supplements traditional bilateral procedures.

Nations may communicate or try to begin to communicate on many different fronts. These efforts—some official, some private—may overlap and reinforce one another. In other instances they may be contradictory. Part of the action is now carried on through new multilateral arrangements: the United Nations and its worldwide system of specialized agencies and programs, regional groupings, and various international organizations. Governments may also communicate through private individuals, or their representatives may meet in unofficial gatherings sponsored by nongovernmental groups.

Despite Truman's wariness of diplomatic amateurs, a number of private efforts, particularly those beginning in the late 1950s and

---

[2] For an extensive analysis of the confluence of national and international factors as they affect the external behavior of nations, see James N. Rosenau, "Pre-Theories and Theories of Foreign Policy," in *The Scientific Study of Foreign Policy* (New York: Free Press, 1971), pp. 95–149.

early 1960s in the area of arms control, contributed to the improved climate of relations between the Soviet Union and the United States. In many of these efforts there was close cooperation between officials and those acting unofficially. Individuals were used to carry messages between the two governments, and in unofficial meetings Soviet and American policy-makers, or persons close to them, could probe for possible new positions or send out feelers about changes that might be possible.

The intent of some of the individuals who initiate private efforts is to prepare the way for intergovernmental action, and often they act with the blessing or at least the knowledge of officials of governments or international organizations. When it suits their purposes governments may support and use private channels. Sometimes nongovernmental actions that are privately initiated and sustained may be viewed with suspicion and regarded by officials, as they were by Truman, as the work of unwelcome meddlers. Private citizens may try to modify or even reverse the official policy lines of their own or foreign governments. Whether they are blessed or unsanctified, supportive of or contradictory to government policies, will in large measure determine how officials respond to private efforts.

We refer to the range of private international relations as "unofficial diplomacy." Within this category fall many different kinds of participants, as well as a variety of channels and approaches. It should be made clear that our concern is not with domestic groups that work to influence only their own government, but with individuals and groups who have contact with private citizens or government officials from other countries as well as with their own government. Furthermore, no effort is made in this volume to deal with cases involving multinational corporations or other commercial ventures.

Unofficial diplomacy does not supplant official diplomacy, either bilateral or multilateral. Although new entities have multiplied on the international scene in recent years, states remain the most important actors in international politics—by their decisions policies are maintained and changed. Many international organizations and some nongovernmental entities, however, influence the policies of governments, and they are becoming an ever more important factor in international politics.

Each chapter in this volume describes a linkage between governmental and nongovernmental elements: governments interact through private citizens or by having their representatives communicate through channels arranged by nongovernmental personnel; a number of these channels are examined in Part One. The supplemental functions that unofficial diplomats perform are aimed at preparing the way for or facilitating the conduct of interstate relations. Unofficial diplomacy may set the stage for official actions and contribute to the possibilities of success once matters are taken up in normal diplomatic channels. In Part Two the special role played by private efforts in time of international conflict is detailed, while Part Three considers some special approaches to particular international problems. Usually these enterprises serve more than one function.

When official channels are blocked or inflexible, governments may move to alternate channels or seek alternate messengers. If the opportunities for quiet communication through formal channels are limited, and governments want to try out new positions without risking commitment or arousing public sentiment, then they may find it necessary to move to private channels. Governments may use private persons to explore new positions. They risk little for these individuals may be disavowed at any time.

The kinds of private efforts detailed in the cases in this volume are not those intended to influence government policy-makers at home and abroad by capturing newspaper headlines, but those aimed at reaching key decision-makers. To overcome the natural distrust of officials, private individuals must demonstrate compelling reasons why governments should "use" them or work with them. Factors determining their saliency might be: a recognized competence in an area of specialization, the prominence of the individual involved, or the prestige of a nongovernmental group that has established an authoritative basis for its work. In some instances, unofficial diplomats may be well-connected because of previous service in government positions, or else may know personally key decision-makers. If government policy-makers seek out specific individuals or private channels, which they sometimes do, it is a pretty good indication that the unofficial diplomats have already established salience as deserving the trust and confidence of decision-makers. The creation of contacts, salience, and trust are the first requirements for successful private efforts.

It is clear that what private individuals or organizations can accomplish is different from what the representatives of governments or international organizations can do—the former can neither make threats nor offer promises. In terms of the resources that government officials control—money, armies, economies—they are feeble. Nevertheless, sometimes alone, other times in concert with official efforts, private initiatives may contribute to the alleviation of problems in communication that may result whenever different nations speak or conduct their relations. By providing auxiliary channels of communication, by serving as intermediaries between governments, by performing various third-party functions, including negotiating and mediating in conflict situations, and by contributing to a climate in which policy-makers can usefully work, private citizens may augment and facilitate official diplomacy.

Adam Curle, writing of the work of the private diplomat, whom he defines as someone who engages in mediation or conciliation of conflict under personal or unofficial auspices, makes it clear he is not describing bumbling amateurs impelled by purely good intentions, but individuals who are as "subtle and experienced as the average public diplomat, although not necessarily in quite the same way, and as well informed, not in the sense of having access to intelligence reports, but in the sense of knowing the people or comparable situations elsewhere, and perhaps in addition, having a high degree of academic competence. . . ."[3] Acting privately the unofficial diplomat has no official base to give weight to his words and he must cultivate in government officials an acceptance of the legitimacy of his actions. It takes special skills and credibility to be effective under these circumstances.

It will soon be readily apparent that privacy and confidentiality

[3] Adam Curle, *Making Peace* (London: Tavistock Publications, 1971), p. 231.

are elements essential to the success of many of these efforts. It is in the nature of probes that in order to be effective they often need to be carried on without fanfare, for publicity can jeopardize the entire operation. The authors in this volume have been able to "go public" because they do not compromise ongoing efforts. Some of the approaches—or those similar to them—have been used in other situations, and others are in the planning stages. Still others we may never know about given the necessity of secrecy if private channels are to be effective and, perhaps more important, used again.

The cases that are presented in this volume are only a sample of the wide variety of approaches that have been developed and used in a number of international situations by individuals from the United States and other countries. In no way are they meant to represent a complete catalogue of such activities.

Moreover, most of the cases deal with security issues of peace and war, although it should be noted that the role of nongovernmental groups in economic and social affairs as described in the section to follow is growing in extent and significance; since World War II this role has become to a great degree institutionalized and in many ways is linked to changes in the international system in the past twenty years.

The Conduct of Diplomacy in the 1970s

Diplomacy has been viewed by students and practitioners as the oldest method states have employed for conducting their relations peacefully with other states. Ideas rather than blows are exchanged, policies are explained, and differences of opinion are accommodated rather than fought over. Through the years, the forms and methods of diplomacy had become remarkably similar around the globe. For the better part of four centuries, the professionals who conducted diplomacy were, in Kenneth Thompson's words, "a small group of leaders who spoke the same language, catered as often to one another as to their own people, and played to one another's strengths and weaknesses."[4] This brand of diplomacy evolved in a Western world made up of sparsely populated, separated states whose governments spoke on behalf of the state—the people scarcely counted before 1789—and who held a near monopoly on information and communication with other governments. Due to an enormous increase in the number of actors, both national and non-national (and in the number of cultures they represent), and to a complicated array of international issues, the international system of the 1970s—and the practice of international diplomacy—have grown increasingly complex.

The Actors

In traditional representations of the international system, which customarily portray interstate relations as the only significant ones, only slight attention is paid to nongovernmental activity. In this widely accepted image of the international system, which Arnold Wolfers called the "billiard-ball" model, the international community is composed only of states, each of which "represents a closed, impermeable and sovereign unit, completely separated from all other states."[5]

The political reality today, however, is that the interactions of governments are only one level of international relations.[6] One student who stresses that fact is John Burton, whose conception of world society—he shies away from use of the term international relations because in his view it represents a system made up of

---

[4] Kenneth W. Thompson, *Christian Ethics and the Dilemmas of Foreign Policy* (Durham, N.C., Duke University Press, 1959), pp. 81–82.

[5] Arnold Wolfers, *Discord and Collaboration* (Baltimore, Md.: Johns Hopkins University Press, 1962), pp. 3–24.

[6] For a detailed discussion of the multiple levels of interaction in the international system of the 1970s, see Donald J. Puchala and Stuart I. Fagan, "International Politics in the 1970s: The Search for Perspective," *International Organization* (Spring 1974), 28:247–66. See also J. David Singer, "The Level-of-Analysis Problem in International Relations," in Klaus Knorr and Sidney Verba, eds., *The International System: Theoretical Essays* (Princeton, N.J.: Princeton University Press, 1961), pp. 77–92.

The senior editor of this volume once proposed in the early 1950s only half-facetiously that a prize be offered for the invention of a word that would describe the present world system as accurately as Bentham's invention of "international" described the system of his day.

states alone—is one composed of many systems of interactions, not just those among states. Among others are communication, tourism, trade, and science. Taken together and superimposed one on the other, the various systems form a cobweb image. World society is a series of overlapping systems and transactions on many levels—domestic and international, governmental and nongovernmental.[7] These levels are not always distinct and indeed may be confused. If we were to posit an official/unofficial continuum, on one end would be traditional bilateral relations and intergovernmental organizations, while on the other side would be nongovernmental organizations composed of private citizens. In between there are institutions that are partly governmental and nongovernmental, and others that are nongovernmental in membership but working very closely with governments.

Complicating the picture of the international system of the 1970s is the great increase in the number—and even in the kinds—of units or actors that initiate actions affecting the international system. Not only has the number of sovereign states skyrocketed—by 1975 the total had reached 150—but there are also nonstate international entities whose activities sustain the international system.

International Organizations

Part of the complexity of official international relations results from the impressive growth in numbers and importance of international intergovernmental organizations. The ranks of these organizations have increased at the rate of several dozen per year,[8] and perhaps of greater significance is the fact that their position has been enhanced, both as vehicles through which much interstate business is conducted and as semi-independent actors. The quantitative evidence now available suggests, moreover, that an increasing volume of diplomatic transactions is conducted through such organizations.[9]

[7] John Burton et al, *The Study of World Society: A London Perspective* (Pittsburgh, International Studies Association Occasional Paper # 1, 1973).

[8] Puchala and Fagan, "International Politics in the 1970s," p. 252.

[9] Donald J. Puchala, "International Transactions and Regional Integration," *International Organization* (Autumn 1970), 24:759–62.

One factor contributing to the growth of international organizations in the 1970s—and to the significant complications in the conduct of interstate business—is the emergence of issues that transcend frontiers of national interest and action. While in the past most matters were handled entirely through bilateral channels, today there are numerous crucial issues that require the action and consent of many nations to effect solutions.

It is true that nations have always been to some degree interdependent by virtue of occupying the same planet, yet issues have emerged in the past ten years that to varying extents affect all nations, and whose solutions are beyond the reach of unilateral or even bilateral action. They have not replaced the issues of 1945 but are added to them. Security, nuclear proliferation, trade, territorial issues, and old problems of war and peace remain important today, yet linked to them in complicated arrays are issues of economic interdependence, resource shortages, and environmental control.

The clear distinctions that used to be drawn between the "high politics" of security and war and the "low politics" of economic and other nonsecurity issues appear of limited value in understanding what goes on in world politics today.[10] Since 1973 key economic issues have been high-priority agenda items in UN General Assemblies once focused primarily on issues of security and war. Moreover, in crises such as that created by the 1973 OPEC oil embargo, economic and political issues are closely related.

The oil embargo of October 1973 brought to a head the question of the relationship between the developed and developing worlds. The General Assembly scheduled the Seventh Special Session on Development and International Cooperation for Sep-

[10] See on this point, Robert O. Keohane and Joseph S. Nye, Jr., eds., *Transnational Relations and World Politics* (Cambridge, Mass.: Harvard University Press, 1972), pp. 378–79; and Stanley Hoffman, "International Organization and the International System," *International Organization* (Summer 1970), 24:401.

Richard Barnet observes that in the nuclear age, since territorial expansion has declined as a means to promote national security, distinctions between economic and non-economic reasons to go to war have blurred: "The increasing economic interdependence of the globe and the increasing dependence of military machines on high technology and scarce mineral resources mean that national security is more than ever dependent upon the state of the economy." See *Roots of War* (Baltimore, Md.: Penguin Books, 1973), p. 160.

tember 1975 and gave it a mandate to consider "new concepts and options [for] the solution of world economic problems, in particular those of developing countries." The continuing "North/South" dialogue between rich and poor countries has been carried on in a number of international frameworks including the United Nations and its agencies and at the Paris-based Conference on International Economic Cooperation composed of eight industrial and nineteen developing countries. The Seventh Special Session opened the way for the Paris talks set up outside the UN system and where negotiations may go on for years to come on issues of energy and development.[11]

Economic and social issues have given rise to other new international organizations and frameworks in the 1970s. Special conferences on a range of issues in which all nations are involved have been organized in the UN system, among them the 1972 Stockholm Conference on the Human Environment, the Conference on Population in Bucharest in 1974, the World Food Conference in Rome in 1974, the 1975 conference held in Mexico City in connection with International Women's Year, and the Conference on Human Settlements (Habitat) held in Canada in 1976, as well as more specialized meetings such as those on the Law of the Sea and the Conference on Crime. New international mechanisms to deal with a number of the major economic and social issues confronting the world grew out of these meetings.

The United Nations and other multilateral arrangements may provide the setting for discreet, exploratory talks, as well as the more formal public dealings. In the corridors, in the dining rooms, and in the lounges of the United Nations, quiet diplomacy goes on. One delegate remarked that, "There is nothing like an unobtrusive face-to-face talk to get diplomatic business done. There is no other place in the world that offers so many opportunities for

[11] For a comprehensive review of the evolving "North/South" dialogue, see Branislav Gosovic and John G. Ruggie, "On the Creation of a New International Economic Order: Issue Linkage and the Seventh Special Session of the UN General Assembly," *International Organization* (Spring 1976), 30:309–46. Experts from a number of developing countries express their views in *Beyond Dependency* (Washington, D.C.: Overseas Development Council, 1975).

this kind of work as New York in the fall."[12] When they are speaking for-the-record in open meetings, delegates have to be very careful. In more relaxed official settings, they may have more freedom to speak and to shade meanings, yet they are still representatives and accountable for what they say. In unofficial gatherings they may feel freer yet to speak frankly of problems at home and of other difficulties.

Nongovernmental International Actors

Also complicating the international picture are the nongovernmental entities that have since 1945 experienced phenomenal growth in number and range. The word "transnational" has been widely adopted to deal with the great variety of nongovernmental international interactions.[13] Transnational actors are as diverse as the Ford and Rockefeller Foundations, multinational businesses, and international professional associations. Some of these, like the foundations, have headquarters in one nation and operations in many countries. Others, like international professional associations, are truly international institutions with citizens of more than one country gathering for annual, biennial, or triennial congresses to discuss the state of their professions or their particular interests. International professional associations include the International Congress of Scientific Unions, the International Political Science Association, the International Association of Universities, the International Chess Federation, to name but a few. These transnational actors all have official contacts—some with international governmental organizations through their affiliation with UNESCO, and others with states—in the sense that all, or at least most of them, make proposals for national legislation to promote an interest or interests of the profession or even for international multilateral action. Although these transnational associations work through of-

---

[12] Paul Hofmann, "In the UN Lounges, Urgent Diplomacy is Conducted," *New York Times*, October 13, 1975.
[13] For a detailed examination of transnational phenomena, see Keohane and Nye, eds., *Transnational Relations and World Politics*.

ficial channels to achieve their objectives, to a certain extent their operations elude governmental control.[14]

Although nongovernmental groups have always been active in international affairs, it is not an exaggeration to say that prior to the end of the second world war, only a limited number of individuals outside the realm of government had contact with individuals, let alone officials of other nations.[15] International bankers and businessmen, a few manufacturing and mining company executives who sought raw materials or markets in foreign countries, missionaries, members of international sports federations, some labor leaders, members of international political and religious movements, and the Roman Catholic Church about exhaust the list of those who engaged in any considerable degree in international activities. A small number of these were influential in world politics in the nineteenth and early twentieth centuries. Transnational political movements—anarchism, socialism, and Zionism—the international labor movement, and peace and humanitarian groups were having an impact on government policies in a number of states. Transnational organizations, such as the International Peace and Arbitration Association located in London and the Interparliamentary Union formed in Berlin in 1888, labored to influence governments to settle disputes peacefully and to abolish war.[16]

Government and private business enterprises began to collaborate closely on economic policy in this period as well. As a result of

[14] For an analysis of the impact and growth of international professional associations, see William M. Evan, "MNCs and IPAs: An International Organization Research Frontier," *International Associations* (Union of International Associations, Brussels) (February 1972), 24:90–101.

[15] James A. Field, Jr. examines the scope of transnational activities in the nineteenth and early twentieth centuries in "Transnationalism and the New Tribe," in Keohane and Nye, *Transnational Relations and World Politics*, pp. 3–23.

[16] Just at the turn of the century, in the summer of 1898, Czar Nicholas II of Russia issued a call to the nations of the world to join in a conference for the limitation of armaments. As the capital of a neutral country, The Hague was selected as the site for the conference that opened on May 18, 1899. In addition to the official participants, among those present at The Hague were observers from unofficial groups such as the American and French Peace Societies. Not only were observers from the Peace Societies present at the second Hague conference in 1907; the socialists, anarchists, and Zionists all held their international congresses in Amsterdam during the conference. Their presence did not go unnoticed by the official conveners and in fact provoked anxiety about public reaction if the conference

the growing recognition of common interests, the international business movement organized a meeting at Liege, Belgium, in 1905—the first International Congress of Chambers of Commerce and Commercial and Industrial Associations. The movement steadily grew and at its international congress held in Paris in 1914, influential businessmen from all leading countries participating adopted a constitution that called for the creation of an executive council and secretariat to carry out the policies formulated at the biennial congresses for common action to protect and expand business interests and "to secure harmony of action on all international questions affecting commerce and industry and to promote peace." [17]

War broke out two months after the Paris conference, and the creation of a permanent international business organization had to wait. But soon after the war businessmen from the Allied countries of Great Britain, France, Italy, Belgium, and the United States met in Atlantic City in 1919 and in Paris in 1920 on the matter of establishing a permanent organization and on the pressing issue of the day—postwar reconstruction.

While the International Chamber of Commerce was one of the few transnational organizations of its day—nonprofit institutions in which citizens of at least two different countries are represented, at least one of whom is not an agent of government or an intergovernmental organization—today it is estimated there are between 2,500 and 3,000 such groups. [18]

Not only did traditional images of the international system depict sovereign states as the only actors, they also represented each state as having full command of all people, resources, and goods

---

should fail to produce significant results. As one delegate observed on the Socialists' presence: "Through the summer the Socialists prowled around The Hague like a cat around a birdcage." See Barbara W. Tuchman, *The Proud Tower* (New York: Bantam Books, 1966), p. 308.

[17] The origins and development of the International Chamber of Commerce in the period 1919–1938 are detailed in George L. Ridgeway, *Merchants of Peace: Twenty Years of Business Diplomacy through the International Chamber of Commerce* (New York: Columbia University Press, 1938).

[18] Kjell Skjelsbaek, "The Growth of International Nongovernmental Organizations in the Twentieth Century," in Keohane and Nye, *Transnational Relations and World Politics* p. 72.

within its territory, although this picture did not always square with the empirical reality. Today it is quite clear that no nation has *total* control over all its people, nor is a government capable of monitoring all the international activities that are initiated from within its borders. The degree of control—and the extent to which nongovernmental groups are free to enter into transnational relations—differs, of course, from nation to nation. In varying degrees individuals and groups within nations may engage in nongovernmental international activities,[19] and a multitude of linkages join governmental and nongovernmental organizations and entities.[20] In libertarian democracies private initiatives are the result of personal concerns or the interest of voluntary institutions, while citizens of authoritarian systems, such as the Soviet Union, who are in contact with representatives of private organizations in libertarian democracies are almost always under the ultimate control of official bodies.

Many of the private transnational institutions recently created in which citizens from more than one country are participants—perhaps active in many professions yet sharing a concern in a particular policy subject—are concerned with issues previously dealt with almost exclusively by governments.[21] Some of these have as their participants or members not only private citizens but officials of various kinds (legislators, government executives, and even high policy-makers) acting in a private capacity, and they may closely cooperate with official institutions.

[19] Karl Kaiser links the spectacular growth of transnational relations with the increasing accessibility of liberal Western societies to the outside world, of which he cites the growth of international investment, trade and movement of persons as evidence. See *Europe and the United States: The Future of the Relationship* (New York: Aspen Institute, 1973), p. 3.

[20] One of the linkages joining nongovernmental and governmental entities involved in international activities is that individuals frequently move in and out of official positions, maintaining contacts and relations with personnel active in official and unofficial institutions. The Fall 1976 issue of *Trialogue*, a publication of the transnational organization, the Trilateral Commission, reported that three members of the Commission since its creation in 1973 were now serving or about to serve in high government positions in trilateral countries: U.S. President-elect Jimmy Carter, Vice-President-elect Walter Mondale, and French Prime Minister Raymond Barre. The prominence of some of the participants in the meetings of the Trilateral Commission and other similar institutions has led to criticism from some who fear they may exert too much influence on policy-makers.

[21] Two notable organizations established before 1945 whose members engaged in international activities were the Institute of Pacific Relations (IPR) founded in Honolulu, Hawaii

One such institution is the Trilateral Commission formed in 1973 by private citizens of Western Europe, Japan, and North America to foster closer cooperation among these three regions on common problems. In the June 16, 1975 issue of *Newsweek* magazine, Robert Christopher reported on the plenary meeting of the Commission held in Kyoto, Japan, May 30 to 31, 1975.[22] He wrote of the theme which "loomed largest" in the Kyoto discussions:

> Somehow the present international system must be changed so as to accommodate in some degree the increasingly insistent demands of the poor nations for a greater share of the world's wealth and power. . . . The movers and shakers gathered in Kyoto had found themselves largely in agreement in their diagnosis of the world's central political problem. As a group, they were in a rare position to press this diagnosis on the world's policy-makers. Any diagnosis, after all, is a necessary preliminary to any cure. . . .

The Trilateral Commission works closely with public international agencies and national governments—while in Japan the group met with then Prime Minister Takeo Miki, and Foreign Minister Kiichi Miyazawa gave the concluding conference address—and the linkages between the organization and international and national governing bodies are extensive. Members of the Trilateral Commission are prominent, well-connected individuals, many

---

in 1925 and the Institute of International Law (IIL) which celebrated its one hundredth anniversary in 1973. The organizers of the IPR hoped that Western understanding of Asia would be improved by bringing together leaders of different nations for unofficial discussions of their differences. By the mid-50s the U.S. leadership of the IPR was defending itself against charges of cooperation with Communism by the McCarran Committee and Senator Joseph McCarthy. See John N. Thomas, *The Institute of Pacific Relations* (Seattle: University of Washington Press, 1974).

The essential conception of the IIL composed of approximately 120 member jurists from 40 countries in every region of the world is that an international body of highly qualified jurists acting independently of government would be able to contribute significantly to the formulation of principles and rules of international law. Many institute members play active and indeed leading roles in official international and national bodies concerned with international law. See Oscar Schacter, "Institut de Droit International. The Role of the Institute of International Law and Its Methods of Work—Today and Tomorrow," *Tribune de Geneve* (June 1973), pp. 2–3.

[22] The activities and the membership of the Trilateral Commission are reported on in its numerous publications. For a report of the Kyoto Conference prepared by the North American segment of the commission, see *Trialogue*, no. 7 (Summer 1975).

being present or former government officials. Because of that fact and the wide range of expertise members can offer, the Commission can expect that its activities and conclusions will receive the attention of high policy-makers. The gathering in Kyoto also captured the attention of the press in many countries. An international meeting of so many distinguished individuals for the purpose of deliberating on the world's major problems is a newsworthy event.

The *New York Times* reported on January 17, 1975, that a new twenty-nation development committee of finance ministers established the previous September by the World Bank and the International Monetary Fund had recommended action toward the establishment of a third lending "window" for the World Bank that would provide funds at a special rate of interest for development in poorer nations. The proposal for such a lending facility had come from a task force of the Trilateral Commission, and, at the request of the World Bank twenty copies of the report were delivered for the deliberations of "The Committee of Twenty" in Washington.[23]

Another transnational institution, quite different in structure as well as in function, is the Stockholm International Peace Research Institute (SIPRI), which was set up on July 1, 1966 by the Swedish Parliament as an independent international research institute. Because of the involvement of a government in its initiation—and indeed funds for operation are still provided by the Swedish government—it may be more accurate to view SIPRI as a semi-official organization. In its operations, however, the Institute works independently of government and responsibility for its governance lies in an international board.

The Institute's policy is to study problems in a pragmatic way and to select issues that are important to international decision-makers. To date the Institute has concentrated its activities on problems of disarmament and arms regulations; it publishes an annual summary of developments in world armaments, as well as books that report on research projects. SIPRI publications are distributed to governments, UN delegations, and other important institutions or individuals in policy-making or opinion-influencing posi-

---

[23] Richard N. Gardner, Saburo Okita, and B. J. Udink, "OPEC, the Trilateral World, and Developing Countries: New Arrangements for Cooperation, 1976–1980," Triangle Papers Series No. 7, (New York: Trilateral Commission, 1975).

tions. The staff is international and represents a wide variety of disciplines.

Nongovernmental Actors
and International Organizations

Through their close collaboration with international organizations, nongovernmental groups, many of them transnational, have come to perform significant functions in international public processes. This development has been encouraged by the United Nations; Article 71 of the charter provided for consultation by the Economic and Social Council (ECOSOC) with NGOs, and ECOSOC itself spelled out relevant provisions for this participation in June 1946. At each major conference dealing with economic and social problems facing the world organized by the United Nations in the 1970s, nongovernmental groups have played important roles.[24]

In addition to the 113 states that participated in the Stockholm Conference, the UN Secretariat and other intergovernmental agencies, as well as 255 international and national nongovernmental associations, were represented.[25] NGOs, many of them transnational actors, were involved in the decision-making process that led to the Stockholm Conference. They sent official observers to the meeting, participated in unofficial meetings outside the formal pro-

[24] One earlier example of close cooperation between nongovernmental groups and an international organization was the World Economic Conference in 1927 in Geneva under the aegis of the League of Nations. Although the League's activities had previously been confined to convening conferences of official bodies, Sir Arthur Salter, a League official and major British wartime official, felt the time was ripe for a world conference to tackle those serious economic troubles of an international character that "do not arise from governmental or intergovernmental action"; Sir Arthur was convinced that "many even of those who, if meeting as officials or government representatives, would feel bound to take a line which would make any useful agreement impossible, would welcome a discussion from a more general point of view and under freer conditions." In addition the conference would serve as a forum of responsible world opinion which would have significant influence on the formulation of national economic policies. Two hundred individuals representing all relevant economic spheres in the fifty participating nations were involved in the deliberations. See Sir Arthur Salter, "A Proposal for a World Economic Conference," quoted in Ridgeway, *Merchants of Peace*, pp. 221, 224.

[25] One study that conceptualizes international nongovernmental organizations as "international pressure groups" acting in the international political system is Anne Feraru's analysis of the role of transnational groups in the Stockholm Conference on the Environment. Feraru identifies the organizations that participated in international environmental policy-making, the functions they performed and their points of access to national and international officials. "Transnational Political Interests and the Global Environment," *International Organization* (Winter 1974), pp. 28:31–60.

ceedings, and were later involved in the establishment of the UN Environmental Program (UNEP).

There was also significant NGO activity during the Seventh Special Session of the General Assembly in September 1975 in New York dealing with economic development. Five hundred participants from 165 NGOs representing the broad spectrum of such organizations took part in the NGO Forum on World Economic Order.[26] The Forum was organized by the NGO community working closely with various UN agencies and with the Under Secretary-General for General Assembly Affairs. There was no detailed agenda for the Forum, and, unbound by the pressures on official planners to narrow the agenda to areas where governmental agreement might be reached, the Forum had more freedom to raise many of the broader issues on various aspects of development.

As was true of Stockholm, the NGOs performed significant functions before, during, and after the Special Session. NGOs participated in preparations for the conference by submitting expert reports, and they also met during the Session to monitor the proceedings. Since the resolutions of the General Assembly are advisory and nonbinding and must be enacted by national governments or other multilateral bodies, NGOs have a significant function to perform in the aftermath of the Special Session on development and of other international conferences dealing with economic and social issues. The implementation of solutions to these problems will require domestic support that the growing constituencies of NGOs—particularly those in Western countries—may help to build. The UN Under Secretary-General for Economic and Social Affairs, Gabriel Van Laethem, underlined the importance of the supporting role of the NGOs in his welcoming speech to Forum participants:

> No one can deny that on such complex and far-reaching issues as those presently under discussion, your contribution to the official debates, originating as it does from a wide range of specialists and

[26] A detailed report on the preparations for, proceedings, and aftermath of the NGO Forum on World Economic Order is *Scanning Our Future* (New York: Carnegie Endowment for International Peace, 1975).

professionals of highly diversified origins, should prove beneficial. No one could deny either that, once official agreements are reached on any of the subjects listed on the agenda of the Special Session, the strong and constant support of public opinion will be essential to ensure significant follow-up to the decisions arrived at. Your organizations can and should be of considerable help in securing such support.[27]

In addition to building support among their constituencies, NGOs perform other functions in international public processes. They can exert influence on national and international levels at times by suggesting that alternative approaches to specific problems exist, or by demonstrating that the constituencies they represent support alternate approaches; NGOs educate their constituencies and wider domestic publics on issues and their possible solutions.

Other functions that NGOs may perform may also expand in coming years. In reflecting on lessons learned at Stockholm, the Secretary-General of the Conference, Maurice Strong, outlined the role NGOs can play in filling the institutional gaps in the international management of environment issues: making arrangements "to organize the necessary research and analysis and monitoring functions, formulating alternative courses of action, and evolving procedures through which conscious choices can be made in the fullest possible knowledge of their consequences."[28] These service and support functions for political decision-making at the highest levels are largely missing.

The role of nongovernmental groups in supporting the efforts of international organizations has to a certain degree become institutionalized and accepted by officialdom. Speaking on the role such groups may play in providing expertise in program implementation, Bradford Morse, then UN Under Secretary-General for Political and General Assembly Affairs, commented at a 1972 meeting in New York that they are a source of "expert advice, information and operative assistance," and that some "are highly technical,

[27] *Ibid.*, p. 3.
[28] Maurice Strong, "One Year After Stockholm," *Foreign Affairs* (July 1973), 51:702.

professional groups, which can contribute substantively to the development and implementation of environmental programmes." [29]

Multinational Corporations

To end any review, however brief, of the growth and influence of transnational actors since the end of the second world war without mention of the category of actors that has had the greatest political impact and received the most attention would be a major omission. Multinational corporations or, as they are sometimes called, transnational corporations control $200 billion in assets and many possess rates of growth higher than in most nations; the activities of such economic giants are bound to affect government policies. [30]

While they may comply with national regulations, the fact that they operate in many countries allows for a potentially large degree of autonomy; their activities often are the objects of intergovernmental concern. Means to regulate multinationals are beyond the purview of any one government; various international institutions—the Organization of American States, several subregional bodies, and the UN itself—are working on the development of regulatory codes of conduct. In 1972 the UN Economic and Social Council created a "Group of Eminent Persons" to study the impact of MNCs on development and on international relations. After holding hearings in both New York and Geneva, the group submitted a report in 1974 on which the UN subsequently took action. In addition, the twenty-four nations comprising the Organization for Economic Cooperation and Development (OECD) adopted a package of voluntary guidelines for multinationals, an action of special significance since the vast majority of MNCs have headquarters and operations in these countries. [31]

[29] "Report on NGO Conference on the Human Environment," quoted in Feraru, "Transnational Political Interests," p. 42.

[30] As not-for-profit activities are outside our stated concern, the international activities of multinational business enterprises will not be examined in great detail here. For one of many discussions of ways MNCs impinge on governments, see Jon P. Gunnemann, ed., *The Nation-State and Transnational Corporations in Conflict* (New York: Praeger, 1975).

[31] The fact that the code is voluntary has brought criticism from some quarters. See Paxton T. Dunn, "Corporate Conduct: When Do the Rules Get Too Tough?" *The Inter Dependent,* September 1976, p. 7.

Traditionally students of international relations have assigned low priorities to the impact of nongovernmental groups on world politics; however, the growth of the multinationals is forcing new analyses because of the great impact of these institutions on governments and international organizations.[32]

The Role of Communications

So far we have examined how new actors and new issues have altered the way nations do business. One other factor contributing to the alteration in the conduct of interstate relations and the crafts and arts shaping these relations is the revolution in communications, including the effects of this revolution on public opinion and the surge in its influence on national and international affairs.[33]

What have been the nature and impact of this revolution?

First, it has played a key role in facilitating the growth of transnational organizations and contacts by allowing for a readier exchange of information between citizens of different countries.

Second, advances in communication have had a great impact on the ways diplomats function, particularly as they have made information on events in distant lands more accessible not only to government officials, but also to private individuals. Although decision-makers normally receive information through diplomatic channels, they tend to be heavy news consumers and even intelligence reports and diplomatic dispatches are dependent on the news media.[34]

One professional diplomat who is also a scholar has noted that the great increase in information flows across national boundaries

[32] Other transnational actors—labor, banking, advertising firms among them—have also been affected by the international activities of multinationals. For an analysis of how labor is faring, see David H. Blake, "Labor's Multinational Opportunities," *Foreign Policy* (Fall 1973), 12:132–43.

[33] See Gregory Henderson, ed., *Public Diplomacy and Political Change* (New York: Praeger, 1973), p. xx.

[34] See on this point, W. Phillips Davison, *Mass Communication and Conflict Resolution* (New York: Praeger, 1974), pp. 16–17.

has changed the reporting function of diplomats. They now must compete with reporters, travelers, and other officials whose views might reach the home government and domestic public before theirs do. In Glenn Fisher's words: "It is the explosion in partici-pation in international affairs accompanying the revolution in com-munication that makes diplomacy in the 1970s so different." [35] In these changed circumstances, the decision-maker and the negotia-tor find their range of alternatives constrained by the moods of at-tentive publics and elites where the press is free to report. [36]

It should be emphasized that only a small percentage of the citi-zens in a country pays attention to international affairs—in the United States and other industrialized nations one high estimate is 15 percent of the adult population are attentive to this informa-tion. [37] On many issues public opinion plays no role in decision-making, yet at other times policy-makers risk failure unless they explain their actions quite fully. [38]

Moods may also affect the day-to-day conduct of relations be-tween nations. When moods are salutary and the state of relations between two countries relatively tension-free, normal diplomatic channels may be open and flexible, and public opinion may not be a significant factor in the conduct of relations through normal bilateral procedures—through embassy personnel, through tele-phone conversations from capital to capital, or perhaps in multilat-eral frameworks.

But if relations are strained, public opinion and attitudes in at-tentive publics and elites, and even in the mass public, can seriously narrow the choices open to governments. In the Middle East, for example, few government officials on either side have

[35] Glenn H. Fisher, *Public Diplomacy and the Behavioral Sciences* (Bloomington: Indiana University Press, 1972), p. 4.

[36] A mood is defined here as both the totality of attitudes relevant to international affairs and attitudes on specific issues.

[37] Davison, *Mass Communication,* p. 19.

[38] Public opinion is, of course, only one factor that may be influential in the foreign policy-making process. Among other significant factors are the individual preferences of policy-makers, party politics, bureaucratic considerations, the legitimacy of the government struc-ture, domestic pressure groups, and the actions of other states. The relative weight of these factors varies from nation to nation and on specific issues within a particular nation.

been willing to risk making public conciliatory statements because of strong public sentiment against such moves. In other disputes—Cyprus, India–Pakistan, the Trieste dispute before it was resolved—policy-makers have been inhibited from even gingerly taking conciliatory steps because of the dangers involved in inflaming public opinion.[39]

Policy-makers often seek to cultivate public opinion, especially when they are constrained by strong public sentiment. In this age of communications, not only do leaders and bureaucrats attempt to form and influence public opinion on international issues abroad as well as at home; private groups, the news media, and even individual citizens have also played a role.[40]

One private citizen who has from time to time been involved in attempts to influence government policy in international matters is the millionaire industrialist, Cyrus Eaton. Although never a government official, he has had many contacts with government leaders, and his prominence and public relations sense assure him of an audience in the United States. In the late 1950s and early 1960s Eaton cultivated friendships with Soviet officials and tried unsuccessfully to promote Soviet-American trade. He helped organize and provided funds for the first Pugwash Conference, which met at, and took the name of, his boyhood hometown in Nova Scotia.

On the occasion of his ninetieth birthday, Eaton in an interview with the *New York Times* spoke of his attempts to create understanding and trade between the Soviet Union and the United States:

> What got me started was the atomic bomb and the realization that our civilization and theirs could be wiped out overnight. I thought I ought to try to do something to prevent this, and I helped put together and financed a meeting of American and Soviet atomic scientists at my boyhood home in Pugwash, Nova Scotia, in 1957 in the hope that they would warn their governments of the perils to

[39] For a discussion of the way domestic public opinion in Italy and Yugoslavia inhibited resolution of the Trieste dispute, see John C. Campbell, ed., *Successful Negotiation: Trieste 1954* (Princeton, N.J.: Princeton University Press, 1976).

[40] Henderson, *Public Diplomacy*, p. xxiv.

mankind. Afterward I visited the Soviet Union and Eastern Europe and was host to their leaders here, with the aim of fostering trade and understanding.[41]

Although they may have no direct impact on policy, visits by prominent individuals to foreign leaders well-publicized in the news media may help to effect a change in the bureaucratic readiness to deal with an issue, since press coverage may raise the perceived importance of an issue. Both the priorities of governments and the agenda of decision-makers may be affected by the mass media.[42] An article in the New York Times or the Washington Post, both widely read by important decision-makers in the United States government and their influential friends on the outside, may nudge an issue slightly higher on the crowded agenda claiming the attention of foreign policy officials.

Less prominent people can also attract the attention of the news media, and as in the case of Abie J. Nathan they may attempt to communicate directly with domestic publics in countries where there is no ready access to the press. The Israeli politician, pilot, and restaurateur gained wide attention in 1966 when he flew alone from Tel Aviv to Port Said, Egypt, in an old airplane, trying to focus attention on starting peace talks in the Middle East. In 1969, Nathan began a five-year effort to launch a floating radio station that he hoped would be a voice of peace in the Middle East. After a great many difficulties in raising the necessary funds to refit the ship and keep it afloat the station finally went on the air in May 1974.

In contrast to the Arab and Israeli state-owned stations, the

[41] Alden Whitman, "Eaton at 90: Still Active and Dogged in Beliefs," New York Times, December 27, 1973. For more on Pugwash, see pages 37–41.

In February 1974 Eaton turned his attention to U.S.–Cuban rapprochement. Returning from a visit with Cuban Premier Fidel Castro, in an interview with the New York Times Eaton reported that relations between the two countries could be quickly resumed if Secretary of State Kissinger were to take up the matter of restoring relations with the Cuban leader. Although Castro gave him no messages, Eaton reported that Castro was aware that he would speak out on the subject of Cuban–U.S. relations, and he did bring back "the clear understanding that the Cuban government and people are favorably inclined toward a resumption in relations with Washington." See H. J. Maidenberg. "Eaton Says U.S.–Cuba Ties Could be Resumed Soon," New York Times, February 14, 1974.

[42] Bernard C. Cohen, The Press and Foreign Policy (Princeton, N.J.: Princeton University Press, 1963), p. 229.

voice of the peace ship was a soothing one which, according to its captain, was intended to try to "create a climate of moderation so that leaders will step down from rigid positions. We don't think we'll bring peace talks ourselves, only the climate for these."[43]

Nathan tried five times to sail through the Suez Canal in a peace demonstration, and after several days of being held under the supervision of the naval base and harbor police at the Canal's northern entrance, the peace ship was given permission by Egyptian authorities to sail through the Canal on January 2, 1977—an occurrence that was reported in the *New York Times* the following day.

Private citizens may also try to change international policies by reaching influential individuals in national policy-making capacities not just in one country. Building upon the ideas expressed in Pope John XXIII's famous encyclical, the Center for the Study of Democratic Institutions in Santa Barbara, California, organized a series of Pacem in Terris conferences for the purpose of enchancing effective international support for the concept of peace. The first two conferences were held in New York in February 1965 and in Geneva in May 1967.

Harry Ashmore, a Center staff member when the conferences were organized, has described the meetings in the following way:

> The design for these Pacem in Terris convocations called for a mixture of political leaders, diplomats, intellectuals, churchmen, and private men of affairs. The hope was that in a public but informal setting where no participant was required or expected to speak on behalf of his government, the inhibitions of normal diplomacy might be eased. . . .
>
> The audience was seen as a primary means of propagating any useful ideas the dialogue might produce. The criterion for an invitation was the recipient's influence in his own country. We would be pleased to have a foreign minister, but we were really after the person the foreign minister listens to. . . .
>
> Our effort was unique only in emphasizing the necessity of reaching beyond the ceremonial chambers and hotel ballrooms where the

[43] Paul L. Montgomery, "Mideast Radio Voice Sought for Peace Ship," *New York Times*, August 9, 1972.

influential are ordinarily assembled. Our goal was not merely to have participants talk freely with one another, but to make the wise and foolish words they spoke available to as many of the world's ordinary citizens as could be reached through the mass communications media. The two convocations were conceived as basic elements in a massive public relations operation on behalf of peace.[44]

This meant, of course, that the advantages of closed sessions, where officials tend to speak off the record with more candor than if their words are being reported by the news media, were deliberately waived.

Among those at the first convocation were an impressive number of the world's movers and shakers, including the Secretary-General of the United Nations, the President of the General Assembly and two former presidents, the Vice-President and the Chief Justice of the United States, an Associate Justice of the Supreme Court, four U.S. Senators, Belgium's Foreign Minister Paul Henri-Spaak, leading officials from Italy, the USSR, Poland, Yugoslavia, two justices of the World Court—all told, more than two thousand participants from twenty nations.

The Geneva convocation was somewhat smaller—fewer than 400 participants—but the number of countries represented had increased to seventy. As was the case with the first convocation, in attendance were a number of ambassadors, foreign ministers, and other prominent people.

In Ashmore's words, "We had never sought any formal blessing for the convocation from the State Department, but we had always recognized an obligation to keep the Department fully informed."[45] At first plans for the first convocation had included an address by President Lyndon Johnson, and after initial encouragement the date was changed to fit the President's schedule. As the date grew near, the President withdrew his commitment to speak, and in Ashmore's view, the administration declared open warfare on the gathering. It so happened the preparations for and

[44] Harry Ashmore, "The Public Relations of Peace," *Center Magazine* (October/November 1967), 1:4−6 and following.
[45] *Ibid.*, p. 16.

the dates of convocation coincided with the build-up of U.S. forces in Vietnam. This quite naturally became a subject of discussion.[46]

Ashmore reports that one government official objected that foreign policy was not a proper matter to be handled in an unofficial forum over which those who had the ultimate responsibility had no control. Moreover, the administration's view was that such gatherings might disrupt official efforts at peace making then going on. Echoing the sentiments of Harry Truman, the professionals expressed fears that amateurs could do damage in an area where they did not belong.

While the first Pacem in Terris conferences ran into opposition from the U.S. government for deliberating on the matter of Vietnam, other unofficial international groups have had more success in raising issues and suggesting solutions to officials of one nation or of international organizations.

It was the Club of Rome, an eminent international group of industrialists, economists, scientists, and others, that published in 1972 an influential study, *The Limits to Growth*, which attempted to forecast the ramifications of continued growth and "progress." The organization was started by Dr. Aurelio Peccei, an Italian industrial manager, in Rome in April 1968, with thirty members. None of the members holds public office, nor does the group seek to express a unitary view, but they are united in the belief that the traditional international institutions are insufficient to deal with the complex problems facing mankind. The club's purposes are "to foster understanding of the varied but interdependent components—economic, political, natural and social—that make up the global system in which we all live; to bring that new understanding to the attention of policy-makers and the public worldwide; and in this way to promote new policy initiatives and action."[47]

The Limits to Growth was translated into a dozen languages, its publication was widely reported in the world's press, and, with the

---

[46] For an account of a trip by Ashmore and another Center Board member to North Vietnam and the difficulties that arose with the Johnson Administration in the trip's wake, see Ashmore's essay in Part Two.

[47] Donella H. Meadows, Dennis Meadows, et al., *The Limits to Growth*, (New York: Potomac Associates Book, 1972), p. 9.

club's influence, placed in hands where its message could stir public debate and have an impact on policy.[48] The club's findings, which challenged the validity of the Western industrial model, set into motion a growth debate that is still raging years after the book's publication. In October 1975 in Woodlands, Texas, a group of scientists, intellectuals, and businessmen convened for the first of a series of biennial reviews of the book and its findings.[49] In a 1976 report which practically reverses its previous no-growth stance, the Club of Rome expresses its current view that the dangers of continued world poverty resulting from no-growth would be greater than those created by selected growth strategies and sets out its concrete proposals for building a new world order.[50]

The club's success in reaching national and international policy-makers is evidence of the growing role of nongovernmental groups in international public processes. Through the greater ease of communications and travel, private citizens from many nations may assemble and publicize in many nations results of their deliberations.

Official/Unofficial Relations

As we have seen, the great increase in the number of actors and in the kinds and significance of issues that must be solved by the action and consent of many nations has greatly complicated international dealings. Many of these problems have been brought on through technological developments, and their solutions require technical or complex scientific knowledge not needed by professional diplomats of past eras. Faced with the complexity of many of today's issues, international organizations and nations may turn to private individuals or groups to provide necessary expertise. Private groups, if they have a true international character, may carry out independent analyses on specific issues without the taint

[48] *Time* Magazine, January 24, 1972.
[49] *The Inter Dependent*, December 1975, p. 1.
[50] Jan Tinbergen (coordinator), *Reshaping the International Order: A Report* (New York: Dutton, 1976).

of national advocacy. Moreover, some of these organizations may provide a forum where government policy-makers (and those close to them) from two or more nations may meet.

It is inevitable that government officials and private citizens should disagree on the limits within which the latter can usefully act, and therefore "interference" from the outside is frequently not welcome. The U.S. government has attempted to control unauthorized intervention by citizens in its international affairs. The Logan Act of 1799 is still on the books. While no one has been convicted under it—and only one person has ever been indicted— it has been used on occasion to intimidate or chastise American travelers who express unpopular views while abroad.[51]

The actress Jane Fonda's open criticism of U.S. policy in Vietnam greatly annoyed many officials when on her well-publicized trip to Hanoi she made a series of twenty-one radio broadcasts. Representative Fletcher Thompson of Georgia in hearings of the House Committee on Internal Security pressed the Justice Department on its failure to prosecute her for violating the Logan Act. Assistant Attorney-General William Olson argued that in order to establish that a person has violated the law, the government would have to prove that the individual, in additon to carrying on conversations with officials of a foreign government in relation to a controversy or dispute with the United States, had also undertaken these conversations "with intent to influence the measures or conduct of any foreign government or of any officer or agent thereof . . . or to defeat the measures of the United States."[52] No court has ever ruled on the constitutionality of the law.

Harry Ashmore and William Baggs also had a brush with the Logan Act following their discussions with Ho Chi Minh in North Vietnam. Alice Widener, a syndicated newspaper columnist, charged they were guilty of a Logan Act violation. According to

[51] For a review of the history of applications of the Logan Act before 1933 see Hope Belsey, "Unauthorized Diplomatic Intercourse by American Citizens with Foreign Powers," *Cumulative Digest of International Law and Relations* American University, Washington D.C. 3, Nos. 12, 13, 14, February 25, 1933. By the time this book is published the status of the act may have changed.

[52] Hearings Regarding HR 16742: Restraints on Travel to Hostile Areas, 92d Cong., 2d sess., September 19, 1972.

Baggs and Ashmore these charges prompted the Associated Press to query the State Department as to whether a violation had been committed: "The AP then compounded its gullibility by circulating a muddled account of the accusations after the Department had confirmed the obvious fact that the law manifestly could not apply to those who acted with its full knowledge and consent."[53]

What these failures to prosecute show, as Ithiel Pool points out, are the "difficulties a free society would face in trying to draw a line between unauthorized diplomatic negotiation and the ordinary practice of free expression at home and abroad."[54] What distinguishes these instances from innumerable others concerning American communications abroad may be the intensity of feelings surrounding them.

When government officials try to shoot down a private effort, the stated rationale may be fear of the harm that untrained hands may cause.[55] But the real reason may be something else: it may be a belief that the aim of the private initiative is contrary to that of the government; or sometimes it may be personal dislike or resentment of "meddlers" who are prone to criticism of official policies and performances. Moreover, officials tend to distrust information from private sources, particularly if it runs counter to official reports.

For example, from the viewpoint of officialdom the information private individuals convey about domestic politics may be inaccurate and misleading. The official negotiator in Paris with the North Vietnamese, Averell Harriman, remarked that the North Vietnamese got their information from some of the Americans who had been invited to Hanoi—some Quakers, people like Tom Hayden, David Dellinger, and others who were strongly against the war. In

[53] Harry S. Ashmore and William C. Baggs, *Mission to Hanoi: A Chronicle of Double-Dealing in High Places* (New York: Putnam, 1968), p. 25.

[54] Ithiel de Sola Pool, "Private and Public Diplomacy," paper presented to the International Studies Association Convention, St. Louis, Mo., 1973, pp. 7–8.

[55] There is the intricate case of the John Doe Associates—two private Japanese citizens—whose intervention into Japanese-American relations in the period preceding the attack on Pearl Harbor in 1941 complicated and perhaps made more ineffectual the talks then going on between Secretary of State Cordell Hull and Japanese Ambassador Nomura. See R. J. C. Butow, *The John Doe Associates: Backdoor Diplomacy for Peace, 1941* (Stanford, Calif.: Stanford University Press, 1974).

his words, "Their opinions have been affected by this, I think. What their actual judgment is, I can't tell you, but certainly they have been exposed to the doves rather than the hawks."[56] Government officials may, for their own purposes, give a false impression of public opinion on foreign policy; they certainly don't like others conveying what they consider false information or views that they believe will in any way jeopardize their ability to influence the policies of other governments.

In Harry Ashmore's view, although professionals may cite reasons for their wariness of outsiders, the main factor is a professional, institutional snobbery that expresses itself in an automatic resentment of outsiders—amateurs—meddling with official business. The ramifications of this stance, according to Ashmore, limit, if they do not preclude, the opportunity to take informal policy soundings "that are simply impossible for those clothed in formal authority and responsibility and shuts off sources of intelligence that are at least as dependable as most of those available internally to the foreign service" (see pages 140–41).

Not all private citizens involved in unofficial diplomacy have had experiences similar to Ashmore's or share his view. There are examples recounted in this volume of the willingness of policymakers to seek or accept help from private citizens—but when they feel they no longer need that help or feel it has turned counterproductive, they may drop private parties like hot potatoes.

As will be seen in the cases to follow, there are opportunities for government officials to take advantage of unofficial assistance, and in a number of instances, though of course not all, unofficial diplomats have made a very real contribution. It will be clearly apparent, we believe, from the selections that follow that dedication, sophistication, and perseverance—plus a realistic assessment of the factors circumscribing success—are the backbone of responsible private efforts.

[56] Interview with Governor W. Averell Harriman, p. 70. Conducted by the Academy for Educational Development, May 17, 1969; deposited at the Oral History Research Office, Columbia University, New York, N.Y.

PART ONE

Unofficial Meetings

OVERVIEW

PART ONE CONTAINS REPORTS on the series of so-called "Dartmouth Conferences" and on bilateral and multilateral seminars arranged by the International Press Institute. These are examples of the kinds of conferences designed to improve communication which, in most cases, is a prerequisite to more effective understanding and possibly negotiation; policy-makers, legislators, other present and former government officials, and private individuals with close ties to decision-makers come together for exploratory, off-the-record communication. Some of these meetings are sponsored by nongovernmental organizations with other programs and functions; others are arranged by organizations or groups that exist only to prepare for and sponsor such gatherings.

For nations whose orientation is essentially friendly, private gatherings may provide a forum where policy-makers and private citizens may meet and exchange information and views in an informal, off-the-record atmosphere. Although official channels may be open and flexible, private channels allow for the kind of exploratory talks often not possible in normal diplomatic arrangements. Particularly if there is continuity, participants may come to know one another and trust each other, thus developing good working relations. Such meetings, moreover, may contribute to an increased awareness of domestic difficulties and an exploration of policy options. It is often possible to dispense with official government viewpoints and to discuss frankly difficulties policy-makers may have in bringing along their home bureaucracies or populace on certain issues.

These meetings may contribute to better communication, even between unfriendly nations. Numerous studies have elaborated on the possibilities for misperception that abound in intercultural communication.[1] Even nations that know each other well in the sense that there are abundant contacts, both governmental and nongovernmental, may suffer at times from the consequences of misperception.

Richard Neustadt in a study of such misperception between two friendly nations—the United States and Great Britain—shows how the two nations managed to get into deep trouble during two crises (the Suez Crisis of 1956 and the Skybolt Affair of 1962) because of misperception occasioned not by gross differences but, in Neustadt's analysis, by small shadings of difference and an inadequate conception of each other's internal political processes and the roles of official personnel. There were plenty of sources for information, both in and out of government, yet what was lacking was, in Neustadt's words, "an adequate conception of the overlapping games in which they were engaged."[2]

If there are risks of misperception between friends with a range of governmental and nongovernmental contacts, then even greater dangers abound in relations between adversaries who have not made strong commitments to accommodate differences peacefully through compromise and normal diplomatic give-and-take. While a case can be made that increasing information sometimes may only harden attitudes and deepen conflict, a stronger case can be presented that in general lack of knowledge is likely to lead to misunderstandings and to possible conflict. When official lines of communication are sparse or talks are carried on in a tense atmosphere, it seems a fair assumption that the probabilities of misperception increase. Without the intent or willingness to improve relations between nations, increasing information may have little effect, yet without channels available it may be more difficult

---

[1] For a detailed review of these studies, see Daniel Druckman, *Human Factors in International Negotiation* (Beverly Hills, Calif.: Sage Publications, 1974).

[2] Richard E. Neustadt, *Alliance Politics* (New York: Columbia University Press, 1970), pp. 79–80.

if not impossible to move in conciliatory directions. Private channels may be used to try out new approaches and to explore ways through which governments may reach agreements. Probing the other side to learn its position without simultaneously risking commitment may be facilitated by private efforts.

When the Pugwash Conference series, bringing together scientists from many nations, began in 1957 and when the Dartmouth Conference series, bringing together prominent Soviet and American persons began in 1960, the miasma of the cold war had by no means been dissipated. The relations between the two nations remained tense and the nuclear threat was growing. In his account of the origins of the Dartmouth series, Norman Cousins recalls this strained atmosphere; one of the key issues facing the two nations and the world at the time was the problem of uncontrolled nuclear testing. In Cousins' words, "The conferences made it possible for both governments to try out certain ideas without penalty." This was true also of the multilateral Pugwash meetings. Moreover, the unofficial efforts complemented and fed into official diplomatic negotiations that were being conducted bilaterally or in the multilateral framework of the United Nations. From an early concern with issues of disarmament, both groups have now taken up other important issues on the international agenda.

Pugwash

In 1955, Bertrand Russell, with the support of a number of eminent scientists, issued a manifesto which was radical; it was to "the scientists of the world and the general public" asking them to urge governments to renounce war as a means of settling disputes. The stated purpose of the manifesto was "to bring men of science of the most divergent political opinions—Communist, anti-Communist and neutral—in a friendly atmosphere in which it was hoped that a scientific spirit would enable them to find a greater measure of agreement than the politicians had found possible." [3]

[3] Bertrand Russell, "The Early History of the Pugwash Movement," in Seymour Melman, ed., Disarmament: Its Politics and Economics (Boston: American Academy of Arts and Sciences, 1962), pp. 18–31.

As an outgrowth of this manifesto, the first conference was held in July 1957 on the invitation of Cyrus Eaton in Pugwash, Nova Scotia, and subsequent meetings have adopted the name of its first location. Up to and including the meetings held in Moscow in the fall of 1960, representatives of the People's Republic of China, along with scientists from many nations, attended the conferences. The Chinese have not yet resumed participation in these meetings.

When the first conference was organized in 1957 it created a thread of contact between scientists where previously there had been none. In the years since it began, Pugwash has become an important channel of communication among scientists for the study and exploration of many complex issues on the political agenda. After the first meeting, a continuing committee of five persons was set up with instructions to organize future conferences.

Pugwash sessions are closed to the press and the public. Joseph Rotblat, the Pugwash movement's Secretary-General for many years, explains why:

> Anonymity is the price paid for bringing eminent scientists together and getting them to talk freely and without inhibition on matters which are of deep concern to them, but on which they are not necessarily experts. Such talks can be effective and generate original ideas, only if participants do not have to worry that what they say may be taken down and published, more likely than not in a distorted fashion. For this reason the meetings are private and the press not admitted. . . . However, although our meetings are private, Pugwash is not a secret society. On the contrary, we are anxious that the public should know who we are, how we operate, and what we talk about.[4]

Furthermore, if sessions are publicized then they may take on the character of public negotiations—posturing, propagandizing—and the possibilities for exploratory discussions may be lost.

In the beginning the goals formulated for Pugwash were to influence governments directly and through the mobilization of public opinion, and to educate public opinion. Although it has not effectively influenced the opinions of a broad public, it has come to

[4] Joseph Rotblat, *Scientists in the Quest for Peace. A History of the Pugwash Conference* (Cambridge, Mass., M.I.T. Press, 1972), p. XVII.

serve as a channel of communication between East and West; many of the discussions at Pugwash have influenced the decisions of governments. On disarmament matters particularly, the Pugwash movement became a useful nongovernmental channel of communication where differing points of view could be discussed in private, without commitment of governments.[5]

In many of the conversations, not only in Pugwash, but in Pugwash-derived contacts, such as the bilateral United States-Soviet Union meetings on disarmament sponsored by the American Academy of Arts and Sciences, there were exploratory conferences on arms control between Soviet and American scientists either holding government positions or with channels to policy-makers. In the beginning the Western contingents included a large number of "ban-the-bomb" scientists who had little or no contact with their governments and who were unsympathetic to government foreign and defense policies. Later on the Western delegations, and particularly the American delegation, included a number of scientists who had experience in political/scientific affairs and knowledge of the defense and foreign policy deliberations that were going on within the government.[6] The Russian delegation also came to include scientists influential in governmental circles and familiar with the deliberations on arms control in their governments.

It is hard to assess with any precision the nature of the contribution of Pugwash, as is the case with many other unofficial meetings. It has been only one of many efforts, both official and unofficial, going on at the same time, yet it appears to have made specific contributions to paving the way for agreements on the official level. Over the course of a number of years new ideas were developed, tried out, and eventually accepted by government bureaucracies. One important aspect of these private, exploratory meetings, particularly on arms control issues, arises from the fact that there is almost always a major battle over policy within government bureaucracies. In such meetings, if they are well-

[5] Eugene B. Skolnikoff, *Science, Technology and American Foreign Policy* (Cambridge, Mass., M.I.T. Press, 1967), p. 145.
[6] *Ibid.*, pp. 144–45.

organized, the nature of the bureaucratic battles and the arguments of various groups will be aired, and what is clearly unacceptable will be brought out.

Arthur Lall has noted the impact of Pugwash discussions on official negotiations at Geneva:

> . . . when the United States introduced its outline of basic provisions at the Eighteen-Nation Committee on Disarmament Conference on April 8, 1962, it departed from its previous position and proposed, in addition to destruction of armaments under international supervision, only partial verification of retained armaments. This was to be done through a series of surprise spot-checks in gradually increasing areas of each country. The system proposed has been described as a zonal inspection system which was first mooted at one of the Pugwash conferences.[7]

One American Pugwash participant and observer believes the greatest contributions have been made, not by Pugwash itself, but by a kind of offshoot of Pugwash—a series of bilateral meetings on arms control issues organized by the American Academy of Arts and Sciences and the Soviet Academy of Sciences that have been going on for more than a dozen years. Over a three-year period of these meetings there were step-by-step changes in Soviet views on the implications of antiballistic missiles and other aspects of arms control.

Although we have emphasized the benefits of such private contacts, it is necessary to add that there are potential hazards in unofficial communication. One of the main hazards is that participants may mislead the other side on whether the views they are expressing are personal or governmental. In one of the side conversations between Soviet and American participants attending the Pugwash meeting in Moscow in 1960, the issues discussed included one related to the official negotiations then in progress on a test ban treaty. When the number of on-site inspections was brought up the figure "three" was discussed as a feasible compromise. The Russians apparently believed that this compromise would be ac-

---

[7] Arthur Lall, *Modern International Negotiation* (New York: Columbia University Press, 1966), p. 309.

ceptable to the American government, and subsequently Ambassador Kuznetsov made a proposal at Geneva along these lines which was then rejected by the American side.[8] Whatever the cause of the misunderstanding, it demonstrates the need to distinguish clearly between personal and official views.

Dartmouth

In his interview in this section, Norman Cousins describes the origins of the Dartmouth Conference series. The meetings, organized at irregular intervals since 1960, were originally the suggestion of President Eisenhower, who believed that private citizens who enjoyed the confidence of their governments might help prepare the way for official negotiations.[9]

From the beginning, conference organizers have kept the U.S. government informed. On the Soviet side, there is a close tie between the delegation and officiaidom; indeed, some hold the view that Soviet participants in Dartmouth, Pugwash and other private conferences and forums are only slightly less than official.

One American observer who has participated in both Dartmouth and Pugwash remarked off-the-record that even though the Russian and the American participants in Pugwash know that the Soviet delegation is subject to greater discipline than the American group, after a period of time a relationship of confidence has developed among participants which lends itself to a degree of infor-

[8] There is some disagreement over where the number three was first discussed. In a conversation with Khrushchev in Moscow, Norman Cousins was told this was the number that Kuznetsov and Dean discussed at Geneva, and that a Soviet scientist attending a private meeting in Cambridge, England, had brought back the same figure. See *The Improbable Triumvirate* (New York: Norton, 1972), p. 94. Arthur Dean has denied that this number was ever discussed with Kuznetsov. See *Test Ban and Disarmament*, pp. 40–41. In his book *Kennedy,* Theodore Sorensen wrote that President Kennedy speculated that the source of the confusion was British Prime Minister Harold Macmillan, since he sounded so much more optimistic than American scientists on seismic identification. See *Kennedy* (New York: Harper & Row, 1965), p. 728.

[9] Norman Cousins, "Dartmouth IX," *Saturday Review,* July 12, 1975, p. 4. Dartmouth X held in Spring 1976 in Rio Rico, Arizona, examined Soviet-American relations in an era of detente. Proceedings are available from the Charles F. Kettering Foundation, Dayton, Ohio, which now administers the American side of the conference.

mal communication; this is seldom true in the more ad hoc operations between East and West, and even less so of official governmental encounters.

Marshall Shulman, an early Dartmouth participant, commented that: "Often times the Russians who are sent abroad are, I imagine, either officials or certain people who are under official instructions. Yet, the faith that keeps one going is that some small corner of a contact may have some utility, and that even though there are carefully chosen and carefully briefed people on the Soviet side, you may nevertheless have some little change in values." [10]

Other Meetings

Aside from the Pugwash and Dartmouth conferences, there have been other meetings bringing together for unofficial talks policymakers and private citizens from friendly and less friendly nations. Some of these meetings are continuing affairs, while others have been organized around specific subjects for one or two gatherings.

The Bilderberg series of conferences originated in 1954 for the specific purpose of trying to alleviate growing mutual suspicion and distrust among the countries of Western Europe and North America. Those who founded it believed that unofficial and private meetings at which there could be frank discussions of difficulties and differences could serve to reduce misunderstandings and tensions.

The conferences have brought together high officers of government and eminent private citizens in finance, industry, cultural affairs, and trade unionism for unofficial discussions of important

[10] *Observations on International Negotiations: Transcript of an Informal Conference* (New York: Academy for Educational Development, 1971), pp. 133–34. Shulman, who attended Dartmouth X as well as earlier conferences, has observed a change in the restrictions on Soviet participants: "While the range of independence among Soviet participants in nongovernmental contacts is obviously restricted, it has nevertheless been widening with experience and the growth of confidence. An important consequence of this is that American participants are able to go beyond the limited printed sources of information on Soviet positions and to become aware of the richer and complex oral levels of discussion of policy issues." See "On Learning to Live with Authoritarian Regimes," *Foreign Affairs* (January 1977), 55:329.

issues on the international agenda. Because of the private nature of the meetings, even members of governments or other leaders in official or semi-official positions can express their personal views on important issues without committing the institutions they belong to. To enable the participants to speak frankly, the discussions are confidential, and no press reporters are permitted to attend the sessions. At the twenty-fourth Bilderberg meeting held in Turkey in 1975, there were 99 participants who came from fourteen European countries, the United States, Canada, and several international organizations. Bilderberg has never attempted or even contemplated direct action, the objective being to draw the attention of people in responsible positions to different currents of thought. No votes are taken and no resolutions are passed.

Another series of meetings bringing together government officials and private citizens in an unofficial framework, is the bilateral German-American meeting sponsored by the American Council on Germany and its parallel organization in the Federal Republic, the Atlantik-Brücke. In the American delegation to the eighth conference held in Bonn in 1975 were fifteen congressional representatives along with academics, business people, and other representatives of professions; the German delegation was similarly composed. Except for opening and closing plenary sessions the discussions are off-the-record and closed to the press.[11]

A similar bilateral meeting is the series of meetings between Germans and Britishers—the so-called Königswinter meetings that occur on a periodic basis.

Another example of private meetings as vehicles for information exchanges are the parallel studies conducted by the United Nations Association in the Soviet Union and in the United States. The two areas that have been jointly discussed are the environment and problems of nuclear nonproliferation. Concerning the latter issue, after discussions between representatives of the two associations, parallel papers on the subject were published in 1972. Contact between the organizations continued and after an agreement

---

[11] For texts of opening and closing remarks of the plenary sessions and a list of participants, see *East-West Issues VIII*, American Council on Germany, Atlantik-Brücke, Freiburg, Verlag-Rombach, 1975.

reached during a visit to Moscow in July 1974 by an American delegation, panels formed by both associations prepared papers on the question of nonproliferation in preparation for the review conference on the nonproliferation treaty held in May 1975 in Geneva. The papers were discussed during a visit to Moscow by the American panel in 1975.

In the preface to the Reports written in Moscow in March 1975 it is noted that while the two documents express the separate and not necessarily identical views of the two associations, "it is the hope of those who participated in the preparation and discussion of these papers that many of the ideas contained in them will commend themselves to the Soviet and American governments and to the other governments participating in the Review Conference."[12]

There are, then, a broad range of unofficial meetings. Participants may include government policy-makers along with private persons, or private citizens alone. The focus may be a specific issue—disarmament or détente, perhaps—or cover a broad spectrum of issues. The organizers of such meetings may bring together members of a profession, in a gathering conceived to make use of certain skills or expertise. Ernest Meyer describes in this section a series of bilateral and multilateral meetings organized and run by the International Press Institute, an independent professional association with close ties to national and international government bodies. Meetings between journalists, the IPI believes, is one way to aid in the elimination of misunderstandings that may often result in conflict, while some of the meetings are arranged to alleviate the misunderstandings that result when a conflict situation already exists. Rather than trying to replace policy-makers, the IPI attempts to aid their work by analyzing a situation, informing participants, and helping to create a climate in which policy-makers can usefully work—functions similar to those of Dartmouth and other unofficial meetings as well.

[12]*NPT. The Review Conference and Beyond,* Reports of the United Nations Association of the U.S.A. and the Association for the United Nations in the USSR, New York, 1975.

TWO

THE DARTMOUTH CONFERENCES

AN INTERVIEW WITH NORMAN COUSINS

NORMAN COUSINS, editor of the *Saturday Review* from 1940 to 1972 and since 1973, was a principal organizer of the Dartmouth Conference series in the late 1950s. In the following interview he talks about the origins of the meetings and their present operation, and other nongovernmental contacts between Soviets and Americans.——Eds.

Q UESTION: LOOKING AT THE INDIVIDUALS and organizations that act in a private, nongovernmental manner to help resolve conflicts between nations, what, in your opinion, are the sources of such unofficial contacts?

NORMAN COUSINS: I think this is largely a product of time and circumstances. I'm not sure it would be possible or even feasible, from a standing start, to make a determination that any given individual could attempt privately to undertake an effort in this direction. When I talk about this being a product of special circumstance, I'm thinking primarily of a total process in which accident plays more than a small part. Some people who are engaged in such efforts are primarily involved in public undertakings. Any person who is an editor of a magazine may from time to time find himself called upon to do things in the nature of informal approaches. This is known as a probe. Without penalty, matters can be explored and government need not be involved.

The process of diplomacy tends to be somewhat limited at times. A government might not wish to take a public position on a certain issue, whereas an individual on his own could take that

This interview was conducted by Maureen Berman and Barbara Rotenberg at the offices of the Academy for Educational Development in New York City on February 14, 1974. The complete transcript is part of the Oral History Collection of Columbia University.

position and get a reaction. The reaction can be important—more important than the position that produced the reaction.

In my own case, there were circumstances which were somewhat special. I had done occasional government work going back to the Office of War Information. I had been editor of *USA* during the war. From time to time there were government assignments. I was sent to places like India, Pakistan, Ceylon, Japan, Africa, West Germany, the Soviet Union, for example, sometimes as government lecturer. When I came back, I might be asked to report to government agencies. Perhaps the most important such experience was the Dartmouth Conference series. It was independent of government but served a public purpose. The purpose of the Dartmouth Conference was to identify areas of opportunity for both countries in reducing tension. Obviously, we relayed the results of each conference to government. The conferences made it possible for both governments to try out certain ideas without penalty.

QUESTION: Does this remain a function of the Dartmouth Conference today?

COUSINS: Yes.

QUESTION: What were the origins of the Dartmouth Conference?

COUSINS: I was sent to the Soviet Union in 1959 in connection with the cultural exchange program, then just getting started. The Dartmouth Conference grew out of that trip. I felt that it might be a good idea to get Russian intellectuals to come to the United States and meet with their opposite numbers. There had been some isolated visits but nothing on this particular scale. My trip made it possible for me to know some Russians and to talk frankly with them. I learned something about the approaches that had to be made in order to set up a conference between Russians and Americans outside the Soviet Union. I just kept at it until finally there was a "yes."

QUESTION: How long was it from the time you first conceived of the Dartmouth Conference until the first one?

COUSINS: Maybe two years.

QUESTION: What were the efforts to get things going?

COUSINS: First, a matter of context. We were then deep in the cold war. The Berlin crisis brought us close to a shooting war. In the talk I had given in Moscow, I tried to make the point that the American people were interested in peace, but that peace couldn't be built on denunciations or fallacies or stereotypes. The talk didn't go down too well, except with a few individuals who sought me out privately while I was there to thank me for having said what I did. These are the individuals who very quietly encouraged me in my attempt to get that first conference started. And it worked.

One of them was a friend of Khrushchev. That helped too, I guess. That played some part in what was to happen later when I was invited to see Khrushchev. The Dartmouth Conference background was helpful in setting the stage for my mission to Khrushchev. The Russians knew, I think, that I was genuinely interested in peace between the two countries. They knew I didn't hesitate to criticize my own country for its approaches to peace outside a genuine multilateral frame.

Then there was the matter of the Cuban crisis at the time of the Dartmouth Conference in Andover. This conference was used as something of an exchange post at a very difficult time. A friend of mine who was very close to the Vatican had come to the Dartmouth Conference to see whether the Pope might have some part to play that was acceptable to both sides in heading both nations off from their collision course.

The Dartmouth Conference in 1962 led to my trip to Moscow several months later as emissary for Pope John.[1] The Pope wanted to explore the possibilities of greater religious freedom inside the Soviet Union and to obtain the release of his friend, Joseph Cardinal Slipyj, from prison in the Ukraine.

The total process leading to my trip to Moscow in 1962 was a complicated one. I come back to your opening question. That's why I said nothing happens from a standing start.

QUESTION: What would you say are the hoped for results of the Dartmouth Conferences?

COUSINS: It's probably incremental rather than fundamental.

[1] For an account of this mission, see Norman Cousins, *The Improbable Triumvirate* (New York: Norton, 1972).

Certain things that pop up might not come to view otherwise. The conferences are valuable, I think, atmospherically. It's quite possible that the Soviets attach considerable importance to it.

Such being the case, they come to it perhaps better briefed by their government than we are by ours. As a consequence, we get a rather good reading on what's going on in the minds of the Soviet government: what their expectations are; what the issues are that they'd like to try out on us.

In this way a number of issues with respect to the test ban were aired very early. There's no doubt in my mind that the Dartmouth Conference had some part to play in the eventual treaty that came about. The same could also be said of the Pugwash Conference and of a number of other probes that were going on. All these efforts, I think, were useful. That is not to say that if there were no Dartmouth, if there were no Pugwash, you would not have had a test ban. Of course you would have. But something else would have had to take their place.

QUESTION: Why is there so much secrecy surrounding Dartmouth? Might it not be more useful if more people knew about the meetings?

COUSINS: There's no attempt to be secret about Dartmouth. Perhaps if I say a word about how the Dartmouth Conference operates and a little more about its purpose, you may be able to understand why we don't seek publicity for it. It's one thing to be secret; it's another thing not to blow a trumpet.

Any probe, by its very nature, has to be very carefully conducted. You don't want anyone to hold back for extraneous reasons. If you had reporters at the conference, you might just as well turn everything over to official diplomacy in the full glare of publicity. If the purpose is to try to get at underlying causes not readily discernible and to try to get people on both sides to be open with one another, you don't want extraneous things to get in the way. There's nothing like a reporter or a photographer in the room to cause people to clam up—or, what is worse, to play to a gallery.

Since you want to be able to inform your government of anything that ought to be explored further on the official level, you don't want to jeopardize that particular undertaking by premature publicity. You can kill off your prospects because the government may not be ready to have public announcements made concerning its position. Later, with progress in that direction, it may be feasible for the government to do so.

Whenever you have a talking partner, any publicity can affect him as much as it affects you. Sometimes it affects him more; only he can decide whether publicity is welcome or useful. On some issues the Russians do not like or may not be ready for public statements concerning their positions on issues before their government has made an open announcement.

At the end of the Dartmouth Conference we do hold a press conference, and we do identify in general outline the matters that were discussed. However, it's not in the nature of this particular conference to seek public attention.

QUESTION: Are there certain types of issues that are best dealt with in the Dartmouth atmosphere?

COUSINS: Yes. I'll give you some examples. On the nuclear test ban, our side at the very start wanted to find out whether there was any chance that the Soviets were genuinely interested. Obviously, countries are eager to avoid public condemnation. But it's quite possible for a government to take a public position on an issue without any real intention of making it official policy. Our job was to find out whether they seriously wanted a test ban apart from what they said publicly.

They were interested in the same question. They wanted to find out if the United States was seriously interested and what the significance was of our insistence on inspections. They were trying to find out whether we were genuinely interested in having a verifiable basis for detecting tests, or whether we were using inspection as a device to accomplish something we couldn't achieve on another level; namely, access to their secrets.

We had been flying over the Soviet Union with our U-2's, as everyone knew. Our military, a number of times, had complained about the fact that the Russians had the advantage; they knew an awful lot about what we were doing and we didn't know as much about what they were doing. There was the implication that this was poor sportsmanship, or that somehow they were obligated to give us parity in that respect. The Russians had no intention of opening up and, knowing that we were being rather petulant about it, didn't want the test ban to become the device for giving us successes in a field in which they had been able to frustrate us officially. Games that nations play.

So this is what they were trying to find out—exactly why we wanted inspection. I think both sides were able to convince themselves that there was a possibility of agreement. We were convinced they really wanted a test ban and they were similarly convinced that we wanted one. The next question was how to get around the specific obstacles concerning inspection. This had to be pursued of course quite apart from the Dartmouth Conference.

We were also useful, I think, in identifying for our government a number of other areas in which agreements might be possible, one being the desire to cool it in West Berlin and not to allow it to become a showdown issue between the two countries. The Soviet Union had its obligations in East Germany, as we had to West Germany, but the Soviet Union was as eager to set limits to those differences as we were.

The big contribution perhaps was in the area of trade. In 1971 trade was very nominal. The list of tradeable items was laughably small. That list had to be withdrawn and a genuine basis for trade had to be established. Here the work done in preparation for the conference was almost as important as what happened at the conference. We exchanged working papers. These papers on both sides, though they originated with individuals, at least on our side, had the advantage of both government scrutiny and government suggestion. We were able to use the facilities available to David Rockefeller[2] to prepare comprehensive statements concerning the possibilities of trade, the difficulties in the way of it, and to indicate how these difficulties might be overcome. Trade, three years ago, under two hundred million dollars, will in 1974 be well in excess of one billion dollars.

It's hard to calibrate the precise part that the Dartmouth Conference has had in that increase, but it's possible we were a factor.

[2] Chairman of the Board and Chief Executive Officer of the Chase Manhattan Bank and a Dartmouth Conference participant.

QUESTION: You might want to talk about how the delegates are selected. At least from the American point of view, is there an attempt to include new people every year, or is there emphasis on continuity?

COUSINS: Both. The thing that we do is to begin with some discussion of what the essential subjects should be. We try to limit them to three or four. Having done so we naturally try to get people for each of those areas. The sequence would be: one, a decision as to whether we want a conference at all; two, if we are going to go ahead with the conference, what the fruitful areas of discussion would be; three, given these areas, who are the people who might be expected to make some contribution?

This sequence is not completed at one time. We might have five or six meetings. The question as to whether to have a conference at all might take more than one meeting—two or three. The question of areas to be covered could be spread over more than one or two meetings. The matter of the participants would involve a process wider than a single discussion. We might begin with some correspondence asking for nominations.

Necessarily these planning discussions take a somewhat different form depending on whether the meeting is going to be held in the United States or the Soviet Union. In the very nature of the case, if we get an invitation from the Soviet side, then the center of gravity for the meeting is over there. If the meeting is going to be held in the United States, then we take the initiative with place, time, and arrangements. By and large the planning tends to be divided into those three parts.

QUESTION: Joseph Johnson, who attended the second Dartmouth Conference, has written that "every time we got a new topic, it was opened by a 45-minute propagandistic cleared speech by one of the Russians—which got awfully damned monotonous." Do you find this still to be the case?

COUSINS: No. The reason we don't is that since so many of us felt as Joe Johnson did after that meeting, we had a very frank talk with the Russians and told them that we didn't think that this particular approach was very salutary. We understood that some Russians were attempting to score points, knowing that they were being rated by one or more of their colleagues. It was terribly time-consuming and, as Joe says, damned monotonous. We didn't go a long way for the purpose of being witnesses to the process by which Soviet representatives score Brownie points in their society. That was why we decided to divide future conferences into working groups, where papers would be exchanged in advance and where we would be speaking to specific things that were already in motion. This is not to say that there are no declamations at all. We take it for granted now, that at some point, most of the Russians are going to seek catharsis. But we can moderate it now somewhat. We don't have the occasion for it as we did before. We are already in motion on papers that have been circulated, so that these things come more in the nature of carom shots than frontal attempts.

QUESTION: Would you say that the conference could hope to change the attitudes of the individuals participating?

COUSINS: It's changed my mind on some things.

QUESTION: The Soviet participants?

COUSINS: It affects them individually, I think. One of the principal benefits is that it gives the individuals a chance to widen their view on what the basic factors are that affect the relationship of the two countries. In their own discussions or considerations of basic issues, I think they develop a more knowledgeable base on which to stand.

QUESTION: Marshall Shulman has written that nothing impresses a Russian more than a Rockefeller as a Dartmouth participant. Could you explain this?

COUSINS: Yes, I think so. The Russians respect power. The epitome of capitalism is the millionaire. The Rockefeller family is the world symbol of family wealth and station. As far back as the 1930s, Joseph Davies, the U.S. ambassador to the Soviet Union, observed that Moscow loves millionaires. Some Russians tend to feel the same way about millionaires that we do about movie stars. The Russians have renounced royalty, but like many people who renounce royalty, there are aspects of it that bulk very large in their sentiments. If you go to the Russian museums now, you see that the way of life of the czars creates a great deal of sympathetic curiosity. The cathedrals are maintained; the palaces of the czars are maintained. This is part of the Russian heritage. There's nothing really inconsistent.

They've got great respect for power and they like to deal with the realities of power. They've got some fixed attitudes about power in a capitalist society. They tend—since this is part of the dogma, and since the dogma tends to exaggerate this aspect of American society—to think they are dealing with ultimate realities, ultimate power.

In addition to being a member of the Rockefeller family, brother of former Governor Rockefeller, David Rockefeller happens to be a very reasonable human being. He tends to be very direct, very open; he is not given to posturing or to tub-thumping. He gives honest answers. There's a combination here of respect for the man as an individual and awe that he's a Rockefeller, and the most capitalistic Rockefeller at that.

QUESTION: Is one part of the process of planning for a Dartmouth Conference consulting with those in official capacity in the United States?

COUSINS: Sometimes. If there are degrees of sensitivity where what we do requires knowledge of context, we try to find out as much about that context as we can. In the present case, as an example, there is a question in my mind whether I ought to resign from the next Dartmouth Conference as chairman of the American side because of the Solzhenitsyn case. If I do resign that would run counter to the purpose of what Dartmouth is all about, which is to accept the fact of differences and to use Dartmouth as the opportunity to make known our feelings concerning these differences.

In the past this approach has worked out very well. For example, with respect to the exit visas of a couple of years ago we were able in a very pointed way to make known the position of American public opinion, and explain that this was not just far-out, unrepresentative voices in the United States. We told the Soviet delegates what the real sentiment was in Congress. We had in the American delegation members of Congress from both parties. The Russians claimed that the exit visa situation was an internal affair. We didn't deny that internal affairs were outside the scope of the conference. On the other hand, if they wanted to know whether they were going to get a most favored nation treaty through the Congress, it was only fair to them to let them know what the considerations were that would affect that particular decision by the Congress. This served a useful purpose. The withdrawal of the exit visa tax may or may not have been related to that exercise.

But we've got a somewhat different issue here, I think, in the Solzhenitsyn case. Sakharov and Solzhenitsyn have said that the only reason they're alive is because of world public opinion, and they've made a specific appeal to intellectuals to support them. This is a somewhat different situation than the one of the exit visas. The battleground here has been rather clearly defined, and I just wonder whether my failure to resign in protest would be harmful.

QUESTION: If you did resign do you think the attitude of the Soviet government toward Dartmouth might be changed?

COUSINS: Possibly.

QUESTION: In some damaging way?

COUSINS: Yes. As I say, the conference is probably a lot closer to officialdom in the Soviet Union than it is here. First, individuals there don't take initiatives the way we do. The Soviet individuals, as individuals, I think, don't enjoy that particular right or even opportunity.

So my resignation could produce an adverse government reaction to Dartmouth itself. This is one of the things I want to think very seriously about. It's a terrible dilemma. If I were an individual participant, I could withdraw from the conference in protest. The question, though, is whether I would be right in jeopardizing a lot of effort that's gone into this—the Kettering Foundation has had a staff working on it; Mr. Rockefeller has his people working on trade matters. So it's not an easy decision.

QUESTION: When the group formulates recommendations do you have in mind the bureaucratic restraints which might limit implementation of the policies that you're recommending to each of the two countries?

COUSINS: We try not to concern ourselves with those limitations, since our purpose is to transcend them in order to operate in ways in which those limitations would be controlling. We recognize, of course, that any opportunities we might perceive for lessening of tensions between two countries may be aborted because of the bureaucratic process. But I don't think this is any reason for abandoning the attempt.

QUESTION: Do you think there's any danger in establishing unofficial contacts?

COUSINS: Yes.

QUESTION: What might those be?

COUSINS: The obvious ones. First, on the level of governments, if this is not done with care, competence, and knowledgeability, false signals might issue from such meetings. From the government point of view, this could be wasteful and harmful. Next, confusion concerning basic purposes and positions could retard efforts of a more central nature. The people in government tend to be rather wary of private efforts because of these reasons. And yet there is a role for citizen action whenever you have basic issues of peace. You can't take the position that governments, left unattended, are the final arbiters of what the peace requires, or are in themselves adequate mechanisms for perceiving and pursuing those opportunities that are essential to advancing peace.

I think that citizens do have a role in a democratic society in working for the best that is possible, as they see it. Governments don't always arrive at the correct answers by themselves. They tend to move in the direction of power. That which adds to power becomes the magnetic attraction for government; that which tends to restrict government power produces in government little enthusiasm. But when you live in a world in which the security of all peoples is represented by the control of power and not by the pursuit of power, then you've got to recognize that officialdom may be more a part of the problem than a part of the answer.

THREE

THE BILATERAL AND MULTILATERAL MEETINGS OF THE INTERNATIONAL PRESS INSTITUTE

ERNEST MEYER

ERNEST MEYER, a French press official, was Director of the International Press Institute (IPI) from 1969 to 1975. He describes the bilateral and multilateral meetings run by the Institute, an independent professional association of journalists with headquarters in Zurich, Switzerland. By organizing meetings at which members of the press from different nations may interact, the IPI attempts to eliminate misunderstandings that often produce international conflicts and those that result when a conflict situation already exists. The rules of the Institute limit membership to countries where the press is more or less free; this means that participants in these meetings cannot consider conflicts, or potential conflicts, where nations do not have a free press.——Eds.

THE INTERNATIONAL PRESS INSTITUTE is an association of 1,900 leaders of the written and broadcasting press and of journalism professors from 65 countries. It has no links to governments or international governmental organizations. Although an independent association operating on its own responsibility, IPI maintains close contact with other professional international, regional, and national associations, and often deals with governments, the United Nations, and UNESCO, especially when controversial matters arise involving journalists and newspapers.

One of IPI's most important aims since its creation in 1951 is stressed in the Preamble to its Constitution:

World peace depends upon understanding between peoples and peoples. If peoples are to understand one another, it is essential that they have good information. Therefore, a fundamental step toward understanding among peoples is to bring about understanding among the journalists of the world.

In accordance with this belief, there is established an organisation to work toward the following objectives:. . . . The achievement of understanding among journalists and so among peoples.

To realize this goal, numerous bilateral and multilateral meetings have been held or sponsored by IPI.

Objectives

The initial idea for arranging these meetings in the early postwar period was that the press might be used to contribute to a better understanding of international problems across borders and to create links between formerly hostile nations. Meetings between editors of different nationalities were considered to be the most appropriate way to overcome basic ignorance of other mentalities and ways of thinking. Such meetings were promoted in various contexts: through the annual General Assemblies, through the organization of bilateral and regional meetings and, later on, through individual contacts and exchange programs. IPI's series of bilateral and multilateral meetings, the focus of this paper, were arranged following a decision made in 1953 that the moment was appropriate for IPI to play a more active part in the improvement of relations across individual frontiers.

Since 1954, the year the first bilateral meeting was held, IPI has run the following meetings:

BILATERAL MEETINGS

Participants	Location	Date
French-German	Strasbourg	January 1954
	Strasbourg	October 1954
	Frankfurt	April 1955
	Rouen	October 1955
	Munich	April 1956
	Marseilles	October 1956
	Köln	November 1957

BILATERAL MEETINGS (Continued)

Participants	Location	Date
	Nancy	March 1958
	Heidelberg	January 1959
	Lyons	February 1960
Anglo-German	London	May 1955
	London	November 1959
	Bonn	October 1960
Korean-Japanese	Tokyo	November 1966
	Seoul	September 1967
	Tokyo	June 1968
	Seoul	April 1969
	Fukuoka	November 1969
Dutch-Indonesian	Zurich	September 1956
French-British	Paris	May 1959
Greek-Turkish	Rhodes	February 1961
Canadian-American	Quebec	March 1965
	Williamsburg	February/March 1968
	Toronto	February 1974
Austrian-Italian	Zurich	April 1970
	Bolzano	April 1971
American-Japanese	Honolulu	November 1970
	Kyoto	November 1971
	San Diego	November 1972
	Tokyo	October 1973

MULTILATERAL MEETINGS

Participants	Location	Date
French-American-British	Paris	May 1957
Canadian-American-British-German-French	Paris	May 1959

The objectives of these meetings divide into two general categories, climate creating and conflict preventing, although at times these functions do overlap. It is, at times, difficult to distinguish these objectives, but, in general, climate-creating meetings are nonspecific and informative in nature, while conflict-preventing meetings deal with specific, controversial issues. Among the meetings described hereafter, the first French-German meetings in early

1954 were mainly directed at the mutual information of journalists in the two countries and resulted in the creation of the first post World War II personal and professional contacts between the two countries. When the problem of the Saar plebiscite came up, with the danger of new and bitter controversies between the two countries, the conflict-preventing aspects prevailed. The Austrian-Italian meeting on the Alto Adige (South Tyrol) dispute between the two countries, on the other hand, is an example of a conflict-preventing meeting.

Content

The seminars differ widely. Bilateral meetings tend to take up the whole complex of relationships between two countries; multilateral meetings are mainly devoted to particular issues, and primarily to their press aspects. When we discuss press councils or give out papers on the free flow of information between East and West, we neglect the relationship of the participating countries and only deal with the political, economic, legal, and communication aspects of problems on the agenda.

The choice of participants and methods of procedure are also very different. In multilateral meetings, experts—not necessarily journalists, publishers, or broadcasters—on specific issues inform the participants on the nature of problems, and, to a certain extent, the discussion that follows is an addendum to the reports. Participants in these discussions are publishers and editors, selected from among those with a particular interest in a problem. Once again for simplification, bilateral meetings are usually round-table discussions, while multilateral meetings are more like panel sessions.

The French-German meetings in 1954 and 1955, the first sponsored by IPI, were run with the intention of bringing together French and German editors to create a climate in which relations between the two countries might improve. As it happened, the meetings were held at a moment when the question of the Saar referendum had brought the relationship between the two countries to a state of critical antagonism. The reports on these first meetings truly reflect the atmosphere of this experiment, which had tremendous importance for IPI:

> Three sessions were held at the Strasbourg meeting. At the first the discussions centered on the shortcomings of the French press, at the second on those of the German, and the final session was devoted to discussion of what could be done to improve the position. At its close the meeting called on the press in Germany and France to eliminate misunderstandings and prejudices. The participants pledged themselves in a gentleman's agreement, to bring to their work objectivity, dignity and an awareness of the responsibilities involved. They urged that the number of foreign correspondents should be increased, that personal contacts between editors should be encouraged and that articles on political issues should be exchanged. And the editors arranged to meet again within the year.
>
> Since that meeting, nine further French-German meetings have been arranged, alternately in France and Germany. In the course of these meetings most of the leading editors of the two countries have come to know one another personally. Both press and political relations between the two countries have, of course, so improved that later there was not the vital need of these meetings which there was originally, but both sides insisted that they should continue to be held at least once a year.

The first meetings, climate creating in nature, were followed by a series of conflict-preventing meetings that resulted in editors from both countries agreeing to print signed articles from editors from the other side on controversial issues. These articles, written for foreign readers, were moderate in tone and content and had the secondary effect of influencing the content of articles written by the same journalists in their home press.

Other bilateral and multilateral meetings, like the Canadian-American-British-German-French meeting, the French-American-British meetings, the American-European Common Market meeting, and the Japanese-European Common Market meeting, were aimed mainly at an exchange of information on important economic and political topics of the participating countries.

The history of the American-Japanese meetings, which have become an annual gathering, is an interesting example of an information-orientated meeting evolving into conflict-preventing discussions. The origin of these meetings is linked to events in 1970—the sudden proclamation of the Nixon doctrine and the emergence of the textile crisis between Japan and the United States. The general reaction of the Japanese mass media—written press and broadcasting—had been hostile and sometimes aggressive. It was felt that an exchange of views between Japanese and American editors could be helpful in improving the atmosphere of the forthcoming intergovernmental negotiations.

This was the moment when IPI was asked by its American Committee to take the initiative for setting up a bilateral meeting, which was held in Honolulu in November 1970. The meeting, a confrontation of some fifteen American, fifteen Japanese editors, was essentially dominated by the Japanese presentation of the contentious textile crisis and the American import tax policy. The impact of this meeting was reflected by the appearance of numerous articles in the American press, in which the American editors demonstrated moderation and an appreciation of the Japanese position.

At the third meeting held in San Diego in November 1972, I introduced the meeting in the following terms which give informally the concept and goals of these meetings:

Two years ago, when we all gathered for the first time and sat down in Honolulu for the first of our bilateral meetings, few of us foresaw the changes and reshaping of East-West (Japanese-American) relations that were to take place less than a year later. And no one, I venture to suggest, anticipated the extraordinary speed of this reshaping.

The events of our time will show that this initial meeting of senior pressmen of the two countries, which tentatively probed the problems and assessed their importance, was perfectly well-timed. And history will show that, if the reasons for holding the first meeting were arguable then, they are no longer so today. Its importance, and that of those that are following, are vital if the press of the two countries is to march in step with the moving diplomacy of the governments of East and West.

In Honolulu we were not entirely sure what we were aiming at, where the target lay and what we were attempting to achieve.

Today, at the third meeting, we know our target with more precision.

In 1970 we spoke calmly of the "Nixon doctrine" in Asia. Last year we spoke anxiously of the "Nixon shocks"—the very phraseology shows that we were shaken out of our belief that we knew what was going on. This year we should be in a position to assess the effects of the last two momentous years. Perhaps this year we shall speak—with confidence this time—of the "press doctrine" in regard to East-West relations.

The last two Austrian-Italian meetings were decided on after a careful analysis of the state of the relationship between these two countries on the question of the South Tyrol, and after detailed negotiations with the South Tyrolean journalists and policy-makers. The two meetings, held with the active involvement of the two governments concerned, represented by their ambassadors, contributed visibly to the efforts made by the two governments to give real content to the "package deal" of laws made in order to end a controversy which had lasted from 1919 and had poisoned the relations between the two countries for the previous fifteen years.

Methods of and Conditions for Bilateral Meetings

Over the years IPI has learned that a number of factors should be considered before taking the initiative for setting up a bilateral meeting. Before a decision is made preliminary studies are needed of:

1. The causes of the dispute.
2. Appreciation of the nature of the dispute.
3. Intranational factors affecting the degree of willingness to proceed to a rational study of the contentious issues.
4. Appreciation of the "influence factor" potentialities of the mass media.

Additionally, an evaluation is needed of background factors that may influence the meeting. These include,

Timing. The unsuccessful attempts over a long period to organize an Austrian-Italian meeting and the initial difficulties in setting up the first American-Japanese meeting demonstrated how important it is to choose the right moment. An initiative taken too early can fail through lack of interest on the part of the concerned policy-makers, or through lack of response from the mass media in one or both of the countries. Choice of the psychologically right moment is a matter of knowing the state of mind of the parties, of making a proper interpretation of the views expressed, and, to a certain extent, of professional intuition.

Evaluation of public opinion. The degree of interest shown by journalists in a bilateral meeting is conditioned by public reaction on controversial topics. The foreseeable results of such meetings must "make news." The press can be mobilized on a political issue only in terms of its news value.

Choice of participants. The choice of participants invited to these meetings involves judgments not only on the individual's personality, but also on his position and ability to effectively transmit views.

Choice of a meeting place. Even in such private meetings, the choice of a meeting place can have a pronounced psychological effect in two ways: the choice itself, which can be seen as an indication of a certain orientation, can influence participation. The site can also affect public interest and media coverage. Before IPI arranged the first Japanese-American bilateral meeting in Honolulu, a location approximately midway between San Francisco and Tokyo, the American Committee had invited members of the Japanese press to meet in San Francisco. This invitation was never answered.

The Agenda. In the case of a meeting aimed at climate creating and at facilitating conflict preventing negotiations, the topics chosen should consider extremist positions on contentious issues in all countries. The agenda should allow for the greatest possible chance for agreement on moderate conclusions.

Semantic problems. Numerous controversies are provoked by semantic errors. The same terms in different languages do not

always have the exact same meaning, which can result in misinterpretations. Careful study of potential semantic difficulties should
precede a meeting.

Detailed special knowledge. Selection of participants should take
into account the need to include persons having special knowledge
of specific problems that may be raised in the course of a session.

Analysis of the Meetings

IPI does not try to replace policy-makers; its goals are not to provide solutions to problems or to act contrary to the aims of government. Rather what IPI tries to do is to analyze a situation, to provide participants with inside information, and most important, to
create a climate in which the policy-makers can usefully work.
Completely independent of governmental influence, IPI attempts
to contribute to the creation of a climate favoring the reduction or
prevention of conflicts, and also to publicize the facts and circulate
the views of the concerned governments, thus giving them an opportunity to expose their views informally without consideration of
protocol factors.

The success of these meetings is explained in part by the fact
that everyone can speak openly. Unless specific authorization is
given, there is no quotation for attribution. Results of these meetings are published in IPI's publications and sent out to all newspapers that are members of IPI. Often results are widely published in
the countries involved in the meetings, thus contributing to the creation of a climate beneficial to conflict resolution.

It is difficult to measure the direct or indirect impact of these
meetings. Sometimes the real effect appears only years afterward,
when the literature devoted to a specific period or event is published, and the findings of these meetings are analyzed by theore-
ticians. Sometimes, meetings are only poorly covered by the news
media, but later extensive treatment appears in specialized periodi-
cals. Other times, on the contrary, media coverage is satisfactory,
but academic appreciation is poor. It is impossible to predict ac-

curately a meeting's consequences, since so many factors influence reactions.

We are independent people—individuals, not organizations—so there is a flexible approach to everything. The basis for whatever authority IPI may have is that we have established a reputation for going deeply into issues. IPI's objectivity cannot be questioned because we have members on all sides of an issue. We are concerned with the credibility of IPI—its moral authority, independence, objectivity, and the demonstration of the influence which it can have on governments. Governments and international organizations have shown an interest in what we are doing, and have at times sent observers to our meetings.

Tolerance, moderation, knowledge, know-how, and the desire to further understanding between the peoples of the world are the characteristics of these meetings, whose usefulness is unquestionable.

PART TWO

The Role of Private Persons
in International Dealings

OVERVIEW

P ART TWO is concerned with the role private persons may
play in international dealings, and the cases in this section
deal specifically with the special role of private efforts in
time of international conflict and in one domestic conflict with international overtones.

States may employ the services of private individuals as intermediaries. Either acting on their own or affiliated with a nongovernmental organization, private individuals may serve as unofficial go-
betweens for two or more nations and convey messages and
gather responses without officially committing a government to
any position. At times the initiative for private missions may come
from outside a government structure, but officials are nevertheless
willing to cooperate and avail themselves of the channel—sometimes with enthusiasm, other times with suspicion.

An example of a private mission initiated from without yet
smiled upon by government officials is the pair of visits to the Soviet Union in 1962 and 1963 made by Norman Cousins, editor of
the *Saturday Review* and an organizer and participant in the Dartmouth Conference series since the beginning.[1] Cousins had been
approached by a representative of Pope John XXIII shortly before
the Dartmouth Conference scheduled for October 1962 in Andover, Massachusetts, about the Pontiff's desire to improve the

[1] For a detailed account of the two visits, see Norman Cousins, *The Improbable Triumvirate* (New York: Norton, 1972).

chances for peace. Through the Soviet delegation at the Conference a request for a Cousins' visit on behalf of the Pope was relayed to Moscow. Word that Khrushchev had given his approval for the visit came through in November.

Before undertaking the mission, Cousins wanted to be assured that the Kennedy administration had no objection, and he was invited to meet with the President shortly before his departure at Christmas time. The President spoke generally of his desire to reduce tensions between the two nations and specifically of his eagerness for an agreement limiting nuclear testing. The issue holding up agreement on this subject appeared to be the need for on-site inspection.

When Cousins met with the Premier in Moscow, Khrushchev raised the issue of inspecting nuclear tests, contending that such inspection might be used as a device for opening up his country to snooping. Cousins replied by stressing the President's genuine desire for agreement.

Upon his return to the United States and before his second visit to the Soviet Union, Cousins reported in detail to the President on his talk with Khrushchev. The official negotiations between Ambassadors Dean and Kuznetsov in Geneva on a test ban treaty had come to a halt on the issue of the number of on-site inspections. The President knew Cousins was planning to return to the Soviet Union and asked him to convey to Khrushchev the possibility that there has been an honest misunderstanding on this issue and that the way could be cleared for a fresh start.

During his second meeting with Khrushchev in April 1963 when the discussion turned to the matter of a nuclear test ban, Cousins assured the Premier that the United States really wanted a test ban:

> I had come to see him, I said, on no official mission; I was a private citizen. President Kennedy, knowing I was to see [Khrushchev], had asked me to try to clarify the Soviet misunderstanding of the American position on the test ban. If [Khrushchev] construed the American position on inspections to mean that we actually did not want a treaty banning such testing, then that interpretation was in error.[2]

[2] *Ibid.*, p. 92.

Khrushchev responded that the United States had made him appear foolish by changing its position on the number of tests after he had gotten agreement from his Council of Ministers, but he did offer to begin the negotiations afresh. Cousins reported back to the President on Khrushchev's offer and his readiness to receive an official initiative from the United States.[3]

The Cousins channel was one of several, both official and private, through which the Soviet Union and the United States were simultaneously exploring the problem of a test ban treaty. Another private effort (which came to be known as the "Angels Project") to facilitate the process whereby the Soviet Union and the United States could begin to agree on ways to lessen the threat of nuclear warfare was initiated by a distinguished scientist, Leo Szilard.[4] His idea was to get around the impasse on disarmament negotiations by finding out in unofficial meetings what might be acceptable to the Soviets. Although the project was never actually launched, in its preparatory stages it overlapped and reinforced other ongoing efforts that helped to clarify issues, to feed new ideas into official deliberations, both within and between the two governments, and to prepare the way for successful official negotiations.

Szilard had helped to create the first sustained nuclear chain reaction and was instrumental in initiating the Manhattan Project for the development of the atomic bomb. From 1942 until the end of the war he conducted nuclear research at the University of Chicago where he participated in the construction of the first nuclear reactor; in 1946 he became professor of biophysics at the university.

After the atomic bomb was dropped on Hiroshima, Szilard became an ardent promoter of peaceful uses of atomic energy and of international control of nuclear weapons. He became chairman of the subcommittee on International Conversations Among Scientists of the American Academy of Arts and Sciences' Committee

---

[3] Theodore Sorensen, Special Counsel to President Kennedy, reports that one of the factors in the President's continued hope for and efforts toward a test-ban treaty was the hint Khrushchev gave to Cousins (and others) that he hoped for a fresh signal from the United States. See *Kennedy* (New York: Harper & Row, 1965), p. 729.

[4] Volume II of Leo Szilard's papers to be published by the M.I.T. Press will contain the correspondence concerning the "Angels Project" between Szilard and Khrushchev.

on the Public Responsibility of Scientists; and also participated in a number of Pugwash meetings. At the August 1962 meeting held in Cambridge, England, Szilard talked about the issue of arms control with a Soviet colleague—a long-time Pugwash participant whom Szilard had met many times.

When he returned to the United States, Szilard discussed this conversation with colleagues and with several people in the administration. What he found in the administration were a number of individuals "on the side of the Angels," willing to give up, if necessary, certain temporary advantages for the sake of ending the arms race. He found those Angels frustrated by their uncertainty about Soviet willingness to accept *any* agreement providing for controls or safeguards. Which approach to this problem the Russians would find acceptable was an even greater unknown. Although those Angels had had, on occasion, very friendly, informal conversations with Russian negotiators, those conversations had not furnished guidance on what kinds of arms control might be acceptable. Although Szilard believed that some of the obstacles to agreement were indeed formidable, he also felt that other impasses might be the result of failures in communication. More profitable exploration of the Soviet position on various forms of control might be carried on in privately arranged conversations, where neither side would feel committed to viewpoints expressed.

In Szilard's view, the Soviet participants would speak freely only if instructed to by Chairman Khrushchev. Szilard had previously met Khrushchev, but before seeking to enlist his support for the project, Szilard again spoke with members of the administration and some potential participants who encouraged him to take the proposal to Khrushchev.

In October 1962 Szilard wrote to Khrushchev asking him to support a project that would bring together unofficially three American "Angels" (selected from the junior ranks of government or from consultants to the government on arms control) and three of their Soviet counterparts for discussions, not negotiations, on a proposal for the first stages of a disarmament agreement. The proposal would commit no one, except those who had prepared it. He received a favorable response.

Although this was to be an unofficial meeting, Szilard viewed the endorsement of the U.S. government as essential. But here he ran into trouble. Misunderstandings over the nature of the project began to arise in the administration. There was concern in high places lest the USSR regard the meeting as a negotiation and the participants as official representatives. With a ruling from the head of the Arms Control and Disarmament Agency that its employees or members of the Advisory Committee could not participate, the project hit another snag. At this point Szilard was now very uncertain about going forward. He specifically questioned the utility of the project unless he—and the Soviets—could be assured that the American participants would be able to convey their conclusions to the President.

In the meantime there had been major developments in official channels of communication. In June 1963 President Kennedy announced that three-power talks (the United Kingdom, the United States, and the Soviet Union) would be held in Moscow. He sent a delegation led by W. Averell Harriman to Moscow in July 1963. Harriman reported that the negotiations were wound up in about ten days and the result was the Moscow Treaty or the Partial Nuclear Test-Ban Treaty which became effective on October 10, 1963. The treaty banned nuclear weapons tests in the atmosphere, in outer space, and under water.[5]

Needless to say, that wrote "finis" to the Angels Project. For any international action there are multiple causes and it would be impossible to identify the exact contribution made by any one approach or effort, official or unofficial. One thing is clear, however. Only governments have the power to alter positions. Szilard and others realized this and therefore aimed their private initiatives on arms control at facilitating official agreement by clarifying positions and by functioning as auxiliary channels of communication. Szilard, sensitive to this political reality, hesitated to proceed without assurances that the results of their meetings would be introduced into official deliberations.

How to end the protracted war in Vietnam was also taken up

---

[5] While the Dean–Kuznetsov talks in Geneva had not led directly to the negotiated settlement, keeping the talks going, in Arthur Dean's view, was valuable for clearing up misunderstandings, clarifying issues, and preparing for the eventual agreement. See his *Test Ban and Disarmament* (New York: Harper & Row, 1966), p. 37.

through a number of private and governmental channels. One of the channels initiated for purposes of communicating probes between the North Vietnamese and the United States government involved the use of a private individual as an intermediary between the two governments.

Within days of President Johnson's announcement on July 28, 1965, that he was doubling the strength of U.S. forces, the United States extended secret feelers to the North Vietnamese concerning a key issue—control of South Vietnam in the aftermath of a U.S. pull-out. One approach was through official channels, specifically both Canadian and French. But President Johnson had also authorized George W. Ball, then Under Secretary of State to put out unofficially a secret peace feeler, provided it was disavowable if anything leaked. Edmund A. Gullion, dean of the Fletcher School of Law and Diplomacy at Tufts University and retired Foreign Service officer who had been posted to Indochina in the 1950s, was selected to be the secret emissary in Ball's words, "partly because he was known to the North Vietnamese leaders as an advocate of Vietnamese independence—both from French and from Communist rule—and also because he was a superb reporter who would obey his tightly written instructions to the letter."[6]

As a private citizen Gullion was able to travel to Washington and then to Paris without attracting much notice. The introduction he used with the North Vietnamese was similar to the one Cousins used with Khrushchev: he was a private citizen who had been in touch with his government. Gullion had several meetings with North Vietnamese officials during 1965, but in the end nothing concrete came of his mission.[7]

Unofficial Diplomats in Conflict Situations

As we have said, effective official international communication becomes difficult, often impossible, in times of conflict—once-open

---

[6] Benjamin Welles, "A Peace Bid that Failed in 1965 Disclosed by Ex- U.S. Officials," *New York Times*, February 14, 1972, p. 3.

[7] For another very different mission, see the essay in this section written by Harry Ashmore.

channels of communication close or are forced to function in a tense atmosphere that multiplies the dangers of distortion. In such situations, nongovernmental groups or individuals may play various third-party roles: providing a setting where parties in conflict may meet; carrying messages; or otherwise attempting to improve faulty communication. Even the mere act of listening to both sides may provide an opportunity for parties to let off steam and spell out their arguments and demands. In addition, private groups or individuals may be able to counteract the accusatory atmosphere that usually characterizes the relationship of parties in conflict and to create an atmosphere more conducive to problem-solving.

Frequently when disputes have reached the crisis stage direct communication between the parties breaks down and third-party intervention may be called for. If and when parties do agree to negotiate directly, this usually, although not always, betokens a willingness to begin bargaining. In traditional third-party roles—mediation, conciliation, arbitration, judicial settlement—a third party enters the picture with the consent of the parties involved for the purpose of assisting them in finding a mutually agreed-upon way to settle their dispute. The third party may be official—e.g., a state not a party to the dispute, one or more representatives of an international organization or grouping such as the United Nations or the nonaligned movement, or it may be a private individual or institution.[8] But without some willingness on the part of the parties to a dispute to settle their differences peacefully, the official third-party intervention is likely to be ineffective.[9]

Private individuals and groups may offer their services or enter conflicts as unofficial intruders. It may be possible to start unofficial discussions, as distinct from official talks, without the need for any official concessions; moreover, at any time the third party may be disowned. In the pre-negotiation stage, before parties have agreed to discuss their differences officially, unofficial diplomats may pro-

[8] Vratislav Pechota, "Complementary Structures of Third-Party Settlement of International Disputes," New York, UNITAR, 1971, p. 3.
[9] There are thresholds of disputes when the parties involved have agreed that a dispute is somewhat negotiable. In that instance the role of normal diplomatic channels or of official third parties is clear. Prior to such a decision it may be impossible for such bodies to take initiatives without being invited to do so by the governments involved.

vide the means through which the parties to a dispute may test the water for concessions and changes of policies, or sometimes serve as channels for communication if none exist. Once negotiations begin, the unofficial diplomat may provide auxiliary channels of communication where parties can test out new positions without risking commitment.

The Functions of Unofficial Diplomats

The range of threats and promises, as we have said, open to a U.S. Secretary of State or any foreign minister differs enormously from that available to private individuals and nongovernmental groups. Private groups tend to be weak in many resources—often even lacking the funds necessary to pay for their maintenance in conciliation activities. Yet despite the resources and capabilities official status confers, official mediators also have limitations. In Adam Curle's view, the advantages and limitations of an official intervenor both derive from the same source— namely, that an official serves a government:

> When the government concerned is the government of a powerful country its diplomats can be very persuasive: they can suggest terms that will be most advantageous to those who will accept them and most damaging to those who will not; they can sponsor complicated bargains and trade-offs to promote their nation's policies; they can put pressure on smaller countries to support them in the United Nations and elsewhere.
>
> At the same time, they are clearly recognized for what they are: the agents of a country whose policy is likely to be suspected in direct proportion to the power of that country.[10]

Powerful nations may be able to offer attractive terms to induce nations to settle a conflict or threaten alternatives that may force nations to settle, but it is difficult to coerce nations into "settling" a dispute; even if that can be accomplished, imposition of terms will not eradicate the roots of conflict. By its nature, Kissinger's role in

[10] Adam Curle, *Making Peace* (London: Tavistock, 1971), p. 228.

the Middle East negotiations of 1974 and 1975 was more than one of mere messenger. With great interests in the outcome of an agreement, the United States promised rewards to the parties and also made threats. The Sinai agreement between Egypt and Israel even calls for the stationing of U.S. civilians on the strategic buffer zones between the two nations. By no stretch of the imagination could Secretary Kissinger be considered a neutral channel of information.

John Burton contends that the 1960s were transition years when it became apparent that only the parties involved in a dispute are in a position to resolve it, and that external coercion has a counterproductive effect. Traditional means of third-party settlement have failed, he believes, exactly because they contain elements of coercion. In Burton's words: "The techniques fail because their objective is settlement by third-party decision-making, or by compromises that do not fully and equitably satisfy the needs and aspirations of all parties. The objective must be agreement which avoids coercion, compromise and third-party decisions and pressures."[11] Others believe that this is too dogmatic and absolute.

Since they have no means of coercion, nongovernmental groups must focus their activities on facilitating independent decision-making by the parties involved to agree to negotiate or, once that decision is made, to resolve their differences through bargaining. The private agent can neither impose solutions nor make offers designed to sweeten surrender or even an unpalatable compromise. Moreover, given the lack of government affiliation, the private party must first establish an authoritative basis for his intervention—why governments should pay attention—unlike government representatives whose authority comes as a consequence of their official position.

In Oran Young's view, the value of nongovernmental entities as potential third parties in conflicts is low because they are weak in resources. In particular, in his view, they lack salience—that is the standing that would convince governments to delegate authority to them. They also, he believes, have low scores in such areas as rel-

[11] John Burton, *Conflict and Communication* (New York, Free Press, 1969), p. 161.

evant information or diplomatic skill, and lack resources and services; in fact their only real strength lies in the area of the basic qualities of impartiality and independence—they favor neither side and are not dependent on or attached to a political entity which has a stake in the outcome of a crisis.[12] In his words, the nongovernmental nature of these institutions and individuals sometimes does allow for substantial detachment from political struggles.

This status of impartiality and independence, however, confers special benefits not always available to government agents. Adam Curle in his analysis of the advantages of private efforts based on first-hand experience in Quaker conciliation efforts in the India–Pakistan dispute in 1965 and the Nigerian civil war in 1968–70, writes that being unattached to an agency of government may give the private conciliator a degree of freedom that an official diplomat can not have. Private individuals may make a unique contribution because:

1. The private diplomat, as a free agent, is not obliged to report back to anyone else or to represent an official policy and can be regarded as an individual with whom people may talk freely without fear of incurring losses if they make admissions of weaknesses.

2. As an individual who is not an agent of government, the private diplomat is free of the constraints that are bound to influence government policies—the need to satisfy the electorate, or special interests—and is free to concentrate on solutions that will work.

3. A private diplomat can move around inconspicuously and without publicity, the diplomatic role often concealed by a personal role such as membership in a religious group or a profession.

4. Private diplomats, as opposed to official diplomats, may find it easier to visit both sides of a dispute.

5. Governments, since they may disavow or ignore private diplomats whenever they want, may be more ready to make use of them.

6. Although he is separate from government, the private diplomat is not necessarily isolated from other groups, and indeed may find ways to collaborate with concerned international agencies, governments, and other private parties.[13]

[12] Oran R. Young, *The Intermediaries: Third Parties in International Crises* (Princeton, N.J.: Princeton University Press, 1967), pp. 108–10.
[13] Curle, *Making Peace*, pp. 231–33.

Third-Party Roles

One authority on international communication contends that "conflict is a breakdown in communication and the chances of conflict increase proportionately as communication decreases."[14] Others would agree that increasing the quantity and quality of communication will not solve underlying causes of conflict and in some cases such causes may be made more apparent as a result of more accurate perceptions. Nevertheless, although communication cannot solve a conflict of interest, it is always a necessary preliminary to finding a solution.

In intense conflict situations there may be no direct communication between the parties in a dispute. One function of third parties is to facilitate communication between disputants and to try to ensure that parties in a conflict receive information in an undistorted form; in some conflicts, however, governments or international organizations playing third-party roles can not gain access to all sides of a dispute. (Secretary Kissinger's success in the Middle East negotiations of 1974 and 1975 was in this respect very rare.) Acting unofficially, either as individuals or attached to nongovernmental organizations, private citizens may possess or be able to open lines of communication to all parties in a dispute. Even when direct or official third-party lines of communication are open, private channels may provide auxiliary means of allowing the disputants to explore ways to ameliorate a conflict situation.

After 1956 there was no direct official communication between Israel and her Arab neighbors until 1974. In this inflamed situation the opportunities for misunderstandings and distortions abound— as do real conflicts of interest. For many reasons, psychological, bureaucratic, and others, these misunderstandings may be perpetuated.[15]

Over the years there have been efforts to establish official communication between the two sides. As special representative of the

[14] James W. Markham, "Communication Research in International Conflict and Cooperation," p. 31, unpublished paper cited in W. Phillips Davison, *Mass Communication and Conflict Resolution* (New York: Praeger, 1974), p. 27.

[15] See on this point, B. Thomas Trout, "Rhetoric Revisited: Political Legitimatization and the Cold War," *International Studies Quarterly* (September 1975), 19:251–84.

Secretary-General in the Middle East, Gunnar Jarring tried and failed to reestablish official communication between the two sides. Henry Kissinger's well-publicized shuttle visited Egypt, Israel, and Syria, often on the same day. He managed to establish official third-party communication, but never with both parties in the same room. This failure is unfortunate because even official intermediaries have transmitted information that has led to misunderstandings on both sides; official third parties have been responsible, whether inadvertently or not, for perpetrating distortions in positions.[16]

Private persons have endeavored to establish or improve communication in the Middle East as well as elsewhere. The Society of Friends and some of its members have been particularly active in this, and two of these efforts are described in this section by Landrum Bolling and C. H. "Mike" Yarrow. Unofficial diplomats may go beyond that as did the Commission of the Churches on International Affairs (CCIA) of the World Council of Churches in the Sudan in 1972: at the request of the government of Sudan in Khartoum and the leaders of the South Sudan Liberation Movement, the CCIA arranged a series of informal meetings bringing together representatives of both sides—meetings which ultimately produced an agreement. Elfan Rees describes this and other activities of the CCIA in conflict situations.

While governments may seek out the services of unofficial message-carriers, private citizens may on their own initiative offer their services. Harry Ashmore details a pair of unofficial visits he made to Hanoi—and the controversy that followed—along with William Baggs (both were then members of the Board of the Center for the Study of Democratic Institutions) with the knowledge but without the wholehearted blessing of the U.S. government.

The final chapter in this section, by Jacques Freymond, is his personal view on the special role played by the International Committee of the Red Cross (ICRC) in time of conflict. As a nongovernmental group intruding upon the delicate matters of state

[16] See Davison's chapter on "Communication in the Middle East," *Mass Communication*, pp. 119–35.

sovereignty, the ICRC must carefully yet forcefully execute its role as humanitarian agent and protector of all victims of conflict at a time when nations are particularly sensitive to outside "interference."

FOUR

QUAKER WORK IN THE MIDDLE EAST FOLLOWING THE JUNE 1967 WAR

LANDRUM R. BOLLING

LANDRUM R. BOLLING, an active member of the Society of Friends and former President of Earlham College, is now President of the Lilly Endowment. Mr. Bolling recounts a Quaker effort in the Middle East in which he played a leading role to fill the communications gap in the area following the June 1967 war. Because of the long-standing Quaker contacts and the Quaker reputation of impartiality, the group had access to both sides, yet Bolling emphasizes that the group's continued credibility in the area very much depended on maintaining its status as a committee of observers—amateurs attached to no government. What they sought to do was to draft a paper that attempted to set forth the views of the parties involved and then to circulate the draft for people to criticize and discuss—both for the purpose of seeing that it was an accurate reflection of views and to initiate a two-way flow of communication.——Eds.

T HE QUAKER EFFORT in the Middle East grew out of an informal search by the American Friends Service Committee to see if anything useful could be done in the Middle East following the June 1967 war. I happened to be going to East Africa about that time and Colin Bell, then head of the American Friends Service Committee (AFSC), called me and asked if I could stop off in the Middle East to find out for what work the Quakers might be welcomed.

I traveled to Cairo, Jerusalem, Amman, and Beirut, asking questions. The conventional things that Quakers have done—working with refugees, children, etc.—did not seem to be urgent needs. Some of these things were already being done by Quakers, and more extensive work of this sort was being carried on by other agencies. By and large, the governments felt they had the situation in hand as far as humanitarian projects were concerned. What everyone agreed upon was that the real nub of the problem was the political conflict situation. We were told Quaker help on this would be welcomed.

What was apparent very early on were the tremendous number of misconceptions so many seemed to have about the nature of the conflict: what the issues were and what the possibilities of solution might be. Certain things became clear to us. One was that many individuals have a tendency to speak in simplistic terms of "the Arab position" and "the Israeli position," or to say "the Arabs" think so and so, and "the Israelis" think so and so. This is all nonsense because there are many Arab positions and many Israeli positions. We found a tremendous amount of misinformation about the nature of the conflict and the points of view of the parties to that conflict.

We began to play with the idea of developing a Quaker statement that would report accurately the points of view of the different parties and would try to make some analysis of UN Resolution 242 and the attitudes of the various groups towards it.

We wanted to see if it was possible for us to develop a paper that would reflect accurately, objectively, and nonemotionally the viewpoints of the parties involved. We set for ourselves the task of trying to be communicators, not mediators, and we constantly had to fight against the accusation that we were trying to be mediators in this conflict. If we took a position of which one side disapproved, they would say, "How can you pretend to be mediators, since you've taken a position on this particular issue?" We would tell them, "We're not trying to be mediators. We're trying to be communicators about what we see as the issues and the points of view of the different sides."

What we then did was to undertake a series of visits around the area. I cannot say exactly how many times I have been around that circuit. We talked with a great variety of people involved in the Middle East problem over these past years, including such top government leaders as Abba Eban, Mahmoud Riad, King Hussein, William P. Rogers, Henry Kissinger, and President Nixon, as well as with a lot of people in the academic world and journalism, lower echelon people in the bureaucracies, Palestine Liberation Organization (PLO) officials, Fatah fighters, numerous student groups, and others.

We then began to write a record of the attitudes we encountered and to pass on our report of these attitudes from one place to another. This was a technique we stumbled onto, and we couldn't dignify it by calling it a deliberate strategy. We began to prepare drafts of a memorandum which we took around to show to different people—usually first academic experts and then government officials.

This technique of circulating a draft for people to criticize, to discuss, and to correct was very useful. It certainly helped to correct many of the misconceptions we ourselves had. Listening to people, I think, is quite an art form. Being able to hear what people are really saying and making sure it is put down just right is a very difficult task. It is always surprising to discover how one has failed to hear what was said at a given moment.

We did, I think, fifteen drafts of the statement. As we were writing, we were unsure what we would do with the memorandum: either to circulate it among Quakers or publish something for general distribution. Eventually we decided we would publish it as a paperback,[1] and it has now gone through a number of English language editions. The paperback has also been translated into Hebrew, Arabic, French, and German. There are probably several hundred thousand copies of the Quaker report now in circulation. It caused a lot of discussion and, of course, aroused considerable criticism from two of the principal groups: the PLO–Fatah groups and the more official hardline elements in the Israeli government. We had some criticism from the Arab governments too, but on the whole these two were the principal critics of the report.

I think to a large extent we were accepted as impartial, well-meaning people. In the beginning from the early drafts we got terrific blasts from both sides. We were accused of not understanding Arabs, of not understanding Jews, of not understanding the cul-

[1] American Friends Service Committee, *Search for Peace in the Middle East* (New York: Fawcett World Library, 1970).

ture, of not understanding the history of humiliation, and so on. We also were told about absolutely unacceptable phrases and references.

The same kinds of objections were raised by each side. We went back and forth with these criticisms, and the fact that we did come back again and again, I think, made many people on both sides believe we were trying to be fair.

In the end, I suppose one has to say this Quaker statement comes out more opposed to the position of the Israeli government than to the position, at least officially taken, of the Egyptian government. I would say, therefore, there are Israelis and American Jews who say we were not impartial and were committed to the Arab cause. We also get some very violent comments from the Arabs. At least we had beratings from both sides as well as kind words from both sides.

I think that the Quaker history of trying to be impartial, fair, and humanitarianly helpful to people in conflict situations has been a great strength to us and helped us gain entree in ways that would not otherwise have been possible.

One of the advantages we had was finding alumni of Quaker-run international meetings everywhere we went. When we went to Cairo, Beirut, or Amman we would usually start with a list of names of the alumni of Quaker seminars. Sometimes this was true not only for the foreign ministries involved, but also in the embassies of various other countries. For example, we had very useful discussions in one capital with the French ambassador, who was known to us in this way. In another capital, we had discussions with the Canadian ambassador, who was also known to us in this same way. In other cases, maybe a second in command was known to us. So these were very valuable contacts. Obviously we did not limit ourselves to them. They in turn helped to pass us on to other people. Admittedly, this was a major asset.

Contacts from other Quaker service projects also proved helpful. For example, after one rather tense discussion with a group of Israelis which included about half a dozen high level foreign office people—and which was the first genuinely substantive, in-depth, no-holds-barred discussion that we ever had with the Israelis—one of them took us aside and said: "Don't be upset by this discussion. You know we have deep feelings about some of these things, but I want you to know we do respect the Quakers, we do trust your integrity, and I want to express my own personal indebtedness to the Quakers. I was a young Jewish boy in Berlin in 1935–36. I had a health problem. It was the Quakers who saved my life then. If some of the American Jews or any of us here give you a hard time, know that you have plenty of friends among us, and that we trust you. We will not always agree with you and we may think you're taking the wrong approach, but keep coming back because we always have a basis for discussion." Such contacts that go back over a period of twenty-five and thirty years are helpful.

As for the attitude of officials concerned with the Middle East, one phase, the paper-writing project, did at one time upset some American officials. But on the whole the officials in Washington concerned with Middle Eastern affairs have been very supportive of our effort, and this has been true of a considerable number of people from other governments. The British were very interested and helpful. We tried to make this a truly international Quaker undertaking, not just an American Quaker effort. However, it was largely American and the initiative came mostly from American sources. We nevertheless had a team that included British and Canadian Quakers as well. As to the United Nations, we kept in touch with UN people about this, and I had no indication of discomfort or unhappiness. Fairly early on, I had a talk with Gunnar Jarring about our involvement. Certainly, he could not have been more cordial about what we were trying to do.

Of what use this effort has been it is difficult to assess. It has certainly provided a basis of discussion for a great many people who are very much involved in these issues. Also, as a result of working on this report, and because we were seeing a variety of people, we were invited back again and again to talk with people at very high levels about these questions.

A question I have agonized over is whether our efforts further solidified the positions of some who were not quite ready to change. I do not know if we have helped some people dig their heels in harder. I think that we have smoked out some issues that previously were obscured in the fog of misrepresentation, but that probably would have been smoked out eventually. I think one might say that in some cases we have encouraged some people to dig their heels in harder.

I am intrigued by the overall question of what the role is of this form of information dissemination in the whole process of peacemaking. The hazard, of course, in trying to do this is that you are bound to displease one side, both sides or all sides of a multifaceted dispute. On the other hand, even if people strenuously argue with you or bluntly criticize you, the fact that such a publication is being circulated apparently does help to stimulate more in-depth discussion of the issues. I think there is little doubt that there has been some greater realism in the discussion of the issues in the Middle East dispute—a realism which is, to a certain extent, attributable to the issues we raised and the reports we gave about the different viewpoints.

Israelis, although very critical of some of the positions the Quakers have taken, have been very courteous and very interested. They have welcomed this particular mission and have invited us to come back. The project has also brought us into contact with a great many people in this country who are interested in the question, particularly American Jewish groups who have extended a number of invitations to me and others in our group to participate in discussions on these issues. I have participated in meetings with the Jewish community leadership all around the country: Los Angeles, San Francisco, Portland, Boston, Washington, and elsewhere.

Many members of Congress are quite interested in these questions and a number in the Senate and the House have invited me in for discussions. I have had easy access to a number of the crucial characters in the drama as far as the State Department and the White House are concerned.

What all this adds up to I really do not know, but it apparently has been of interest to the people in these governments to be able to talk to private individuals who have access to government officials on the other side. We would be asked, for example, our impressions of what the other people were saying and thinking. In reply we would get back correctives to these interpretations. We have been able to operate as an informal supplementary link in communications, and various governments seem to feel our efforts may have been of some value.

We have also become increasingly involved in general public information and have been encouraged by expressions of appreciation for the pamphlet studies which the Quakers have produced on various international topics. Over the years the Quakers have put out a number of pamphlets about such issues as China policy, relations with the Soviet Union, Vietnam, and this one on the Middle East. All of these reports fall somewhere in between scholarly writing and journalism—a semi-journalistic research project. One of the major foundations became interested in our effort, and said that they think the main value of this effort has been our developing a form of semi-journalism which many busy but interested people will take the time to read. This will therefore help to increase and broaden understanding of what the issues are.

We have tried some other things too, none of them successful, I am sorry to say, although it is hard to know what will happen in the long run. We had a conference in California with a group of Israelis and Palestinians and a few Americans, talking about the Arab–Israeli conflict and what kinds of solutions might be viable. The Middle East Institute attempted something like this in February 1971. That conference, however, was a complete shambles, primarily because the Palestinians finally came under the influence of a PLO belligerent who pressured everyone except one brave Palestinian woman to withdraw. There was also an effort to prevent or disrupt the Quaker conference in California, but apparently that attempt did not succeed. The people did stay and they had on the whole some good discussions.

One side project which we attempted for a few months following the publication of the little book was to develop working papers presenting some alternative approaches—conceptual approaches—to some of the specific issues in the Arab–Israeli dispute. We had a few international lawyers working with us who had a good deal of knowledge about this subject. We circulated some of these papers to both sides. These papers had enough effect at one point to get serious consideration by the PLO.

One of the arguments we put to the PLO was that we felt their dream of a binational, secular, unified Palestine was romantic nonsense. It was not going to get anywhere. And their tactic of guerrilla warfare as a way of reaching any settlement of the problem was, from our viewpoint, a wrong one. Therefore, we urged them to consider the possibility of trying to develop some political options. We presented some papers for consideration to them and to the Israelis and others. The PLO had very serious discussions on this. They translated the papers into Arabic and put them on the agenda of a central committee meeting of the PLO held in Cairo. They turned the suggestions down, but at least they began talking about some specific political options.

We therefore felt this technique might have been useful. I do not know what the long-run value of this has been, but I think that at a time when the PLO was in a state of trauma, following the civil war in Jordan in 1970, we certainly helped to bolster the hands of those in the PLO who were arguing for more flexibility and for more of a political approach.

As I have said, this activity was a very haphazard kind of Quaker amateur happening. It is not social science, but it has been an experience for those of us who participated in it that certainly has added to our knowledge of the area and of the problems, and has given us a deeper understanding of the emotions that lie behind the policies. Whether we have contributed anything to the thinking of other people or not, we just do not know. At least, both sides continue to speak kindly to us, if not always in agreement with us, and they have asked us to come back.

One of the touchy moments in this effort came when we were accused in Jerusalem of trying to be an official spokesman for the State Department. We told everyone we were not speaking for the State Department, the White House, or for anybody, and that we were just a bunch of meddling Quakers. We would really have been ruined if we had been unable to make clear the fact that we had no official connections. It did take some rather harsh cables from Washington to clear this up. I must, however, reiterate that it was terribly important to the credibility of our whole mission that we be what we were, and never tried to be otherwise; we were simply a group of outside observers, interested amateurs, who were not speaking on behalf of any government.

FIVE

QUAKER EFFORTS TOWARD CONCILIATION IN THE INDIA–PAKISTAN WAR OF 1965

C. H. "MIKE" YARROW

C. H. "MIKE" YARROW is a Quaker who served in the International Affairs Division of the Americans Friends Service Committee from 1963–72. Mr. Yarrow describes Quaker efforts at conciliation during the India–Pakistan war over Kashmir in 1965. Like other Quaker efforts, including that presented by Landrum Bolling, the mission could draw upon long-standing contacts and the Friends' reputation of impartiality to gain initial access to the disputants. To maintain the confidence of the parties, however, required the special approach that Yarrow labels "balanced partiality"—while establishing their position as favoring neither side, team members at the same time had to be sympathetic listeners on both sides—a role not easy to play. Yarrow explains how the Quaker functions evolved during the effort.——Eds.

QUAKERS HAVE LONG URGED that men should "deny all outward wars and strife and fightings with outward weapons, for any end, or any pretence whatever." [1] Stirrings of inner guidance have led Quakers beyond this negative witness against war to positive efforts for achieving the conditions of peace. Both the acts of withdrawing support for war and of making peace arise from a religious assumption stated by George Fox in 1650: "I told them I lived in the virtue of that life and power that takes away the occasion for all wars." [2] Interpretations of the basic testimony have varied from century to century,[3] but in all

[1] From "A Declaration from the Harmless and Innocent People of God, called Quakers," presented to Charles II 1660.

[2] John L. Nickalls, *The Journal of George Fox* (rev. ed.; London: Cambridge University Press, 1952), pp. 4–5.

[3] For a recent exposition of the history, see Wolf Mendl, "Prophets and Reconcilers," Friends Home Service Committee, London, 1974.

periods various efforts have been directed toward reconciliation. These efforts have included major relief operations, such as the child-feeding program in Germany after World War I; rehabilitation programs, such as the Rasulia Village Project in the Madhya Pradesh province of India; lobbying at the United Nations for better rules of international conduct; actions in a situation Quakers consider one of injustice, such as British rule in India; and, finally, conciliation between hostile groups, such as we are considering here.

Under the heading "conciliation" come many efforts to promote better communication and understanding by bringing people together in seminars and efforts to work with opposing parties in a specific international conflict. The definition given by Adam Curle for conciliation appropriately describes Quaker assumptions: "Activity aimed at bringing about an alteration of perception (the other side is not as bad as we thought; we have misinterpreted their actions; etc.) that will lead to an alteration of attitude and eventually to an alteration of behavior."[4] Similarly, Kenneth Boulding writes of the way in which messages between hostile parties pass through an intense emotional field and are likely to be distorted. The conciliator is outside the field and can help point out the distortions.[5]

Conciliation, thus defined, is most appropriate if conflicts arise primarily over differences of perception. Other conflicts arise primarily from gross injustice between parties of unequal power and the quarrel is not so much over perceptions, which are real enough, but basic human rights. In these latter situations conciliatory activity may blunt a necessary confrontation. Quakers have not always been successful in limiting conciliation to the first category, although they have reserved for situations of injustice the quite different methods of witness or advocacy. In this essay we are dealing with a conflict in which conciliation was judged an appropriate role. Each side, of course, in the standoff between Pakistan and India over Kashmir wanted the Quakers to be an advocate of its position, and yet each accepted in good spirit the intermediary role the Quakers chose to play.

[4] *Making Peace* (London: Tavistock Publications, 1971), p. 173.
[5] *Conflict and Defense* (New York: Harper & Row, 1962), p. 319.

The Dispute Over Kashmir

The dispute over control of Kashmir, a former princely state, was not resolved at the time of partition of the subcontinent in 1947, and India and Pakistan were soon locked in an undeclared war. Through the initiative of the United Nations, the Kashmir war of 1948−49 ended in an uneasy truce with a UN-patrolled cease-fire line dividing the state into two parts—one under Pakistani jurisdiction, one under Indian jurisdiction. In the fall of 1965 the smouldering hostility that had prevailed between the nations broke out into open warfare. At the root of the dispute were the contradictory nation-building concepts of the two nations in the subcontinent. According to the Pakistani ideal of a Muslim state, the Muslim majority of Kashmir could not exist happily in a predominantly Hindu nation. India's theory of a secular pluralistic state insisted they should and could. These mutually exclusive assumptions were not just theoretical derivations, but were a strong source of identity for ordinary citizens, a ready basis for mob action, and a guiding principle of popular journalism.

At first fighting in the 1965 conflict was confined to skirmishes between Indian army units and bands of so-called infiltrators crossing into Indian-controlled territory from the Pakistani section of Kashmir. Then the Pakistani army made major incursions over the cease-fire line into the Indian sector, and the Indian army retaliated by crossing the internationally recognized boundary between India and Pakistan with a pincers movement directed at Lahore.

For Quakers who had participated in the birth pangs of the two nations, the news from Kashmir brought fears of a renewal of the terrible days of partition when fighting between religious communities took a deadly toll in human spirit and life. Many Friends who had participated in efforts to help village development in the two countries realized how drastically even a short war would set back plans for improvement. Quaker organizations sponsoring communication efforts across the boundaries saw the barriers raised higher than ever.

Such thoughts and feelings brought forth a major concern in the Meeting for Sufferings in London on September 3, 1965. This body was set up originally at the time of the persecutions of Friends in the seventeenth century, and came to be the interim executive organ between sessions of London Yearly Meeting. Although it is hard to identify any specific decisions at this meeting, the airing of views stimulated later action by staff and committees in London.

An India–Pakistan subgroup of the Peace and International Relations Committee, one of the regular committees of London Yearly Meeting, was formed and met first on September 14. The group included several persons with wide experience in the subcontinent. The chairman was Horace G. Alexander, who had played an important role with the India Conciliation Group in interpreting the Gandhian revolution to the British people. Meeting frequently during the next five months, the group sent emissaries to confer with the Commonwealth Office, the British Foreign Office, and the High Commissioners of India and Pakistan, arranged meetings with experts to discuss the issues, and made recommendations to the Peace Committee.

On the other side of the Atlantic, the staff and committees of the American Friends Service Committee in Philadelphia were also studying the crisis situation and deciding what action could be taken. Figuring prominently in the deliberations were urgent messages from field staff in the subcontinent—especially those from Warren Ashby, then director of the Conferences and Seminar program based in New Delhi. Warren Ashby was in Pakistan from August 23 to September 3 to obtain clearance for Pakistani participation in a conference of Asian leaders planned for Nepal from September 22 to 30. This conference was part of a series of Quaker international conferences begun in 1950 bringing together in separate meetings students, diplomats, and young leaders. A promise of clearance was obtained from Pakistan's Ministry of Foreign Affairs, but not long afterward the accelerating war forced the cancellation of the conference. Warren Ashby reported back to the AFSC that a main cause of war was the struggle for national identity in each country. Moving back and forth between the two nations he had become acutely aware of the distortions, delusions and falsifications with which each nation looked at the other.

The Idea and Purpose of a "Mission"

The first allusion to a possible "Quaker mission" came up spontaneously in the September 3 Meeting for Sufferings mentioned above. John Dennithorne asked for a Quaker mission to India and Pakistan at the earliest possible moment in the following words: "Such a mission would invite the leaders of these nations to realize that this political problem could be solved only by raising the spiritual awareness of their peoples and of themselves. The principle of 'holding by letting go' was the principle to be held out to them and it was appropriate that Friends as 'a spiritual people' should do this."[6]

Such a message arising from the prayerful spirit of the Meeting, when reduced to cold print in the minutes, took on the semblance of "spiritual imperialism," although the speaker would be the first to deny any such intention. There were Quakers in India who took this message as an indication of a "holier than thou" attitude. One of them wrote a letter which appeared in the October 8, 1965 edition of *The Friend,* a publication of London Yearly Meeting, explaining why India could not possibly "let go" of Kashmir and criticizing meddlers who did not know the Indian scene.

With such criticisms in mind, subsequent thinking about a mission was low-keyed and more politically sophisticated, although the original inspiration was never missing. Across the Atlantic there was reluctance to using the label "mission" because of the inflated connotation from diplomatic usage, as well as the confusion arising from the term's religious usage. The words "team" or "visit" were favored, but eventually the group itself chose the name "mission."

Indeed, there were good precedents for using the term. The Quaker group that went to East and West Germany in 1963, seeking conciliation between the two Germanys and between East Germany and the United States, had called itself a "mission." There had also been several "missions" of Friends to communist countries in the 1950s, seeking to break the barriers of Eastern iron curtains and Western ostracism.

[6] Report in *The Friend,* September 10, 1965, p. 1082.

Most of the missions of the past had stressed conciliation between "us" of the Western world and "them." Now the committees were talking about conciliation between two countries, neither their own. The first suggestion on September 28 by the London-based India–Pakistan Group was for a visitation by different individuals to each side for the purpose of listening and reporting back. Leslie Cross was picked to go to India, because of his experience there dating back to 1942. It was suggested that Roger Wilson and Adam Curle visit Pakistan. Roger Wilson had been an adviser on social welfare for the government of Pakistan some years before, and had been followed by Adam Curle who served as an adviser on social affairs. The importance of the conciliatory aspect of the mission was first stressed in a letter from Roger Wilson to Adam Curle written on October 11, 1965: "The essence of the operation is that if Friends go they should be able to say that their opposite numbers are engaged in a similar effort to understand the other side of the frontier." The Philadelphia response was highly favorable to the idea of a Quaker visit and the suggested team members, but asked why all the participants should not constitute one team and visit both sides in order to enhance the conciliatory possibilities.

The board of directors of the AFSC at its October meeting in Philadelphia created the Pakistan–India Advisory Group. The group's name, in reverse order to the London committee, was chosen in order to distinguish the two groups and to emphasize the parity of the two countries in Quaker considerations. The group formed was eminently knowledgeable in the affairs of the subcontinent. It included two persons in the State Department, a high official in the World Bank, three professors, and a foundation director—all Quakers acting in a private capacity.

The Pakistan–India Advisory Group first met with staff October 20, 1965. The members worked over a statement of purpose and gave full support to the idea of at least two, preferably three, persons to visit both countries. The following excerpts from the minutes show the care in the discussion and the desire to avoid pretence:

The primary purpose of a visit should be to listen sensitively in a quiet and unobtrusive way, in order to learn and understand what is going on in the minds of Pakistanis and Indians. This attitude would reflect a friendliness to the people of both countries, and a profound concern that they not follow down the road of mutual destruction. The approach then would be one of listening, but with questions to present. Much thought would need to be given to the right questions. Our questions would probably not relate to the central political issue. For example, questions involving the joint interests of the people of both nations, which are very important, are not being asked any more. One of the most important objectives would be slowly to create situations where such questions of mutuality can be raised, in order to legitimize the very function of asking them. These might relate to water resources and uses, exchange of persons, cultural relations and other such. Success in obtaining attention to such mutual problems and approaches would be a marked achievement. While the immediate situation is urgent, any plans of Friends should be developed on the assumption that we have time to do what is right to do. While contacts with high-level government people have value, there was a feeling that it is especially important to have conversations with middle-level people, in private situations which would not embarrass them.[7]

The final blessing for the visit was given by the board of the AFSC on October 29, 1965 with a $7,500 funding and by the Meeting for Sufferings in London on December 3 with an appropriation of £500.

The statement of purpose was modified several times, with the intent of expressing in the fewest words possible modest, but not-too-limited expectations. The formulation agreed to on both sides of the Atlantic was summarized in the final report of the team:

First, the members of the mission were simply to inform themselves on the situation so that they might carry back to Friends and others concerned a rather clearer picture of a complex and dangerous situation than might be available from the press. Second, they were to see if there were any helpful roles they could play in this situation.

[7] Report of the Pakistan-India Advisory Group Meeting, October 20, 1965, in AFSC Archives.

Third, the mission was to concern itself with ways in which Quaker activities could be best directed towards the development of better relations between India and Pakistan and towards making a more effective contribution to the needs of the countries themselves.[8]

Although not intended for publication, the statement was to be used as the basis for an oral presentation explaining the purpose of the mission to the governments and individuals the team would see—thus underscoring the unofficial, off-the-record character of the visit.

Early in the process of considering this visit, it became clear that the advice of government officials was important, and that clearance from the two governments involved was necessary. Staff and some committee members in London and Washington sought out government and embassy officials. A Pakistani diplomat in the United States, favoring in principle a visit by Friends to Pakistan, cautioned the committee in October to wait for a more propitious time and to select persons acceptable to his government. An officer in the Indian embassy in Washington said that such a visit of British and American Quakers would be warmly received in India. Their good offices, he thought, might even usefully convey ideas that governments could not put into more official channels.

The process of selecting the team was carried out by unrecorded telephone communication and letters across the Atlantic. The committees in London tended to stress as a qualification the strength of Quaker background, while the committees in Philadelphia stressed knowledge and experience in the subcontinent. Consensus was readily achieved, however, since both sides recognized the importance of all these qualities. Leslie Cross was a unanimous choice. He had gone to India in 1942 starting out with the Friends Ambulance Unit in relief and welfare work and staying on with other organizations through partition until 1950. He was chairman of the Asia Committee of the Friends Service Council and manager of several charitable trust funds benefitting the old, the poor, and the sick.

Roger Wilson was unable to go, but Adam Curle was available.

[8] Report of the Pakistan-India Mission, February 1966, AFSC Archives.

Though not long a member of the Society of Friends, Adam Curle did have wide experience in Pakistan, having served not only as an adviser on social affairs to the Pakistan government from 1956 to 1959, as has already been mentioned, but also as a consultant on education from 1963 to 1964.

Since both Leslie Cross and Adam Curle were British, an intensive effort was mounted by staff in Philadelphia to find an American. This effort resulted in the selection of Joseph W. Elder, associate professor in the departments of Sociology and Indian Studies of the University of Wisconsin. Somewhat junior to the other two, he nevertheless had five years of experience in India in the 1950s, spoke Urdu and Hindi, had written many articles on Indian village and religious life, and had been an active Friend for many years.

Before the second meeting of the Pakistan-India Advisory Group in Washington, December 21, 1965, arrangements and schedules had been roughed out for a team visit starting in mid-January. The group supplied the team members, two of whom were present at the meeting, with many suggestions on procedure and substantive issues, but avoided restrictive instructions. Prominent in the deliberations was the plan of moving back and forth between the two countries. The team was asked to work closely with the resident staff in the two countries and to bring back recommendations for ongoing work in the future.

Work of the Quaker Mission

The timing of the Quaker mission was the result of practical requirements rather than either clairvoyance or a scientific assessment of the phases of crisis. January 17 was the first date that all three team members could meet in London to begin the trip. As it turned out this was probably the most propitious time for a visit.

The intense fighting of August and September had been followed by a lull, leaving the Indian army at the gates of Lahore and the Pakistani army bracing for siege and counterattack. The strenuous efforts of the UN Secretary-General, U Thant, led to the passage of a cease-fire resolution in the Security Council on September 22. The resolution was accepted by both sides, but the situation remained highly inflamed. In Karachi on September 21, 30,000 students took to the streets attacking the embassies of India and the United States and some UN offices. Debates in the Security Council failed to produce any progress on agreement on the withdrawal of troops. Then India, on November 23, and Pakistan, on November 25, announced they had accepted the Soviet Union's offer to conduct talks at Tashkent. This led to the Tashkent Declaration of January 10, 1966, a nine-point agreement to restore relations, withdraw armed forces, repatriate prisoners, and end hostile propaganda.

Although the central issue of the war, the status of Kashmir, had not been settled, the basis for a cooling-off period had been established. The time was ripe for the intervention of an unofficial, unpublicized third party to strengthen the forces of moderation on each side and to promote thinking on the terms of a longer-lasting peace. The Quaker group was the first and only attempt of this kind by an unofficial party as far as is known.

The itinerary of the team of three involved a week in Pakistan, a week in India, and then a return visit to each state for a week and a half. A final week in Pakistan for writing and conferring brought the total to six weeks. Pakistan was put first on the agenda because of the tendency of the people in Pakistan to feel they received less attention from the West than India.

The team went to the subcontinent with a sense of great urgency, but also with minimal expectations of what might be accomplished. In the Quaker tradition their reason for going was the rightness—even necessity—of doing what they could for the goal of peace, whether or not success was assured. They were well aware of the need to move cautiously and of the danger of making matters worse instead of better. Nevertheless, they soon found their role progressing from one of gathering information, to one of serving as a channel of communication across the lines, to one of giving their own assessments on certain aspects of the situation, and finally to one of playing a highly tentative and modest role of proposing measures that might bring peace.

I have studied the team's changing role from the record of the interviews and the remembrances of the participants, and I shall try to summarize the process and results, employing the categories Oran Young uses in his book *The Intermediaries*.[9] Although his treatment applies primarily to official intervention in which the intermediaries are governmental bodies whose activities are officially acknowledged by the parties in conflict, his categories are nevertheless useful in analyzing the Quaker operation in which the intervenors were self-invited and entirely unofficial.

Establishment of Confidence

The first necessity for a third party entering into conciliation between parties in conflict is the establishment of confidence, and the basic qualities needed to establish and maintain credibility, according to Oran Young, are impartiality and independence.

Impartiality

A third party must be seen by the protagonists as not favoring either side. The Quaker team members were impartial in that they were willing to assess the pros and cons of each side's position, and if they started with any preconceptions of an easy or one-sided solution, they soon learned better. Yet impartiality implies an aloofness or indifference that does not adequately describe the Quaker approach. A more appropriate though paradoxical description might be "balanced partiality"—that is, they listened sympathetically to each side, trying to put themselves in the other party's place. The evidence is clear that they were perceived as sympathetic listeners on both sides. A good indication of this balanced partiality is the wording of the mission's report. Under the headings "The Pakistan Viewpoint" and "The Indian Viewpoint," the team carefully worded the historical facts and judgements as an insider on each side would, rather than as an outside observer. Readers of the report on both sides expressed satisfaction in later interviews with the way the Quakers had described their side of

[9] Oran R. Young, *The Intermediaries: Third Parties in International Crises* (Princeton, N.J., Princeton University Press, 1967).

the situation, although they raised grave doubts about the statement setting forth the other side's view.

Another aspect of balanced partiality is the Quaker concern for all people involved in a situation. The Quaker team emphasized the need to maximize the gains that might accrue to both sides through a settlement. Time and again on both sides they raised questions about the burden of the arms race and the futility of military means as shown in the recent fighting. The history of Quaker services in humanitarian relief and development helped to give weight to their words in the passionate advocacy of peace.

In an exercise of "partiality to each side," there is the danger of grossly misleading a discussion partner into thinking that he has been successful in convincing the Quakers of the justice of his plea. How does the sympathetic listener preserve his integrity in his own eyes and in the eyes of the advocate? The answer is in the nonverbal communication of the conciliator as well as the words he uses. The Quaker tradition of speaking the truth can be helpful but nothing can replace a personal quality of transparent honesty that does not necessarily come with membership in the Society of Friends!

The team members underscored their balanced partiality by reminding their discussion partners that they were hearing different views on the other side. An occasional question concerning views held on the other side was also helpful. The fact that all three were involved in all of the interviews was also important.

Independence

It is frequently easier for a nongovernmental group with no political power to establish the quality of independence than a governmental one. Because the Quakers have a reputation, deserved or not, for internationalism and peacemindness little explaining on this score was needed. A question of this kind came up only in relation to the nationality of the team members, and it was fortunate that the team was composed of individuals from both Britain and the United States. At that time, 1965–66, Pakistan was inflamed against the United States and India against Britain. Thus the first entree was made easier on several occasions because the Pakistanis felt freer to talk with the British and the Indians with the

American. In one interview, an Indian talked only to the American after strongly criticizing British policy.

Other Resources for a Conciliatory Role

Oran Young speaks of "ascribed resources"—that is, resources that are attributed to the conciliator by the parties through circumstances of history and prior contact, rather than resources that are intrinsically possessed or acquired. Under this heading he lists "salience, respect, and continuity." The Quaker team did not have salience as widely recognized mediators in many conflict situations. However, as the result of Quaker conferences for diplomats in thirteen prior years, there were people in the Foreign Office of each country who knew about the Quaker organization, and even some who had participated in conferences. The conference program also provided the resource of respect, especially the type that Young calls "affectual respect"—the feeling that the third party will give a fair hearing and be warmly motivated toward the protagonists. As for continuity, Quaker efforts in the immediate past did not involve direct conciliation between highly placed officials, but there was continuity in facilitating communication between the two countries in various seminars and in continuing contact in London, Washington, and at the United Nations with representatives of the two countries. Behind these recent activities of the Quakers lay the work prior to 1950 of the India Conciliation Group, which added a further dimension to these resources.[10]

Personal Qualifications

Knowledge of political/military affairs and economic and cultural aspects of a dispute are all very important for an intermediary. On this score the team had extensive firsthand experience in India and

[10] The India Conciliation group, an informal loosely organized body that operated from 1931 to 1950, was a channel of communication between the Indians and British in the preindependence era. Although it was not officially sponsored by Quakers, throughout its existence Quakers were in leadership roles in carrying messages, bringing key people from the two parties together, and undertaking a public education job in Great Britain.

Pakistan and keen acumen in political analysis. Each brought different talents whose sum was impressive. Although such a private effort could not match the resources of a governmental enterprise in which researchers would supply background papers on every aspect of the situation, nevertheless the committees and staff in the United States and Britain and the staff in the field provided significant assistance. In addition the team added to its knowledge of the situation by talking with a number of well-informed contacts in the two countries. The team spoke with nineteen observers on the scene, including a French journalist, a British High Commission officer, a Harvard University adviser to the Pakistan government, and a United Nations resident representative. Gathering information in the field is easier for an unofficial team whose activities may go completely unnoticed by the public—an official conciliator must be constantly aware of setting off rumors by his actions.

In this Quaker enterprise the personal qualifications of individual conciliators were enhanced by the team approach. The three members were quite different and yet complemented each other in remarkable ways. Leslie Cross, the elder statesman, had a special understanding of the problems facing those in power. Adam Curle and Joseph Elder, on the other hand, both believed that any political figure should do more than he was doing for peace. On the dispute's central issues, Adam Curle had a strong sympathy for the Pakistani search for national identity that sought "liberation" for the Muslims of Kashmir, and Joe Elder had experienced quite directly the village flare-ups between Indians of Muslim and Hindu communities that were continually ignited by the Pakistani press. The team's range of ages was valuable in relating to a variety of discussion partners. Adam Curle would present the case to the younger, brasher, more skeptical persons; Leslie Cross would do the honors with the older, more senior people.

With such differences one might expect tension, but there is unanimous testimony from team members and observers that there was no sense of rivalry or jealousy in their relations, no jockeying for position in the interviews, no pride of paternity in an idea or a phrase, and no post-mortem criticisms. This harmony of teamwork arose largely from a sense of common dedication to an important job and from a sense of the group's strong support in the two home countries. It is also clear that none of the three required large ego-satisfaction from this exercise, such as a future reputation at stake, a book to write, or an individual hypothesis to prove.

The three men lived closely together for six weeks and spent a considerable portion of their long days discussing the mission. Before any important meeting they would consider their approach, the issues to be raised, and sometimes which one would pose a particular question. They also considered how the meeting related to those held in the past or planned for the future. They used their differences, depending on the fact that each one could do certain tasks better. In the preparatory sessions for important interviews, Adam Curle stressed the importance of role-playing. He would typically play the part of the person to be interviewed, challenging the team members on the purpose for their visit, misinterpreting statements made, and finding suspicious undertones in the phrasing of questions. In addition to being fun, these exercises helped the participants to avoid mistakes in the real interviews, and to gain greater understanding of the full dimensions of feeling and logic of the persons whose roles they represented.

In one preparatory session they had a meeting for worship. As Joseph Elder described it in a letter written on November 30, 1972:

> Our most serious meeting came, I believe, when we learned that we were going to be able to see Ayub Khan. We decided that we would have a three-person silent meeting for worship to prepare ourselves for whatever we would encounter. The meeting was one of the most moving I have ever participated in—in Leslie's room I recall, with each of us sharing our own sense of inadequacy at what we were trying to do, and yet each of us sensing something like a "Quaker legacy" that we had been drawing on throughout the trip that provided a power well beyond what any of us individually possessed.

This description of the Quaker emissaries and their operations must of necessity be based on the one-sided testimony of the team members and close associates on the staff. Exactly what the Pakistanis and Indians thought of them is unknown, but there is one bit of evidence on this point. The following year a Quaker couple saw nearly all of the persons the team interviewed, and in not one case was there a negative reaction about the purpose and functioning of the team. Moreover, in most cases there was a strongly positive reaction. The mission report sent to all persons interviewed and dealing with highly controversial issues was well-received, bringing strong but friendly criticism from only a few individuals.

The Process of Conciliation

Having considered the make-up of the team, the way in which the members worked, and the way in which they were accepted, we must now analyze the record on the types of conciliatory functions they performed. As stated earlier they progressed from listening, to channeling communication, to offering evaluations, and finally to proposing.

The Listening Function

The importance of this function was indicated by the degree to which the team was used as an audience. Time and again after the team members introduced themselves and their purpose, the person they were talking to would list the many grievances against the other side. After a while team members could predict the exact facts and history that would be given. This was particularly true on the Pakistani side, where there was a great sense of grievance and injustice. Although eventually totally familiar with these recitals, the team members felt it was necessary to listen, nod their heads dutifully, and occasionally raise some pointed questions.

Carrying Messages

Listening was the main feature of the team's activity during the first week in Pakistan, but following this, on the first trip to India, the team found there was interest in what was being said "on the other side." During later visits to Pakistan and India the function of reporting back and forth grew. It is hard to estimate the value of this communication function. But it is clear that each side had been limited to one-sided reporting in its own partisan journals and, with the objective channels shut off, the team was able to bring reports that were news. These reports were eagerly solicited and accepted as accurate by both sides, and the team was seen as reporting not its own views but the views of the other side.

An example of this reporting dealt with the matter of aggression. It was easy for the team to point out that each side was firmly convinced that the other was the aggressor, and to detail which events in the sequence of attacks and counterattacks were singled out by each side. For some this kind of information was a moment of awakening: "You mean they are saying the same thing we are?" It must be said, however, that some reacted by saying that it was merely an indication of the depravity of the other side that they would commit such bald aggression and then justify it as "self-defense."

Thus for some the report reinforced their prejudices. In many cases the message-carrying was personal, since some knew the persons on the other side to whom the team had talked or would talk. In one case the team talked with two brothers, each highly placed on his side of the border. The team tried to enhance the feeling that common problems could be dealt with by sensible and open-minded persons on both sides.

Assessment and Evaluation

As time went on the team members were asked more frequently what they themselves thought. Thus the next level of functioning was conveying their own assessments of the situation.

They sedulously avoided taking sides on the interpretation of history and confined themselves to conclusions regarding present and future. On this score their message to Indian leaders was that Ayub Khan was the most moderate leader Pakistan was likely to have, and that he was having a hard time convincing the people that the Tashkent Agreement was anything but a complete defeat. Since Tashkent provided no settlement for the Kashmir issue, the objective of the fighting was, in Pakistani eyes, lost. The team also reported in India that the Pakistani public believed they had won the war, stopped the Indian army in its tracks, shown great restraint in not going on to capture all of Kashmir, and that the leaders of the Pakistani government were in a way trapped by their own biased press. In this connection the Quaker team reported the snubs that President Ayub Khan had received, the defection of his own protégé, Foreign Minister Z. A. Bhutto, and the great difficulty in which the Information Service of the government of Pakistan found itself.

In talking to Pakistanis the team emphasized the difficulties which Indira Gandhi faced in the rising clamor of the extreme rightist Jan Sangh Party, which thought Tashkent was a sellout. While Mrs. Gandhi could ignore this extremist minority she could not ignore the same strong views in her own Congress Party. The Quakers reported that the death of Prime Minister Lal Bahadur Shastri just after the signing of the agreement in Tashkent was widely considered as the only thing that prevented widespread protests about the signing of the cease-fire agreement.

Proposals

The process of evaluation moved naturally into the next stage—proposing or transmitting measures for ameliorating the situation. The team used great ingenuity in making proposals, all the way from very small steps for improving the climate, such as a cricket match between the two countries, to major steps for resolving the Kashmir dispute. Some of the proposals were their own; some were suggested to them. The mission report fully lists the various ideas. We will consider here two suggestions.

A highly placed Indian official suggested that Pakistan participate in the Gandhi centenary celebration to be celebrated in 1969. This idea was tried out on a former Gandhian in Pakistan, who was then vice-chancellor of a university. His answer was that the idea was unwise, since Gandhi had opposed partition. Moreover, he suggested any such step would be impossible until India made a major move toward conciliation on the Kashmir issue.

On the Pakistani side the suggestion was made that a reduction in the Indian arms budget, which had quadrupled since 1962, would be seen as a major sign of relaxation. When this message was conveyed to a highly placed Indian the matter was seriously considered, but the threat of China was used to explain the high military budget.

Many specific proposals for resolving the major issue came to the team from foreign observers and parties in the dispute. But the team soon saw that none of these was likely to be considered in the near future, and they did not try to develop a comprehensive formula for settlement. Tashkent brought an uneasy truce that was not popular on either side. In India, Kashmir was seen as an integral part of the Union. Indians were willing to discuss other issues with Pakistan, but not Kashmir. In Pakistan, the leaders insisted that India carry through its earlier agreement to a plebiscite. In their view no other issues were worth discussing. Faced with these rigidities the team tried to probe for possible means to soften positions. Was there any way in which the situation could be defused and cooled off enough so that some settlement of Kashmir involving consultation with Pakistan could be considered in the future? As they labored with this they came to formulate what they privately labeled "The Question." In talking with the Vice-President of India it was first phrased in this way: "Should we tell the Pakistanis that the cease-fire line was the international line; there was no more point raising the issue; or should we say that if they simply let up the pressure for five or ten years the status of Kashmir might change?" In later interviews this question was raised again and again in various forms.

On the Indian side although the usual answer was that the status of Kashmir in the Indian Union was non-negotiable, at high levels of government the answer was more conciliatory. For the present, it was indicated, the issue was closed. Pressure and threats from Pakistan would be of no avail, but if there was a long enough period of peace and if India could count on Pakistan not to commit aggression, then it might be possible at some future time to consider some mutual arrangements for Kashmir.

In posing "The Question" on the Pakistan side the team explored unilateral steps and promises that might be made by India to improve the climate and encourage the Pakistanis to wait patiently for a later resolution of the Kashmir issue. One question they often posed was, "If you were Indira Gandhi, what would you do?" The usual answer of governmental as well as unofficial leaders was that no promises or gestures on other issues would count if India made no moves on Kashmir. The least Mrs. Gandhi could do, they said, was to have the issue of Kashmir discussed at a ministers' meeting. At high levels of responsibility in Pakistan, however, there was an openness to conciliatory signals from the other side, and a series of unilateral actions that would help restore confidence was suggested for the Indian side. It was suggested that India refrain from any further steps to integrate Kashmir into the Indian constitutional and legal framework, provide decent treatment for people displaced by the war, and reduce the grossly inflated military budget.

On the team's return visit to India, the suggestions brought back were seriously considered, and reasons given why most of them could not be implemented. Returning to Pakistan, the team conveyed Indian reactions to the various proposals to the government. At this point the team members believed they had done all they could and that further messages would be better channeled through official avenues.

Summary

As one reviews the activity of listening, message-carrying, assessing, and proposing, one is impressed by the perseverance and ingenuity of the Quaker go-betweens who kept up hope in a situation that was almost completely blocked. As one probe after another ended in disappointment, they saw that neither side was in a position to move. There was no breakthrough in the stalemate because even minimal proposals were unacceptable at the time. Yet one can discern great value in the total effort.

The value most clearly evident is the support given to the position of moderates on each side. The team interpreted the practical reasons behind seemingly irrational statements of opposing leaders, and explained the phenomenon of inflamed and uninformed public opinion on both sides. Most important, they helped to change the perceptions of the opposing leaders by demonstrating to each side that their counterparts were also reasonable and well-meaning people, motivated by similar ideas and pressures. Although at the time the process of changing perceptions was ineffective with the extremists, the important job to be done was to strengthen the voices of moderation and support the truce against the strong forces of extremism on both sides.

In this case the Quaker effort was only a small part of the total picture. The major operating forces were beyond the influence of the Quakers. The great powers, especially the United States and the Soviet Union, for their own reasons did not want strife. The leaders of the Pakistani and Indian armies were more realistic about the chances of success in renewed fighting than the newspaper writers and readers. On the political scene, although Tashkent was a burden for both heads of government, renewed war was not viewed as a way out. Serious economic, political, and minority problems in each country put a premium on each retaining an outside enemy, but a renewal of armed conflict would only have made matters worse.

So it was that although the Quaker mission did not assist any major breakthrough, it did play a more important role than was anticipated, coming at a crucial time to give aid to the cooling-off process.

Other conflicts in which Quakers have done similar conciliatory work in recent years are: the strained relations between the two Germanys after the Berlin Wall of 1961; the Nigerian civil war of 1967–70; and the Middle East after the June 1967 war. In each case, but in differing ways, diverse Quaker enterprises—United Nations Office, conferences for diplomats, international work camps and seminars, and relief work—have played a part. In each case individuals were assigned for short or long terms to work directly on conciliation in the particular conflict.

In some of these other instances Quaker involvement was greater and more sustained than in the India–Pakistan case. In Nigeria, for example, three Quaker representatives were looked to by the governments of Nigeria and the secessionist Biafra for an important function of message-carrying over a period of two years. The members of this Quaker team consulted closely with two outside governments, two regional organizations, and several private parties in the many efforts to find peace. The value of these other undertakings is not any easier to measure than that of the India—Pakistan effort described here. In any case, however, there can be little question that Friends consider these efforts important parts of their ongoing work for peace.

SIX

EXERCISES IN PRIVATE DIPLOMACY

Selected Activities of the Commission of the Churches on International Affairs

ELFAN REES

ELFAN REES, long a member of the staff of the Commission of the Churches on International Affairs of the World Council of Churches, and now a consultant to the organization, writes of certain of its activities. Since its formation in 1946, the operating principle of the Commission has been to bring a balanced and informed Christian judgment to bear on international political problems. The Commission's authority in religious matters and the standing with officials that that authority confers have been factors contributing to the effectiveness of the Commission's political activities. At times this has meant drawing upon substantial Christian communities on different sides of a dispute to look at a shared political problem in the context of a shared Christian faith. This has included both international problems, and, as in the case of the civil war in the Sudan, internal problems with international overtones.——Eds.

SINCE ITS ESTABLISHMENT IN 1946, the Commission of the Churches on International Affairs (CCIA) of the World Council of Churches (WCC) has consistently sought a balanced and informed Christian judgment on international affairs and to advise the WCC, its committees, officers, and member-churches accordingly. On a number of occasions the CCIA has acted as a private diplomat in various attempts to aid in the handling of international disputes.

The problem with attempting to relate activities in this field is that written about (and even unconsciously) boasted about, they cease to be discreet and, at that point, lose some of their diplomatic character. The only approach out of the dilemma, therefore, is to confine oneself to the past and to give examples that will neither flutter contemporary dovecotes nor inhibit current or future exercises of the same kind. That is why this essay takes an historical and reminiscent approach, drawing upon examples from the history of the CCIA.

I am fortunate in having at my disposal some notes especially provided by Sir Kenneth Grubb, chairman of the CCIA from its creation in 1946 until his retirement in 1968, and the unfinished and unpublished memoirs of the late Dr. O. Frederick Nolde, director of the CCIA from its foundation until his retirement in 1969. Dr. Leopoldo Niilus, the present director, has been discreetly indiscreet, at my request, in regard to one example which is more contemporary but not, I think, dangerously so. Sir Kenneth has chosen, out of a multitude of examples of private diplomacy in his experience, Cyprus and religious liberty in Spain and Portugal. I can do no better than to quote his notes in extenso and without amendment or correction.

Cyprus

"The 'fifties, when nations were recovering from the exhaustion of war, saw a crop of new international tensions. One of these is still (1974) very much in the public eye, namely the status and government of Cyprus. Cyprus was then a British possession administered through the Colonial Office. The agitation of those years was not a new thing, but a revival. "Enosis" (union with Greece) had raised its head vigorously between the World Wars, but it does not seem that any church agency existed then, equipped to concern itself responsibly with the issues at stake.

"It was not an easy case for the churches and the Commission of the Churches on International Affairs in particular. The organized ecumenical movement was young and little experience had been gained in the handling of delicate international disputes. The Orthodox Church of Greece had been a member of the World Council of Churches from its beginning. The CCIA has never existed, however, to be a mouthpiece only for its friends. In any case, it would have been plainly silly and repugnant to good judgment to assume that the Christian Greeks were right and the Moslem or secular Turks were wrong. Such situations are never so simple.

"The chairman and director of the Commission visited Greece, Cyprus, and Turkey. These visits included lengthy discussions with cabinet ministers, heads of State and leading personalities of public influence, whatever their outlook. In Cyprus the chairman and director met with the community leaders such as Archbishop Makarios, Mr. Clerides, Mr. Kutchuk of the Turkish community, as well as the Governor and many others in the Administration of those days. Passions were already running high, perhaps higher than at any subsequent time until the recent outburst in July 1974.

"The concern of the CCIA for Cyprus was maintained steadily so long as the situation remained acute. The extensive discussions briefly recounted here had a mediating influence; of that there is little doubt."

Religious Liberty in Spain and Portugal

"The familiar but urgent question of freedoms and rights, particularly in the field of religious beliefs and practices, occupied the CCIA throughout the 'fifties and 'sixties. All members of the staff were involved; much of the necessary negotiation was in the hands of the chairman and director. Many questions of this order arose in the 'Latin' countries, that is in Latin America, Spain and Portugal, and the Portuguese overseas territories. Indeed the chairman was for many years also chairman of the special international committee of Protestant interests concerned with religious minorities in Spain.

"It is hard today to recall with any vividness the acute disaffection and disabilities of the non-Roman Catholic minorities in Spain. The task of cooperating with them when such cooperation was requested—which happened often—in seeking to obtain reasonable freedom, and of struggling to obtain a liberalization of legal restrictions which were plainly incompatible with the standards of the United Nations, was for many years depressing and difficult. It was made no easier by the suspicion of intervention by foreigners which the Spaniards nourished. Only too often do modern nations claim the benefits of internationalism and membership in the UN, but, domestically, decline to adopt and apply liberal standards.

"Those were years when Protestant ministers were imprisoned on the flimsiest grounds. Minorities could not openly diffuse their beliefs; even the circulation of the Bible was limited to a derisory degree. Publications on religious or public questions involving a discussion of freedoms and rights were severely restricted and often penalized. Heavy fines were imposed on very slight cause. Church life, activities and meetings were kept under narrow and disturbing surveillance, and any form of witness and work other than services of worship was almost stillborn, if born at all.

"The handling of these questions was not eased by the divisions between the Spanish evangelical churches, but it cannot be said that the policy of the World Council of Churches was always wise; this was partly because of the difficulty of obtaining really reliable information and evaluations. The World Council did succeed in arousing wide protests over the forced closure of the United Evangelical Seminary in Madrid, but this issue was not of crucial importance, a fact that a few well-informed persons had perceived from the start.

"The chairman of the CCIA made repeated visits to Madrid and constant discussion went on with leading public figures in Spanish politics, the press, the Roman Catholic Church, Opus Dei, and the influential professions. The embassies principally interested, such as the Dutch, the American, and the British, and not least the Papal Nuncio were consistently helpful.

"Similar discussions were also held in Lisbon on repeated occasions, different as the Portuguese scene was from the Spanish. Here the main matter for concern was the rights and freedoms of individuals and of organized communities, such as churches and missions, in the Portuguese territories in Africa. The going was not always easy, but from time to time real progress was registered. Discreet contact was meanwhile maintained with the local 'freedom' revolt.

"In these situations there is much which cannot be said publicly. It is particularly true in Spain and Portugal that the extreme sensitivity of government implies a standing ambiguous hazard for the negotiator. On the one hand regimes such as those then in power may be painfully sensitive to criticism, even when the criticism is serious and well-argued and is presented by persons whose general friendship is well known. On the other hand, injudicious publicity and any impression of moral censoriousness, albeit inadvertently left by a hurried visitor, may be quite fatal. The manner of a protest is of prime importance and fluency in the languages involved is always useful and commands attention."

Dr. O. Frederick Nolde

Fred Nolde's enterprises and adventures in the field of private diplomacy were so many and so diverse that I have had to exercise stern self-discipline in my selection of examples, omitting many outstanding ones simply for lack of space. In the end I have selected Indonesia, Korea, and the Peace Observation Commissions.

I chose Indonesia because it is a good example of action based on the fact that there were substantial and influential Christian groups in each of the two contending countries. This has so often been the basis of effective CCIA mediation in an essentially political situation.

Indonesia

Prior to granting independence to Indonesia in December 1949, the Dutch had initiated military action. A short time thereafter agreement was reached to convene what came to be called the Hague Round Table—a meeting held in August 1949 between representatives of the Netherlands and Indonesia where the Dutch agreed to transfer sovereignty to Indonesia later that year. While Indonesia is predominantly a Muslim country, there are substantial numbers of Christians there, and Christian leaders in both countries—both lay and clergy—had been working fairly closely with the CCIA for some three years.

Consequently, prior to the convening of the Hague Round Table, Nolde sent contacts in each of the two countries a request for a memorandum interpreting the situation as they saw it, asking each to remember that there were Christians in the other country. In other words, we solicited from our people in Indonesia and in the Netherlands separate memoranda compiled within the dual context of political expertise and Christian community. Very considerably to our surprise, the memoranda arrived with more than usual promptness. We then crossed them, sending the Indonesian memorandum to leaders in the Netherlands and the Netherlands document to those in Indonesia—in each instance asking that a group be called together to study the other's point of view.

When the Hague Round Table met, our commissioner in Indonesia, then Deptuy Prime Minister and formerly Minister of Health, was a member of the official delegation of Indonesia. The president of our commission and the head of the Ecumenical Institute at Bossey were advisers to the Dutch delegation. While one must not exaggerate the value of the conversations that took place apart from the formal meetings of the Round Table, there is no question that certain issues were moved more readily to solution because of the relationship that had been established in the process of looking at a common political problem in the context of a common Christian faith. Whether called a technique or an area of activity, here is a type of situation where Christians organized on an international plane can make a contribution to the reconciliation of differences or to the solution of problems.

Korea

The conflict in Korea and its possible escalation into world war became a deep concern and preoccupation of the CCIA when war broke out in 1950. Although they expressed it in differing—and sometimes contradictory—ways, the churches throughout the world showed grave perturbation about what was happening in Korea and about what it could lead to in a wider world.

Two messages from the National Council of Churches situated in the United States sent to the U.S. Delegation to the United Nations are indicative. In November 1951 the National Council sent a message which stated: "We commend the action of the UN in resisting aggression in Korea. We are gratified that 51 members of the UN are associated in resisting the aggression in Korea, and that 41 members have offered specific assistance to this collective endeavor. We are saddened by the many thousands of casualties resulting from these operations." The National Council expressed its views again to the U.S. Delegation in an October 1952 letter which stated: "While the National Council reaffirms its support of the United Nations in resisting aggression in Korea, it urges your Delegation to do everything possible to bring about a speedy and just armistice. It supports the United Nations in refusing to repatriate forcibly prisoners of war to North Korea and China. It favors a full and frank discussion of the Korean problem in the General Assembly. It urges your delegation to help spread relief and rehabilitation efforts in the Republic of Korea."

Negotiations between the United Nations and the Communist commanders had begun on July 10, 1951. Three main issues prevented an agreement: the Chinese demand that all troops leave Korea, the question of the boundary between the two Koreas, and the prisoner return issue. On this last issue negotiations had been deadlocked and then broken off.

The Central Committee of the World Council of Churches also deliberated on the Korea question. At Lucknow, India, on January 7, 1953, the Central Committee authorized its chairman, the Bishop of Chichester, to address by cable the following letter to the President of the Seventh General Assembly of the United Nations with copies to all member governments:

The Central Committee of the World Council of Churches meeting at Lucknow has requested me as its chairman to express to you as President of the General Assembly of the United Nations its deep concern at the growing deterioration in the relations between the rival groupings of powers and to make an appeal to the United Nations. It is profoundly distressed at the widespread sense of frustration over the increasing bitterness which affects relations between the powers. In addressing you it believes that it not only speaks for the delegates from the churches of many lands but also reflects the great body of Christian opinion throughout the world. . . .

The Central Committee wishes me to say how greatly it appreciates the efforts of the United Nations to overcome what is apparently the one remaining obstacle to the conclusion of an armistice in Korea. It regrets that no plan has so far been found acceptable to all parties. It most earnestly urges that the United Nations persevere in its efforts to resolve the conflict by a truce which will safeguard prisoners of war against forcible repatriation or forcible detention.

The question of repatriation may not be the only obstacle to the conclusion of agreements to end the fighting and other steps may have to be taken. The Central Committee therefore welcomes the expressed willingness of the highest authorities of certain great powers to hold personal discussions and trusts that the essential preliminary conditions of successful consultation may be satisfied.

The immediate object for which the United Nations intervened has been fulfilled. There now remains the settlement of the Korean question with a view to the unification and independence of Korea. The Central Committee is far from underestimating the difficulties. But it is convinced that the only way to end the bloodshed in Korea and so hasten the solution not only of the Korean but also of wider questions is through negotiated settlements. A deep sense of responsibility therefore prompts this appeal to the United Nations to guard against any extension of the conflict and to persist unceasingly in the promotion of negotiations until success is achieved. It commends the more widespread use in international conferences of an umpire.

The Central Committee of the World Council of Churches is also aware that the serious economic needs of many countries in different parts of the world, especially in Asia, cry out for attention. It appreciates the notable work done through technical assistance and in other humanitarian ways by the United Nations and urges the nations unitedly to devote their resources to meet this call. But in this grave and perilous hour the breaking of the deadlock in Korea is the immediate and essential step to these wider constructive activities. . . .

President Dwight D. Eisenhower who, following his election in November 1952, had proceeded to Korea on a tour of inspection, was bent upon obtaining an honorable truce which perforce had to safeguard prisoners of war against forcible repatriation or forcible detention. Among the obstacles to the conclusion of an armistice was the opposition of South Korean President Syngman Rhee with his avowed intention to march his armed forces to the Yalu. The situation which prevailed in the spring of 1953 was indeed uncertain and precarious.

On April 9, President Rhee addressed a letter to President Eisenhower frankly criticizing the Communists' recent offer to resume peace negotiations. He stated that if a peace agreement should be arranged allowing the Chinese to remain in Korea, South Korea would feel justified in asking all her allies to get out of the country except those who would be willing to join in a drive northward to the Yalu.

In his reply to this letter, President Eisenhower expressed sympathy with the aspirations of the Korean people, but emphasized the following points:

> First, the action taken by the United Nations in Korea was to assist your valiant country in repelling the armed attack directed against it initially by the North Korean regime and subsequently by the Chinese Communists. This has successfully been accomplished.

> Second, the task of repelling the armed attack having been accomplished, it would not be defensible to refuse to stop the fighting on an honorable basis as a prerequisite to working out the remaining issues by peaceful means.

> Third, the United States and the United Nations have consistently supported the unification of Korea, under conditions which would assure its freedom and independence. Neither the United States nor the United Nations has ever committed itself to resort to war to achieve this objective. To do so would be a complete negation of the basic tenets of this country and the United Nations.

> Fourth, any agreement to stop the fighting on an honorable basis presupposes a willingness on the part of both sides to discuss the remaining issues and to make every reasonable effort to reach agreement thereon. As I said in my address of April 16 an honorable armistice "means the immediate cessation of hostilities and the prompt initiation of political discussions leading to the holding of free elections in a United Korea." [1]

A few days later armistice negotiations were resumed. The thorny issue of repatriation remained unresolved and was viewed as a test of the good faith of the Chinese Communists. On May 30, President Rhee again addressed a letter to President Ei-

[1] Dwight D. Eisenhower, *Mandate for Change* (Garden City, N.Y.: Doubleday, 1963), p. 182.

senhower in which he opposed any armistice agreement that would allow the Chinese Communists to remain in Korea.

In his reply, President Eisenhower gave assurances that the United States would continue its effort by all peaceful means to bring about the unification of Korea; that at the conclusion of an acceptable armistice he was prepared to negotiate a mutual defense treaty; and that the United States government would seek to continue economic aid to the Republic of Korea.

On June 4 the Communists submitted a prisoners-of-war proposal which seemed favorable and which a few days later turned out to be so in that it provided for voluntary repatriation of prisoners of war. Reaction from around the world to steps in the armistice negotiations was highly favorable. While President Rhee did not oppose the progress in forthright fashion, demonstrations against the armistice continued in Seoul, and Rhee stated that if he felt Korea had to take military action on its own he would do so.

The promising progress toward an armistice was suddenly brought to a standstill by the "escape" of 25,000 North Korean non-Communist prisoners and the admission of complicity in this incident by Rhee's government. Since the United Nations High Command was contending that prisoners of war should not be repatriated against their will—and this the Communists had conceded—the action of Syngman Rhee sabotaged the very basis on which the armistice was to be built. (Negotiations were broken off in consequence of this act on June 18, but later resumed on July 20). The Secretary of State, John Foster Dulles, sent a sharp letter to Rhee, taking him to task for his actions and advising him that Assistant Secretary of State Walter Robertson would come in person. The negotiations which had to be undertaken in Seoul with President Rhee, whom President Eisenhower called "this fiercely patriotic but recalcitrant old man," [2] required tact, fortitude, and patience.

It was at this stage that Fred Nolde became convinced that something more than Chrstian statements was required. When June of 1953 brought threats of a unilateral march to the Yalu, the

[2] *Ibid.*, p. 187.

time seemed to him to have come when someone should convey personally to Korean Christians the views which prevailed within the Christian fellowship round the world—namely, that the time had come for a truce, if it could be honorably negotiated.

In short he decided to board a plane for Korea, no easy achievement in itself at that time. He went with the full support and the anxious prayers of all his colleagues in the World Council of Churches and with the knowledge, and in fact approval, of John Foster Dulles.

In a memorandum dated June 25, 1953, Nolde defined his venture in the following terms (which may be viewed as guidelines for the private diplomat):

1. My visit must be ostensibly and in reality as Director of the CCIA representing the churches and not in any way connected with any government or the United Nations.

2. The normal assistance of the U.S. government in facilitating the trip by way of military clearance and visas can be accepted.

3. While certain officials in Korea will be informed of my visit, contact will be initiated by me.

4. My primary purpose will be to seek within the Christian fellowship better understanding in face of known differences and to decrease the area of difference with a view to promoting agreement. I shall accordingly hear the views of our Korean colleagues and shall present the views of the CCIA.

5. As far as contacts with government officials outside our church groups are concerned, I shall be guided by our Korean colleagues and by the situation in which I find myself.

6. Because of the anticipated opposition to the objectives which I seek and to protect those with whom I establish contact I am authorized to raise certain questions in behalf of Church World Service pertaining to personnel, extensive shipment of dried milk released by the U.S. Department of Agriculture and clothing shipment.

7. Little can at this time be said as to how I shall actually proceed. No advance preparations have been possible and I shall have to make my own way.

8. The expense of the trip will be met by the CCIA—if necessary as now seems to be the case through extrabudgetary funds. This we shall face in due course.

The full story of Nolde's Korean enterprise is too long to be reported in this brief essay. His first task had been to discover how deep-rooted was the popular agreement with President Syngman Rhee's opposition to a cease-fire. His provisional conclusions were that the public demonstrations in support of the President "were not forced but were well-organized," but that there was a good chance that public opinion might just as readily fall in with any change in official policy. The climax of this enterprise finally came when, by devious routes, all of them Korean, an interview was arranged with the President. It is worth recording that this meeting immediately followed one between the President and Walter Robertson, who was there as President Eisenhower's special emissary.

The interview began on an unpromising note. It needs to be remembered that South Korea at that time was dominated politically by staunch but somewhat fundamentalist Christians of whom President Rhee was one. Taking direct aim at Nolde, whom he knew to be both an American and a theologian, President Rhee opened by referring to his Bible reading of that morning. It was the story of Joseph and his betrayal by his brothers. He interpreted this literally and figuratively and saw in Korea the younger brother being betrayed by his elders. Affairs improved after this opening gambit, and finally the President announced his intention of proclaiming a Day of Prayer. At the President's request Nolde drafted a proclamation, but, apparently because of administrative confusion, it was never used.

As a result of the Robertson negotiations—Nolde had been in discreet touch with Robertson throughout—Dr. Rhee assured President Eisenhower that he would not obstruct in any way the implementation of an armistice. At the same time he expressed again his misgivings about the long-term results. A truce was finally signed on July 27, 1953.

Nolde's own assessment of his venture was: "As far as the efforts of CCIA are concerned, it should not be concluded that this procedure followed in connection with the Korean armistice would be applicable in other situations. Yet it is not amiss to say that the good offices of the Commission have potential worth, with necessary adjustments, in a wide variety of tensions and conflicts."

United Nations Peace Observation Commission
The idea of the United Nations Peace Observation Commission germinated in the Korean crisis. Concerned about the future of peace and security in Korea and with a view to aiding the unification and independence of Korea, the General Assembly on December 14, 1947, by a vote of 43 to 0 with 6 abstentions adopted a resolution wherein it established a United Nations Temporary Commission on Korea. On December 12, 1948, the General Assembly by a vote of 48 to 6 with 1 abstention, adopted a resolution establishing a Commission on Korea composed of seven member governments to continue the work of the Temporary Commission.

The following year, on October 21, 1949, the General Assembly by a vote of 48 in favor to 6 against with 3 abstentions resolved that "the United Nations Commission on Korea shall continue in being." The Commission was authorized to "observe and report on any developments which might lead to or otherwise involve military conflict in Korea," and "have authority . . . in its discretion to appoint observers, and to utilize the services and good offices of one or more persons whether or not representatives on the Commission." It was with this mandate that the Commission was operating when hostilities broke out in Korea.

The important role played by this Commission in June 1950 convinced Nolde that if a Commission of this kind, set up temporarily for a particular area, could identify an aggressor, there would be merit in a permanent system of international observer commissions under the United Nations, with the purpose of deterring aggressors or of identifying the aggressor in the event that aggression was perpetrated.

At that time John Foster Dulles—long active in the USCC, an original Commissioner of the CCIA, and a long-standing friend of Nolde—was an adviser to U.S. Secretary of State Dean Acheson. Accordingly, early in 1950, Nolde wrote to Dulles raising the question, inter alia:

Would it be possible for the United Nations, perhaps through the General Assembly, to establish Commissions to observe in areas where a clear international responsibility continues to exist as in Germany and Austria; and further to send a Commission to any country which believes itself to be in danger of aggression and seeks assistance from the United Nations?

This letter was followed up by a long consultation between the two men and, on July 26, 1950, Dulles wrote Nolde:

I was able to talk at lunch with Deputy Under Secretary [H. Freeman] Matthews and with Assistant Secretary [John] Hickerson, who is in charge of United Nations matters. I told them of my talk with you and of the idea which we had discussed, of the United Nations Assembly proposing to have observers at the various points of particular tension between the "two worlds" and to make acceptance of such observers a test of nonaggressive disposition of the various member states.

Both of them thought the idea was excellent. As you know, we had been thinking along these lines but not with quite the same generality.

They both thought it would be a very good thing if your commission would somewhat develop this thesis and then get the idea out through the various national adherents.

With this substantial encouragement there was no stopping Nolde. He readily secured the support of the President and Chairman of CCIA—the late Baron van Asbrek and Sir Kenneth Grubb. A letter was addressed to our commissioners on national commissions in thirty-three countries, the main substance of which was:

By a comprehensive system of International Observer Commissions, objectively conceived and operated, the United Nations would:

1. call upon all Member Governments to cooperate in this measure at a time when international peace and security are dangerously threatened;

2. make the extent of cooperation by Member Governments a test of their nonaggressive disposition and of their readiness to bring their conduct under international scrutiny;

3. serve as a deterrent to aggression, on the assumption that governments will not want to risk the stigma of being named the aggressor by an impartial agent;

4. facilitate objective identification of the aggressor in the event that aggression is perpetrated.

We are convinced that a plan of this kind can work in the interest of peace and will commend itself to our constituent members. We therefore suggest that the appropriate Department or Commission of the Churches in your country give serious consideration to the proposal for a system of International Observer Commissions. If agreement is reached, representation to the Foreign Office of your Government may serve to encourage support for such a proposal at the forthcoming session of the UN General Assembly.

The issue was now in the hands of enough Foreign Ministries to make possible, if they were in agreement, positive affirmative action by the United Nations.

On November 3, 1950, fifty-two member states voted for a resolution entitled "Uniting for Peace," a measure which they held as a "good policy of insurance against a Third World War," as a "turning point in the history of mankind," and as "the most constructive action since the founding of the United Nations." Two countries abstained, and five, led by the USSR, voted against, but all agreed on the crucial importance of the resolution.

The earlier vote on the section dealing with the Peace Observation Commission was adopted without opposition. It reads:

3. **Establishes** a Peace Observation Commission which, for the calendar years 1951 and 1952, shall be composed of fourteen Members, namely: China, Colombia, Czechoslovakia, France, India, Iraq, Israel, New Zealand, Pakistan, Sweden, the Union of Soviet Socialist Republics, the United Kingdom of Great Britain and Northern Ireland, the United States of America and Uruguay, and which could observe and report on the situation in any area where there exists international tension the continuance of which is likely to endanger the maintenance of international peace and security. Upon the invitation or with the consent of the State into whose territory the Commission would go, the General Assembly, or the Interim Committee when the Assembly is not in session, may utilize the Commission if the Security Council is not exercising the functions assigned to it by the Charter with respect to the matter in question. Decisions to utilize the Commission shall be made on the affirmative vote of two-thirds of the members present and voting. The Security Council may also utilize the Commission in accordance with its authority under the Charter;

4. **Decides** that the Commission shall have authority in its discretion to appoint sub-commissions and to utilize the services of observers to assist it in the performance of its functions;

5. **Recommends** to all governments and authorities that they cooperate with the Commission and assist it in the performance of its functions;

6. **Requests** the Secretary-General to provide the necessary staff and facilities, utilizing, where directed by the Commission, the United Nations Panel of Field Observers envisaged in the General Assembly resolution 297 B (IV).

Although the Peace Observation commissions subsequently had a checkered history, the underlying concepts for their creation constituted an early step in the peacekeeping history of the United Nations. John Foster Dulles, who had been so cooperative, was correct when he wrote Nolde, "I think you have hit on something that may be constructive for peace."

The Sudan

The 1972 "Operation Sudan," a go-between service undertaken by the CCIA at the request of the parties concerned, is an interesting and promising example of how a private, or nongovernmental, agent can act as a catalyst at the instance of one or both of the protagonists. It was so successful that both Leopoldo Niilus, director of CCIA, and Burgess Carr, secretary of the All Africa Conference of Churches, were decorated with the Order of the Two Niles (first grade) by Sudanese President Nimeiry at the conclusion of the operation.

While there are various and sometimes contradictory analyses of the origins of the tense division between northern and southern Sudan after the country's achievement of independence in 1956, it seems clear that the conflict was partly a consequence of the stupidity of colonialism and partly a consequence of the colonialism of missionaries.

Although the detailed argument need not detain us here, it is important to note that when Sudan became independent it was a nation divided religiously, ethnically, regionally, and historically.

The African nation largest in area, Sudan is populated by Arabs in the north and by black Africans in the south. Arabic, the official language, is spoken in the predominantly Muslim north (where Khartoum, the capital, lies), while various tribal languages are spoken in the south. Following independence successive regimes in the north were unable to pacify the distrust and fears of the southern tribes, and guerrilla warfare was waged in the south against the national government.

Both the World Council of Churches and the All Africa Conference of Churches had been concerned with Sudan problems since, at least, 1965. The WCC was mainly concerned with aid to refugees, particularly the thousands who had fled from the south to neighboring countries, and the AACC with the succor and sustenance of the church life of the south.

By 1970 it had become clear to both Councils that their efforts meant little or nothing so long as the basic political issues, resulting in virtual civil war, remained unresolved. This was underlined by the continued confrontation of the forces of the Anya-Nya, the military arm of the South Sudan Liberation Movement, with the Sudan armed forces.

After much quiet negotiation and considerable, though discreet, encouragement from the Sudanese ambassadors in Kenya and Ethiopia, a joint WCC/AACC mission was invited by the Sudanese government to visit Khartoum in May 1971.

The main objective was the channeling of aid, but the question of reconciliation was by no means ruled out. On the contrary, it happily became the major issue of discussion and agreement. The delegation reported back as points of agreement:

1. Reconciliation
   a) The Government is in favor of the delegates making contacts with representatives from the South with a view to establishing direct contact for talks on reconciliation.
   b) Groups to be represented are those who have influence on people in the South and among the refugees.
   c) Talks could take place anywhere.
   d) The Government would agree to a "cooling off" period if no security danger is involved.

e) Details of regional autonomy within one Sudan would be
discussed.

f) The question of under whose auspices the talks would take
place would be discussed later.

With this encouragement the CCIA immediately renewed its
contacts with the representatives of the South Sudan Liberation
Movement in exile in London. This resulted in the following letter
from Niilus written in late 1971:

We are pleased that following several conversations with you as the
delegated representatives of the Anya-Nya in Europe, during which
you informed us of the present position of your movement; and following the visit of the joint World Council of Churches/All Africa
Conference of Churches mission to Khartoum, where we were given
the Sudan Government's position on reconciliation and relief, we
are now able to help make your journey to Africa possible. This we
do out of our sincere interest that a peace be established in the
Sudan which will make possible a creative use of the relief assistance
to the suffering Sudanese which the churches stand ready to give as
soon as it can be determined that such assistance can be properly
supervised and distributed.

You have been fully informed about our visit to Khartoum, where
we were asked to enter into conversations with you which might
lead to negotiations between the two parties in conflict. It is our understanding that, despite the events which have occurred in the interim, these positions remain firm and can be considered those of
the Khartoum Government. We have a standing invitation to return
to Khartoum for further discussions in which we would hopefully be
able to faithfully represent the views of the Southern Sudanese leadership. We therefore look forward to having a report of your visit on
your return. We hope that it will include a) the reaction of your leadership to the positions stated by the Khartoum Government, b) the
obtaining of a list of Southerners whom Anya-Nya leaders would
want to be involved in any negotiations; and c) the obtaining of letters of credance stating whom in fact Col. Lagu wishes to authorize
to deal with the WCC/AACC on behalf of the Anya-Nya.

Allow me to repeat that the WCC has offered its services to you
and to the Khartoum Government as a politically disinterested international humanitarian organization. Our sole motive is to best serve

the people of Sudan, North and South, for which we understand that a lasting peace is indispensable.

The rest is history. A series of "informal" meetings between the Sudan government and the SSLM/Anya-Nya leaders with the CCIA invited as "observers" but acting as mediators culminated in the meeting at Addis Ababa in February 1972 where formal agreement was reached and ratified a month later.

This successful outcome of a skillfully handled mediation is a good note on which to conclude this essay. I suggest the experience in Sudan described here is evidence that there is need, from time to time, for a private or nongovernmental organization to act as handmaiden, or even midwife, in tense and seemingly unreconcilable situations. Other efforts are not always as successful.

The CCIA's involvement in the examples recounted here has been a mediating influence. But in such claims modesty is the best policy—the formulation and acceptance of peaceful resolutions of conflicts require the concurrence of many approaches, of which the church background is but one. And even when settlements are effected, they do not always endure. Publicity on these occasions is apt to hinder rather than to help. Often publicity cannot be avoided, and it does tend to precipitate at too early a stage the assumption of firm positions which cannot later be adjusted and not infrequently leaves misunderstandings. Nevertheless, when the right conditions prevail an outside entity, having the respect and confidence of the parties involved, can, as these examples show, help contribute to the peaceful resolution of conflict.

SEVEN

AN EXERCISE IN DEMI-DIPLOMACY: THE CASE OF VIETNAM

HARRY S. ASHMORE

HARRY S. ASHMORE, a journalist by profession, has been active for many years in the Center for the Study of Democratic Institutions in Santa Barbara, California, and was its Executive Vice-President from 1967 to 1969. With his colleague William Baggs, a Florida journalist, he twice traveled to Hanoi. In Ashmore's view the purpose of their visits in 1967 and 1968 and their limitations were clearly understood by responsible officials of the U.S. government at the outset; as private citizens they had no official status and therefore could not negotiate or in any way represent the government. But in the end the government refused to make use of the channel Ashmore and Baggs had opened with Hanoi. The Ashmore/Baggs visits and the controversy that then developed about them demonstrate the limitations of outside initiatives.——Eds.

I N 1964 THE CENTER FOR THE Study of Democratic Institutions, a privately financed organization located in Santa Barbara, California, saw in Pope John's 1963 encyclical, Pacem in Terris, an opportunity to participate in a vital effort to thaw the cold war. With much encouragement from the United Nations and the initial approbation of the new administration of Lyndon Johnson, the Center, directed by its founder and president, Robert M. Hutchins, employed the papal message as the basis for assembling a distinguished international group for three days of protracted talks in New York in February 1965, and a repeat performance with a different cast in Geneva, Switzerland, at the end of May 1967. The design for these Pacem in Terris convocations called for

---

For the more detailed account of this exercise on which this article is partly based, see Harry S. Ashmore and William C. Baggs, *Mission to Hanoi: A Chronicle of Double-Dealing in High Places* (New York: Putnam, 1968). See also Harry S. Ashmore, "The Public Relations of Peace," *Center Magazine* (October/November 1967), vol. 1.

a mixture of political leaders, diplomats, intellectuals, churchmen, and private men of affairs. The hope was that in a public but informal setting, where no participant was required or expected to speak on behalf of his government, the inhibitions of normal diplomacy might be eased.

In August 1964 the incident had occurred in the Gulf of Tonkin that is now generally accepted as marking the crucial turning point in the Vietnamese War. In the first wave of reaction to a reported attack by North Vietnamese patrol boats against U.S. Navy vessels, President Johnson got the blank-check resolution from the Senate he would later use to justify taking the air war across the neutral zone. On February 4, 1965, dispatches from Saigon reported that the lid was being taken off the heretofore limited war. By the time Pacem in Terris I convened in New York on February 17 the aerial bombardment of the North was under way.

From that time forward the bombing of North Vietnam provided an obligato to the Pacem in Terris effort. In June 1965, three Under Secretaries of the United Nations, along with veteran diplomats from a half-dozen foreign countries, came to the Center in Santa Barbara to help evaluate results of the New York convocation. The mood of the gathering was dark. Escalation of the war in Vietnam, they reported, was already imperiling the fragile East-West detente that had made possible Pacem in Terris. Unanimously they urged that the Center try again, with the main effort this time on bringing in the mainland Chinese.

A year later, at the Palais des Nations in Geneva, the Center assembled advisers from ten nations and the United Nations—all persons who had participated in the first convocation or were familiar with the undertaking. Hutchins put two questions to them: How could we persuade Peking to participate in Pacem in Terris II? If we could not, was there any point in going ahead? The first question drew a variety of suggestions, all admittedly doubtful. The answer to the second was yes. And the participants on their own motion added an item to the agenda.

The senior Russian at Geneva, N. N. Inozemtsev, observed that while those present might agree among themselves that Vietnam was only one among urgent issues of coexistence, the world no longer thought so; the fighting in Southeast Asia was bound to dominate any program we might devise for Pacem in Terris II. This suggested a concentrated effort to bring Hanoi into the convocation, and thereby to initiate a direct American contact that conceivably could open the way for diplomats to make a formal move toward peace negotiations. The French participants, headed by former Premier Pierre Mendès-France, agreed to arrange with the North Vietnamese legation in Paris to transmit to Hanoi a letter suggesting a meeting with representatives of the Center.

In late August 1965, under a Prague postmark, there arrived in the ordinary mail a polite letter to Hutchins in Santa Barbara saying that such a meeting was not possible at that time, but pointedly leaving the door open. It was signed Ho Chi Minh.

The Center's overture to the People's Republic to consider participation in Pacem in Terris II was borne westward in October 1966 by a remarkable Mexican intellectual, Luis Quintanilla, now teaching at the University of Mexico after a distinguished diplomatic career. In Peking Quintanilla got as far as an audience with Foreign Minister Chen Yi, from whom he received a lengthy lecture on the inevitability of World War III, and the certainty of the ultimate Chinese triumph. He read this correctly as an indication that the Center's invitation to Pacem in Terris II would not be accepted, but he did wangle permission to leave China by way of Hanoi. There he was granted a private audience with Ho Chi Minh, in the course of which the President indicated that he would consider receiving U.S. representatives of the Center for further discussions. Quintanilla subsequently informed Ho that the Center would send me (I was then executive vice-president) and a member of its board of directors, William C. Baggs, editor of the *Miami News.*

Hanoi's acceptance of this proposal automatically produced a new relationship with the State Department. The Department could grant us clearance to join our Mexican colleague in a mission to North Vietnam only by acknowledging the legitimacy of the undertaking. When we were asked to keep the trip secret as long as possible, and to clear our passports at the U.S. consulate in Hong Kong to avoid any possibility of a news leak in Washington, the

Department was recognizing that we might open up a useful channel of communication with the North Vietnamese. Finally, we were asked to make a number of inquiries in Hanoi on the Department's behalf.

We agreed to the conditions, although secrecy could be only temporary, since it was understood that Baggs ultimately would write a series of articles for his newspaper, and that at some point Hanoi's reaction to the Center's invitation to Pacem in Terris II would require a public announcement. This, however, was all to the good in the Department's view, since it would provide an excellent cover in case of premature publicity.

In the weeks before our departure we talked with Under Secretary of State Nicholas deB. Katzenbach and William P. Bundy, the Assistant Secretary for East Asian and Pacific Affairs and some of the Vietnamese experts in his section. We had two lengthy background briefing sessions at Foggy Bottom, more than a month apart. After the first briefing session we prepared a confidential memorandum for our principals at the Center setting forth our understanding of the U.S. position as it had been presented to us. Copies of this went to Katzenbach and Bundy, noting that we wanted to make certain that we had not inadvertently done violence to their views. This written summary was before them when we met again in late December for our final session before departure, and no demurrer was indicated.

The memorandum made clear our understanding of the nature and limitations of our mission, in which we would "function as private citizens, with no obligation to our government except to keep the State Department informed." We added that, "we could foresee no eventuality in which we would be in a position to do more than transmit information and impressions, that if anything in the nature of a specific proposal emerged in our conversations it would of necessity require some official action on both sides, at which point we would fade from the scene."

We arrived in North Vietnam on January 6, 1967. As we progressed through the schedule laid out for us, we began to note that the propaganda content was dropping day by day. For the first three days we were taken regularly to the villa occupied by our

host, the DRV Committee for World Peace, or to the headquarters
of an appropriate agency, and exposed to a series of specialists
called in for what were evidently set briefings. It appeared to us
that the cast of characters at these affairs was steadily becoming
more political, and so was the tone of the conversation. This
turned out to be the build-up for a meeting with Ho Chi Minh arranged the day before our departure. Ho cut short the pleasantries
and moved straight on to business. "Please forget protocol," he
said in English. "Please feel at home. Can we talk among ourselves—in confidence?"

We assured him that we could, subject to the understanding that
we would report the conversation in full to the high officials of the
State Department with whom we had talked before beginning our
journey. We had no official status, we emphasized, no authority to
negotiate or act as agent for our government, but we thought we
could adequately report the prevailing views in Washington and
accurately convey his in return. Ho indicated his understanding
and approval, and then spoke with us for two hours.

Neither we nor Ho were under any illusions that we were
engaged in anything that could possibly be construed as a negotiating session. I am sure he regarded us as no more than a direct
conduit to the State Department through which he could, without
binding himself in any way, convey broad general terms as the
preliminary basis for negotiation and modify one sticky condition
he had previously set—that he would not be bombed to the negotiating table. In effect he had altered the position he had previously
taken in public to say that he would agree to negotiate in advance
of a bombing cessation on the understanding that the bombing
would halt before the actual negotiating took place and would not
be resumed so long as the negotiations continued.

I did not then, and do not now, see that Ho had anything to
gain by making his offer if he did not mean it. Nothing was going
to happen until and unless the United States accepted the feeler
and moved to enter into formal discussions of a settlement—at
which time the official negotiators of the actual terms of settlement
would take over and Baggs and I would be wholly out of the picture, with neither side committed in any way to any of the substan-

tive matters, such as a loose federation rather than an immediate coalition government, mentioned in passing by Ho, I thought, primarily to demonstrate how unlimited an agenda he was prepared to accept.

As it turned out, the story of our visit broke while we were still in North Vietnam. Harrison Salisbury, then of the *New York Times,* had been cleared just ahead of us and departed from Hanoi the day we arrived. He picked our names off the manifest of the weekly International Control Commission plane which provided the only means of entry for U.S. citizens.

By the time we got back to Los Angeles on January 15, Salisbury's articles had already created a furore. By documenting the extent of civilian casualties produced by saturation bombing of some North Vietnamese cities and towns, Salisbury had refuted official U.S. claims that the air attack was confined to military targets. The initial Washington reaction was a concerted effort to discredit Salisbury by attacking his veracity and, in the case of some administration fuglemen in the press, his loyalty.

As professional observers who had covered most of the ground Salisbury described, and some he did not, we found ourselves in considerable demand. At the State Department's request, however, we managed to hide out for some days after our return, and to meet privately in Washington with the Department's top echelon. These briefings went on intermittently for a day and a half, and covered in detail the two-hour conversation we had had with Ho Chi Minh. A memorandum summarizing our report concluded: "In the circumstances, the remarks of Ho impress us as an offer to come to the table and the elements of the offer are simple enough: we stop the bombing and he will talk."

I then returned to Los Angeles to meet the press and deliver a considerably expurgated report on the Hanoi tour at a public meeting of the Center's Founding Members. In Miami, Baggs began a series of articles for the *News,* which were distributed nationally by the Associated Press. Our reports were a vindication of Salisbury, and as a result we encountered the first private signs of what would later become a public monument of official displeasure. But, as we had agreed to do, we continued to avoid any suggestion that we had had any but routine contacts with the State Department or had opened up any significant new channel of communication with Hanoi.

In fact, our dealings with the Department had begun to take on a pronounced schizoid quality. There were those in high places there and elsewhere in the administration who seemed to regard our open channel to Ho Chi Minh as valuable and who sought to use it, not as an instrument of negotiation, but as a means of exchanging exploratory views without compromising the official position of either side. But there were also those of equal or higher rank who seemed to be opposed to any kind of exchange with Hanoi.

We had not brought back any hard proposal from Ho Chi Minh, beyond the reiteration of his unqualified commitment to enter into negotiations if the United States halted the bombing of North Vietnam. This could not on its face be said to meet the stated American requirement of a reciprocal gesture of reduced military action by Hanoi. But Baggs and I offered our judgment that the tone of the conversation had been deliberately conciliatory and that Ho seemed prepared to consider a specific proposal based on a formula of mutual de-escalation.

Moreover, no real risk was entailed in finding out whether this was so. Ho had understood that we would report our conversation to the State Department, and had made arrangements to have any response sent directly to him. We were in position to pursue the matter through another exploratory round without any official obligation on Washington's behalf.

For the next few weeks, while our report presumably bounced back and forth in the State Department, Baggs and I held to our agreement to stay out of the news as much as possible. At the State Department's request, we also rejected invitations to testify before committees of both Senate and House. In the course of explaining our declination to Senator Fulbright, then chairman of the Senate Foreign Relations Committee, Baggs was asked if we had reported our conversation with Ho Chi Minh directly to the President. Senator Fulbright expressed surprise when he was told that we had not. At a White House function not long afterward he voiced the same view to President Johnson.

While he thought it would be unwise for him to see us and run the risk of starting a lot of speculation, Mr. Johnson said, he wanted Senator Fulbright to be absolutely satisfied that we were being taken seriously and treated properly. He would personally see to it that we had access to anybody in the administration, and to make sure that Senator Fulbright was satisfied that this was so, he wanted the Senator to sit in with us at our next session at the State Department. The meeting with Katzenbach, Harriman, and Bundy turned out to be something of a confrontation. He was present, Fulbright began, only because the President had asked him to be there, and he thought he was wasting his time and theirs. He continued:

> The trouble is that I believe we ought to negotiate a settlement of this war in Vietnam and you don't. You're all committed to a military victory, and all this talk about being willing to go to the table doesn't mean a damned thing and you know it. . . . Over the years I have spent many hours questioning the Secretary about what we are doing in Vietnam. I know what Dean Rusk thinks, and that's what you've got to act on—and so we go ahead treating this little piss-ant country as though we were up against Russia and China put together . . . I say you're caught in a trap and you can't get out because you won't do the one thing you've got to do—admit you're wrong and start off in a new direction.
>
> That's what I mean by the arrogance of power, and I'm prepared to bet that you're going to prove me right by hanging so many conditions on whatever reply you send to Ho Chi Minh you'll make sure he'll turn you down, and then you'll use that as an excuse to step up the bombing even more.

Perhaps because of the stringency of the Fulbright attack, the letter to Ho we finally drafted in collaboration with Bundy was in fact quite conciliatory. It expressed the views of "senior officials of the State Department" indicating that it might be possible to suspend the bombing and initiate negotiations without specific concessions, beyond an agreement that neither side would use the occasion to improve its military position. The letter also suggested that Baggs and I could return to Hanoi for further informal discussions, or that arrangements could be made to phase us out if it were desired that the matter proceed directly to the official level.

The page-and-a-half letter went out over my signature on February 5.[1]

Fulbright, however, turned out to be a fully vindicated prophet. This conciliatory feeler was effectively and brutally canceled before there was any chance to determine what response Hanoi might have made. On February 14, after a temporary cessation of the bombing for the Tet holiday, the aerial attack on North Vietnam was resumed and escalated. Later it was revealed in Hanoi, and confirmed in Washington that the President, under date of February 2, had already dispatched an offsetting message to Ho Chi Minh over his own signature. This was transmitted from Moscow on February 8, the day the bombing was suspended and received in Hanoi on February 10. It was certainly in Ho's hands when ours arrived.

The Johnson letter set forth as a condition for continuing the bombing pause the most stringent demands yet made for advance assurance that Hanoi would halt infiltration of troops to the south. The uncompromising tone of the presidential message thoroughly disposed of the careful tempering of our letter. When Hanoi made this correspondence public on March 21 the State Department was moved to disclaim the virtually unanimous press interpretation that the President's blunt demand for advance evidence of a halt to infiltration actually constituted a new condition for negotiations, and that the letter was, as the *New York Times* described it, "designed to convey a hardening of the U.S. position." That, however, was the way the recipient read it. Under date of February 15, Mr. Johnson got from Ho Chi Minh a sharp, negative reply. Ours came a little later, a simple, unexceptionable statement that there did not seem to be any point in our coming back to Hanoi at that time.

After Baggs and I reviewed the experience in light of what had transpired with some of the principals involved in this episode, we concluded that the dim prospects for a negotiated settlement could not be harmed, and might possibly be improved, by exposure of the high-level double-dealing in which we had been involved. I in-

[1] For the full text of the letter, see Ashmore and Baggs, *Mission to Hanoi*, pp. 70–71.

cluded an abbreviated account of the dispatch of the two contradictory letters to Ho Chi Minh in an article for the *Center Magazine*.[2] When the text of this article was released to the press on Monday, September 18, it produced a sharp reaction in Washington. The blunt charge of presidential duplicity produced headlines in the morning papers across the country and that afternoon the administration felt it necessary to send forth William Bundy to try to put out the fire. The State Department also issued a lengthy "White Paper."

In the course of a long press conference, Bundy characterized the Ashmore–Baggs channel to Hanoi as one of little consequence. In response to a question asking for his views on the Ashmore article, Bundy replied, "I will comment to say that it's again obvious to any student of the relative weight to be attached to the channels as of that time that the direct channel in Moscow was by far the most important. I think Mr. Ashmore yields to an understandable personal feeling that his own was the center of the stage. I think the account I have given makes clear that it was not, and in the nature of things could not be."

Despite all this, we were to go back to Hanoi again at the end of March 1968, and again we arrived bearing messages from the State Department. Although we had no forewarning, we were there when Lyndon Johnson made his surprise announcement that he was pulling back the bomb line from central North Vietnam, was prepared for a negotiated settlement, and to facilitate it was withdrawing from the presidential race. The happenstance that we were in Hanoi at the time Johnson made this dramatic cease-fire proposal may have been instrumental in persuading the North Vietnamese not to reject the offer; at least we tried hard to convince the high-level functionaries available to us that this had to be taken seriously as a bid for a new opening by the beleaguered President, and we came out of Hanoi with a message indicating their acceptance, which went into official channels when we reached the U.S. Embassy in Vientiane, Laos. Our information was urgent enough to have us booked at highest priority directly to

---

[2] Ashmore, "The Public Relations of Peace."

Washington, and again we were involved at the upper levels in the State Department during this sparring over a meeting site that finally was resolved with the agreement on Paris.

Ours had been an uncommon vantage point. If our unofficial, and usually suspect, status denied us access to a good deal of pertinent information in both Hanoi and Washington, it also left us free of the inhibitions that attend official envoys. We were messengers and observers, not negotiators, and we never departed from that role in our actions, or in our minds. We were paying our own way, or the Center was, and we asked nothing of the State Department except clearance. As private persons we had no personal stake in the larger policies that hedged about the essentially procedural questions of contact between the two parties which we considered ourselves authorized by the State Department to discuss.

To the Vietnamese we provided an opportunity for frank discussion with Americans who could be presumed to present to them a fair estimate of prevailing public opinion and political reality in the United States. Similarly, some, at least, of the American officials with whom we dealt accepted our ability to report and appraise the views expressed to us by Ho Chi Minh and his associates without any undue coloration or personal bias.

The summary conclusion I drew from our experience in the course of these two excursions to North Vietnam is that ideological predispositions, although important, probably counted for less in the frustrating experience than what seems to be a systemic paralysis of the decision-making process. In regard to Vietnam—and in other foreign policy areas as well—once a policy line was locked in, and there was no indication of reconsideration at the top, it was considered imprudent for anyone in official position to even discuss serious alternatives, let alone bring outsiders into the deliberations.

It is understandable that there exists a professional, institutional snobbery that is often expressed as automatic resentment of outsiders—"amateurs"—meddling with official business. Long before I had had any public differences with Lyndon Johnson and could still be regarded as an active supporter of his administration, I went to the White House following up on an invitation to the President to address the Pacem in Terris I convocation in New York, which he had tentatively accepted when Supreme Court Justice William O. Douglas and I had called on him months before. I asked McGeorge Bundy, who was then still heading the National Security Council, why we could not get a reply. He said the responsibility was his—that he was recommending against acceptance because he did not feel that foreign policy was a proper matter to be handled in an unoffical forum over which those who had ultimate responsibility had no control. In theory this seems to me an indefensible policy under a democratic system, and in practice it has been disastrous.

This sort of cavalier attitude limits, if it does not preclude, the opportunity to take informal policy soundings that are simply impossible for those clothed in formal authority and responsibility and shuts off sources of intelligence that are at least as dependable as most of those available internally to the foreign service. I would have expected Lyndon Johnson and Dean Rusk to have been wary of our possible policy prejudices, but it seemed to me very near dereliction of duty that they did not take the opportunity to cross-examine the only two professional American journalists to have seen Ho since the war began.

EIGHT

THE INTERNATIONAL COMMITTEE OF THE RED CROSS AS A NEUTRAL INTERMEDIARY

JACQUES FREYMOND

JACQUES FREYMOND, Swiss historian and director of the Graduate Institute of International Studies in Geneva, was a member of the International Committee of the Red Cross (ICRC) from 1959 to 1972 and vice-president in 1965 to 1966 and 1969 to 1970. From January to June 1969 he served as acting chairman. While the agencies of the Red Cross movement agree in the abstract on the basic function of protecting the victims of conflict, there is less agreement at the level of specific action. Many of the issues raised here by Professor Freymond on the special role of the ICRC in conflict situations concerning the development and application of humanitarian law are currently being debated in Red Cross circles.[1] Not all in the ICRC share Professor Freymond's view about the scope of its protective role; many raise such questions as: Should the ICRC concern itself with political prisoners? Should the ICRC be involved with the victims of kidnappings and highjackings? Should the ICRC be concerned with the individuals in situations that might be considered either civil wars or internal conflicts?——Eds.

D ESPITE SUGGESTIONS TO THE CONTRARY,[2] the International Committee of the Red Cross does not consider itself a "conflict manager." Up to now, it has resisted the temptation to play a political role that would destroy its position as a neutral intermediary whose sole objective is to protect all victims of conflicts.

[1] For an examination of many of the currently debated issues on the ICRC's special role in conflict see the Background Paper prepared for the committee of representatives of various Red Cross bodies formed in 1973 to reappraise the role of the Red Cross movement by David P. Forsythe, "Present Role of the Red Cross in Protection," Geneva, Henry Dunant Institute, 1976.

[2] See, for example, Glen H. Utter, "The International Committee of the Red Cross as a Conflict Manager," paper presented at the Annual Meeting of the International Studies Association, St. Louis, Mo., March 20–23, 1974.

An action aimed at reducing human suffering can, of course, greatly affect military operations and political issues. In a period of history when wars have become totally destructive, when it is nearly impossible to make a distinction between "combatants" and "noncombatants," any intervention on behalf of the victims is a direct challenge to the parties in conflict. Peace—internal peace as well as peace between nations—is the only alternative to war that cannot be conducted in a "humanitarian" way. Therefore, the entire Red Cross movement, which means all those actively committed to defending and promoting the values embodied in the Red Cross, must be excluded from any category of conflict management. The Good Samaritan is not a conflict manager.

This position should not be construed as a total rejection of differing views expressed by scholars who are examining the institution from the outside. There is no doubt that the cool analysis of the outsider can be helpful, at the least by encouraging an institution too prone to romantic narcissism to view itself more realistically in the framework of international organizations. The ICRC occupies a position and plays a role in the international system which the scholar has a duty to examine critically and to compare with other organizations. The insider will quite naturally underline the *sui generis* character of the ICRC as an institution that is in danger of being progressively caught up in a web of governmental, intergovernmental, and nongovernmental international organizations.

What has been forgotten is the revolutionary content of the message delivered by the ICRC's founder, Henry Dunant. While negotiating with governments whose support he needed for the protection of victims, Dunant did not in any way condone conduct leading to armed conflicts. He was not a partner to an international venture that associated governments to alleviate the evils of war, but rather a protector of the victims—a protector whose actions were oriented against wars and violence. And this is still—and should remain—the position of the Committee.

As has been the case in the past, the ICRC has to negotiate with governments and parties in conflict as an advocate of the victims. It needs the agreement of the parties to operate, but it is not their instrument. It needs their financial support and should be able to demonstrate that funds allocated have been properly spent. But it is not constrained by any political commitment.

This task is extremely difficult in a world ridden by conflicts, divided by ideologies, and maintained in a state of permanent confusion by the accumulation of contradictory recipes proposed by too many men of good will. The Committee has been subjected to severe criticism. Its usefulness—its very continuation—has been questioned. Some raise doubts about its neutrality. Others do not recognize the need for a "uninational" international organization; they wonder why the Swiss are maintaining their monopoly. But these criticisms neglect the decisive factor: that the world needs, more than ever, an institution whose only mission it is to define a humanitarian policy in order to ensure the protection of the victims of violence by reminding governments and parties in conflict of their obligation to respect and to apply the Geneva Conventions,[3] and by extracting from them new measures better adapted to the evolution of warfare.

An institution like the International Committee could be set up by recruiting outstanding individuals from various countries. There is not the slightest doubt that all over the world there were—and still are—people who have dedicated their lives to promoting the ideas of the Red Cross. The main problem, then, would not be finding the right people, but selecting the countries from which they should be chosen; the selection would unavoidably be guided by the desire to ensure representation from a diversity of nations and ideologies and, therefore, by political criteria. This would mean that a member of the Committee, as independent as he would be, still could not easily "detach" himself from his nationality. By creating too great a distance from his country, a member might cut some ties which could be in the interest of the institution

[3] The first rules of war protecting wounded and sick members of enemy forces and medical supplies and personnel were drawn up by representatives of twelve nations at a diplomatic conference held in Geneva in 1864. These first Geneva Conventions have been significantly revised and expanded three times since 1864. Protection was extended to victims of warfare at sea in 1906, to prisoners of war in 1929, and to civilian populations in enemy-occupied territory in 1949. The four Conventions of 1949 have been ratified by 135 nations.

to maintain. The opposite stand could put him in a position of dependence, which would be incompatible with the neutrality required for the institution.

As has been demonstrated on several occasions, multinationality and neutrality are not easily reconciled in a world torn by national and ideological contradictions. There are situations, therefore, in which a "uninational" international organization could be beneficial, and members of this organization should be recruited from among nationals of a neutral country. Although it could have been Sweden or Austria, it happened that, thanks to Henry Dunant, Switzerland took the initiative. There are, therefore, no convincing reasons for a transfer of nationality, at least as long as the Swiss Committee gives serious proof of its capacity to assume the leadership of the Red Cross movement and to render the services expected from it.

Defining a humanitarian policy is precisely what was forgotten during the preparation for the diplomatic conference on humanitarian law held in Geneva in early 1974.[4] The participants forgot that, although this was a "diplomatic" conference, priority should have been given not to determining the legitimacy of the parties in conflict, but to identifying the victims of these conflicts and examining measures to ensure their protection. The rules governing a diplomatic conference on humanitarian law should have been derived from those used on the battlefield, where the Red Cross worker ignores the fronts and helps the victims without questioning the origin, nature, and legitimacy of the war in which he is involved. Consequently, all parties in conflict should have been invited to the conference with the stipulation that the invitation did not imply *de jure* recognition or a judgment on the merits of their causes.

Further, all discussion of just or unjust wars should have been

---

[4] At the invitation of the Swiss government, 117 nations met to update the four 1949 Conventions on the protection of victims in view of changes in warfare since the Conventions were adopted. The two additional draft protocols would provide extensive protection of civilian populations against becoming direct victims of hostilities and ensure civilized treatment of captured guerrilla fighters and other rebels in civil conflicts. Slowed by procedural disputes over recognition of nationalist groups and insurgent movements, the conference adjourned with no agreement on amending the 1949 Conventions.

discarded, because there are, for the Red Cross, no just or unjust victims. Also, the ICRC should not have been used as an international secretariat that prepares conference papers and is consulted for its expertise. Rather it should have played to the full an independent role as advocate of the victims.

By focusing on the role the ICRC should play, I do not underestimate the influence of governments. I simply call attention to the need for a division of labor. Although delegates to a diplomatic conference on humanitarian law are, no doubt, fully aware of the plight of the victims, the situation in prison camps, and the effects of some weapons—they are even eager to apply the Geneva Conventions and to refine their interpretations—nevertheless they must also consider their national interests. Any protection extended to the victims of a conflict is bound to interfere with the freedom of the military and provoke adverse reaction from those responsible for military aspects of national security. In the very delicate process of balancing national interests and the protection of the victims, delegates will be tempted to agree that raison d' état comes first, although they may perhaps disagree on the permissibility of certain weapons or kinds of warfare.

Attempts to codify humanitarian law, although intended to reaffirm and extend existing Conventions, can therefore lead—and are now leading—to a restrictive interpretation of humanitarian principles. Nations are adapting humanitarian law to suit the changing nature of war, rather than altering the nature of war to conform with humanitarian principles. Yet it is imperative that priority be given to reasserting the spirit of the Geneva Conventions.

Hence there is a need to reaffirm the independence of the International Committee of the Red Cross in the interests of the world community. In a diplomatic conference on humanitarian law the ICRC should be treated like a government; this means as an actor responsible for implementing the Geneva Conventions, accredited and entitled to engage in dialogue with all governments. It should be understood that, because the ICRC is entrusted with the mission of protecting victims of violence it should have the final word on invitations to attend the conference. Members of the ICRC, who too often behave like dilettantes in humanitarianism, need to be reminded that they must fight on the battlefront for humanitarian principles by telling governments that they are not free to wage wars according to what is considered military efficiency.

This is not so unrealistic as some have said. Governments that take a narrow view of their national interest in terms of victory or defeat neglect two important aspects of the conduct of foreign policies. First, they forget that peace should come after war, and that wars should not be allowed to degenerate to the point where there is no possibility of reestablishing peace. Second, they forget that it is always a mistake to trade short-term security achieved by repressive measures involving cruelty and mistreatment for long-term security. The ICRC's duty is to prevent a degeneration of wars by suggesting to governments that it is in their interest to apply humanitarian laws and principles because this behavior projects a positive image of their policies. Many examples could be drawn from history to show that cynicism does not pay off in the long run and that repression accelerates the spiral of violence.

Some will quite naturally object that governments do not like to be lectured to by a bunch of self-elected moralists and will simply not listen to them. To this serious objection there is only one answer: the ICRC, having been entrusted through a long historical process with the role of advocate of the victims, has no other choice but to take their side, to plead their cause, and to propose means to ease the gravity of their plight. The possibility—and perhaps the probability—that governments, commanders-in-chief, and leaders of revolutionary movements will not respect its resolutions, advice, and recommendations is not a sufficient reason for the ICRC to relax its pressure. Intransigence on fundamental principles should be the basis of a humanitarian policy.

Intransigence on fundamental principles does not exclude using subtlety and flexibility in conducting what could be called humanitarian diplomacy. Strategy and tactics should be complementary, and the only criterion of skill is the capacity to balance these two aspects in a single operation. A rigid strategy that could suppress a possible tactical maneuver or arrangement or compromises endangering the strategy should be avoided. A humanitarian diplomat should know where and when to speak strongly and when a soft, conciliatory tone is preferable. Between the narrow, stubborn attachment of lawyers to the letter of the Geneva Conventions or the pedestrian approach of a small town politician on one side and the romantic paranoia of some Red Cross workers on the other, there is room for a diplomacy reconciling long-range goals and short-range objectives.

The ICRC must take a firm stand and exert leadership in all discussions, all conferences of experts, and even diplomatic conferences on developing humanitarian law, because in these forums the long-range goals and general characteristics of humanitarian policy are defined. The ICRC may express its views in direct and public exchanges without taking too great a risk of antagonizing one or another government, because in this setting the discussion has a general character. Multilateral diplomacy provides very good opportunities to criticize certain types of behavior as not in accordance with accepted humanitarian law or recognized humanitarian principles, without being too specific. And it should never be forgotten that an international conference can be used as a forum to mobilize public opinion. Indeed, it gives the ICRC a unique occasion to make its position, views, and recommendations known to a broad public.

Bilateral diplomacy, on the contrary, must be conducted in a discreet manner. When delegates of the ICRC negotiate with governments during international conflicts and/or internal troubles, they must remember that they are touching on delicate problems affecting the national interest and the sovereignty of the state. They enter what could be called a *domaine reservé,* controlled not so much by armies, as by the state apparatus entrusted with national security.

If he wants to obtain substantial results, the neutral intermediary should not enter through the front door and should refrain from any publicity during negotiating. Official visits made by presidents and members of the Committee—who played the contemporary game of traveling diplomacy, sometimes with pleasure, sometimes reluctantly—have not, in most cases, gone beyond courtesy calls.

Some good arguments have been advanced in favor of a "policy of presence." Some maintain, for instance, that ambassadors' salons and ministers' offices are the necessary antechambers to the battlefield. The best that can be said in favor of this traditional method is that cocktails, lunches, dinners, and even communiqués do no harm in peacetime. But many examples demonstrate they are of no use and can even be counterproductive in periods of crisis. If the ICRC wishes to assert its presence, it should do so only through a good delegate working unobtrusively in close and friendly contact with the officials in charge of those whom he, as a Red Cross worker, considers the victims. Hospitals and prison camps are his target. Many examples could be given of the excellent preparatory work done by delegates who established contacts with the right persons at the right time—before the opening of a crisis—and therefore made possible prompt intervention when the conflict, external or internal, exploded. These include Dr. Georges Hoffman in Nigeria; Serge Nessi in Latin America, with the cooperation of Eddi P. Leemann and Jacques Moreillon, the latter presently engaged in the same type of activity in Africa; Marcel Boisard in Egypt; Michel Barde in Indochina, where he got extremely efficient background support from Alexandre Casella.[5]

These Red Cross workers did not attract the attention of the general public. Because their names did not appear in the press, they could continue to get into areas that no administration in the world likes to open to foreign visitors. Behavior to gain access to the backdoor differs from the kind that should be adopted to gain entry through the front door.

But discretion does not mean secrecy. The neutral intermediary does not have to hide secrets and should even avoid burdening himself with secrets. His interventions, the most delicate of them, should appear as manifestations of his day-to-day routine work. It is only through the unassuming approach of a person totally dedicated to his duty that a neutral intermediary can hope to overcome the normal reserve of representatives of parties in conflict. Discretion and impartiality are the bases on which credibility is established. Manifesting impartiality is particularly important when a delegate—a Swiss citizen with all his prejudices, his ethnocentrism,

---

[5] These are instances of "preparatory work" before a crisis. Needless to say, a whole chapter could be written on the work of some ICRC delegates in times of crisis.

his semi-Cartesian, semi-pragmatic training—is working in societies that cannot be understood by applying his own criteria. A Committee delegate should be honest and should project, despite his own internal contradictions, an image of honesty, which is particularly difficult in periods of tension and crisis nurturing suspicion. This is the only way to overcome the deep distrust born out of the difference of cultures, ideologies, and mind-sets. Because the representative with whom the neutral intermediary works is involved in a tense situation, emotion and anger could prevail even if the intermediary's approach to problems seems to be cool. This argument also supports discreet diplomacy, which allows for coolness and objectivity.

The neutral intermediary should also meet other requirements. First, his actions should enable the parties in conflict to recognize his neutrality or, in other words, his ability to handle problems more objectively than others because he is not tied by any political commitments. For this reason, a Committee delegate, if he wishes to maintain his neutral stand, must insist upon maintaining his position as intermediary between the Geneva Conventions and one or another party in conflict. He is not a mediator. He is not an arbiter. He does not—and should not—recognize reciprocity as a rule. Each party in conflict is bound by its signature to recognize the rules of the Conventions. The delegate should, of course, welcome any positive gesture made by one side as an encouragement for the other to reciprocate and offer his service for exchange of prisoners. But he should refrain from any action that would involve the institution in any political deal. It is necessary to give only one example—the disengagement of the ICRC from the negotiations after the highjacking of planes in Zerka in September 1970—in order to demonstrate that using the ICRC as an instrument in a political confrontation should be avoided. The cost would have been the loss of any possibility of protecting Arabs in Israel or Israeli-occupied territories. On this occasion the ICRC could only plead for the liberation of all hostages. It tried, and it failed.

It failed because passions were too high for any rational arguments to be heard. This leads us to reaffirm what was said earlier:

the only service the Red Cross or any other humanitarian institution may render in the cause of peace is to intervene on behalf of *all* of the victims, to reduce tensions, and to create a process of deescalation of violence. Thereby it can establish a climate where the spirit of negotiation will prevail.

PART THREE

Special Approaches

OVERVIEW

IN a variety of special activities unofficial diplomats have endeavored to prepare the way for or facilitate official action by creating a context in which problem-solving efforts can take place, increasing the clarity of officials' perceptions, and even on occasion actually putting forth proposals, however tentative. In this section participants report on a number of special approaches: two carefully designed unofficial gatherings are described by Phillips Talbot and John Goormaghtigh; Herbert Kelman and William Foltz analyze the use of problem-solving workshop techniques; and Lincoln Bloomfield and Michael Harbottle report on the use of simulation in international settings.

Creating a Problem-Solving Context

Herbert Kelman compares international negotiations with other negotiations, such as labor−management collective bargaining. In the latter there is generally a built-in understanding that the outcome will be some kind of compromise on a quantitative dimension. In international negotiations, this understanding hardly ever applies, since it is very rare that a dispute will center on a quantitative issue. Moreover, in Kelman's view,

> Compromise itself is an important part of the issue. Winning versus losing as such is much more important in most cases than specific outcomes in terms of some kind of resource or territory or what have you. The issues are often seen as incapable of compromise, or at

least they are presented as nonnegotiable, whether or not they really are so. What is particularly important is that the negotiators are dealing with varied and complex constituencies. As a result, public positions that they take have terribly important short-run and especially long-run consequences both domestically and internationally for the negotiators.[1]

The way issues are defined has a major impact on what kinds of solutions are possible. In many international negotiating situations, the stated goals of the two parties are incompatible and, as a result, the conflict is defined as incapable of solution. If an issue can be redefined or reformulated it may be possible to discover that goals are not as incompatible as they originally appeared and that joint solutions can be found.[2] This is not to say that all international conflicts result from misperception or misunderstanding; very real conflicts of interest may be brought into sharper focus through increased communication. Nor should it be forgotten that nations may put out signals designed to confuse the receiver about intentions and future actions. Yet at other times it is possible to try to change a dispute from a zero-sum one—that is, one in which one side takes all and the other side loses all—to a non-zero-sum where both sides give up something in order to gain other benefits. The task, then, in Kelman's view, is to create a problem-solving orientation which would provide an opportunity for the participants to learn from each other, to explore each other's motives, goals, perceptions, and anxieties, and to engage in a "playful" process of exploring various possibilities.

In the usual diplomatic negotiations, there are a number of factors that interfere with a problem-solving orientation. If negotia-

---

[1] Herbert Kelman, Remarks at a conference sponsored by the Academy for Educational Development in Bellagio, Italy, July 1973, p. 451; transcript on deposit at the Oral History Research Office, Columbia University, New York.

[2] Kelman describes a classical example of this approach presented by Mary Follett in her book, *Creative Experience*, published in 1924, which involves two people who are in conflict about whether or not a window should be open or closed. As long as they argue on that basis, one person will win and the other will lose, or there will be some sort of compromise. But if they can reformulate the issue, discover that what one really wants is fresh air, and what the other really wants is to avoid a draft, they can open a window in another room and open the door, and the one could have his fresh air without disturbing the other. Kelman transcript, p. 451.

tions are conducted publicly, then negotiators must act with the knowledge that they are being observed by members of their home governments and domestic publics. In such situations they are inevitably forced into hard-line uncompromising stands. They may be required to work under precisely formulated instructions that inhibit them from seeking ways to reformulate issues and to learn about opposite number's positions. To counteract these tendencies, unofficial problem-solving approaches are conducted away from public view as much as possible. The outside organizers or observers may suggest new ways to formulate issues and also point out misperceptions of goals, motives, and even of shades of meaning. This was the purpose of the unofficial working group described by Phillips Talbot, assembled to assist the official negotiators representing the Greek and Turkish communities in Cyprus in working out possible means to resolve the long-standing Cyprus dispute.

Controlled Communication

John Burton draws from his insistence that only the parties involved may resolve conflicts that a new relationship acceptable to all parties must be freely negotiated. As a result "communication" must be established between the parties.[3] The technique of controlled communication he has developed as described here by Herbert Kelman gives the parties involved an opportunity to explore their relationship and to assess accurately the costs and values. Thus alternate means of achieving goals may be brought out.

In Burton's view, controlled communication—direct meetings between parties in conflict in the presence of academic observers—may result in an alteration of perceptions. The scholar's role in this confidential meeting is to inject into the discussion insights about the parties' behavior in the conflict situation.[4] The

[3] For a fuller account see John Burton, *Conflict and Communication* (New York: Free Press, 1969).

[4] As with other private efforts publicity may be inimical to these initiatives. In 1966 Burton arranged a meeting on the Cyprus question involving people very close to the decision-making structure. Leaks about the meeting appeared first in the Turkish press and these

function of such meetings is not to mediate but to control communication between the parties. The underlying hypothesis is that conflict is subjective and therefore alterable and that experience and knowledge may alter the components of conflict, differences in values, goal attainment, and assessments of values.

Controlled communication as a stage prior to negotiation, may be an exploratory way that underlying causes of conflict can be revealed. In Burton's words, there are "some advantages in having around a table officials and even private persons who, as persons, are freer than politicians could be to explore, to examine critically their stereotypes and generally to stand back from the situation so as to look analytically at the reactions of their political leaders."[5]

Problem-Solving and
Process-Promoting Workshops

The underlying rationale for the problem-solving and process-promoting workshops that William Foltz reports on is that behavioral science techniques may be used during face-to-face communication between parties in conflict, to provide, at a minimum, greater cognitive and emotional understanding both of one's opponents and one's own situation and values and to promote greater openness and competence in communication.

Even if a workshop is successful in changing perceptions of participants there still remains the problem of translating those changes into new policies. Although participants may learn something, there is no guarantee that policy changes will result. These special approaches embody the creation of artificial environments. If decision-makers have not been direct participants they may not share the willingness of participants to adopt new attitudes. Nevertheless improving the quality of openness of communication by

were then picked up in the Greek press. The stories finally ended up in the Turkish, Greek, and English press on Cyprus. The participants in this meeting, incorrectly portrayed as an ultrasecret top level negotiation, were put into a difficult position, and the Greek Embassy in London, the site of the meeting, was furious because it was not consulted.

[5] Burton, *Conflict and Communication*, p. 42.

means of unofficial techniques may help to create a problem-solving context.

Simulation

Political games were originally developed as national projects, relying on national participants. They were played essentially for purposes of government policy planning, for the development of contingency plans, and for the training of a country's own decision-makers stationed both at home and abroad. Only in the last decade has the technique as described here by Lincoln Bloomfield been used with international teams of players under private auspices.

As the Helsinki exercise reported on by Harbottle illustrates, an international group of individuals assembled for a nongovernmental game may shed their real-life roles and nationalities and share the lessons of the interaction. The lessons may relate to the resolution of specific issues, to theories regarding policy-planning and decision-making, particularly in times of crisis, or simply to the sharpening of personal negotiating and mediating skills. Summing up his experience from all the games in which he has participated, however, Bloomfield views them not chiefly as a way to provide specific solutions to specific policy problems, "but to affect the policyman, to loosen up his assumptions—particularly if he exchanged roles and played the role of another bureaucratic element or another government—and to strengthen the sense that there were options other than the chosen or favored or preferred option that were present in the existing position paper." [6]

Interaction during the game is intended to produce constructive ideas and possible solutions to the problems under consideration, particularly if the given scenario closely resembles reality. Participation in the game also should provide a learning experience for the players and the opportunity to experience involvement in a multinational forum. The experience may help them to perfect

[6] Lincoln P. Bloomfield, in *Observations on International Negotiations. Transcript of an Informal Conference,* Academy for Educational Development, 1971, p. 84.

their skills in international negotiation and mediation and to sensitize them to differing national and cultural points of view.

Private Cooperation with Public Agencies

Apart from the problems that may result from misperception or the way issues are defined, the resolution of international problems may be inhibited by the structure of international organizations. A particularly successful private effort is described in the last selection in this volume; John Goormaghtigh details the role of the European Centre of the Carnegie Endowment for International Peace in helping bring about new international legislation governing the terms of the Office of the High Commissioner for Refugees, a UN institution. Itself incapable of adapting its structure (because "formal United Nations procedures are notoriously unsuited to bringing about operational revisions"), the High Commissioner's Office turned to the Endowment for assistance in overcoming the inhibitions of formal institutional machinery. The result of close cooperation between the official and unofficial institutions was a new official protocol.

NINE

THE CYPRUS SEMINAR

PHILLIPS TALBOT

PHILLIPS TALBOT, president of the Asia Society in New York, is a former Assistant Secretary of State and U.S. Ambassador to Greece. Ambassador Talbot reports on a seminar, "An Inquiry into the Resolution of the Cyprus Problem," arranged in 1973 by the Center for Mediterranean Studies in Rome of the American Universities Field Staff. At that time negotiations on a new constitution between official representatives of the Greek and Turkish communities on Cyprus had gone on intermittently without substantial results. By arranging for these two men to meet in the presence of an unofficial international working group of experts, the organizers hoped that helpful ideas and proposals to surmount barriers would emerge. This was a unique private approach to feed new ideas into official deliberations, even though immediate results came to naught due to the outbreak of further violence on Cyprus.——Eds.

A MONG THE MANY APPROACHES to conflict resolution one of the most unusual and interesting in which I have been involved was held in Rome from November 19 to 24, 1973, to consider constitutional dimensions of the Cyprus problem. Organized under the auspices of the Center for Mediterranean Studies of the American Universities Field Staff as a private seminar, the effort brought together the two principal Cypriot negotiators and a group of Greek, Turkish, British, continental European and American personalities, each with personal experience of the Cyprus problem but without current governmental responsibility. For a week they discussed ways in which the existing negotiating logjam could be broken, and offered concrete suggestions to the negotiators. I know of no similar approach to stalemated negotiations.

A number of essential conditions had to be met to make this effort fruitful. First, nothing could have been attempted had not the

Cypriot negotiators had confidence in the private sponsoring organization. The American Universities Field Staff is a remarkable organization whose staff members are area specialists of unusual talents and experience. Its Center for Mediterranean Studies has developed a reputation for seminars that bring together persons influential in their respective fields to consider major issues of the Mediterranean region. Nothing like the Cyprus seminar had previously been organized by the Center, but the Center proved an ideal base for the development of the concept over many months as its director, E. A. Bayne, discovered and encouraged the Cypriot negotiators' interest in such an approach.

Bayne was peculiarly qualified to stimulate this experiment. A staff member of the AUFS for twenty years with wide contacts in the Middle East and eastern Mediterranean, he had previously held a variety of positions during and after World War II in aid and development programs sponsored by the United States and other governments and by United Nations agencies. He had long maintained an interest in Cyprus and knew well both the leader of the Turkish-Cypriot community, Rauf R. Denktash, who in 1973 was Vice-President of the Republic of Cyprus, and the parliamentary leader of the Greek-Cypriot community, Glafcos Clerides, president of the Cypriot House of Representatives. Bayne had talked frequently with each of them about the problems encountered in their long negotiations (which had been going on since 1968, with frequent breakdowns along the way) to produce a new constitution for the Republic of Cyprus. His perceptions and his independent views were respected by both of them. Their trust in him made it possible for them to consider and ultimately accept the idea that they might jointly present their positions to an international private panel assembled by him, in the hope that the panelists could contribute constructive ideas to help overcome the impasse which the negotiators had reached.

A second factor crucial to the utility of this exercise was the personal relationship existing between Denktash and Clerides, spokesmen for opposing viewpoints who had known each other since boyhood, were personally friendly, and had explored their own and each other's positions so closely that each one had come to be able to perceive the slightest intimation of a shift by the other. Knowing their cases so well also gave them confidence in exposing themselves to a panel of concerned outsiders.

The third requirement for fruitful discourse was the existence of, and Mr. Bayne's success in assembling as a panel, an international group of public figures and scholars who had had intense personal experience of the Cyprus problem at earlier stages but now held no governmental positions. These individuals were, therefore, both knowledgeable and free to apply their minds to the Denktash—Clerides difficulties without the need to adhere to the policies of any government.

Preparations for this seminar, "An Inquiry Into the Resolution of the Cyprus Problem," had gone on for more than a year. In his discussions with Clerides and with Denktash from late 1972 through much of 1973 Bayne perceived with increasing clarity that their more than four years of discussion, which several times had temporarily reached a dead end, were moving into a new stalemate. Neither the negotiators themselves nor outside official influences seemed able to get negotiations moving again. The United Nations, which had a peace-keeping mandate in Cyprus, would have been the natural outside agency to apply the necessary stimulus, but Denktash was repeatedly making the point that it was no help to the talks.

At first quite informally, therefore, and later more formally during successive visits to Cyprus and in correspondence, Bayne raised with each of the Cypriot negotiators the question of whether they were at a stage of their discussions at which some outside nongovernmental comment might be pertinent and helpful. He and they considered the sorts of panelists who might be useful. They came to like the idea of a possible mix of persons who had had official responsibilities in their respective governments or in international agencies in connection with the Cyprus crises of 1964 and 1967, when war between Cyprus and Turkey was narrowly averted, but were now free of governmental discipline, and scholars and others closely acquainted with the problem. Gradually, the conception of such a gathering began to appeal to each of the negotiators, and they approved Bayne's organizing the seminar.

To ensure against even the appearance of domination of the seminar by big-power interests, the Cypriot negotiators suggested that a Yugoslav be found to serve as chairman. On Bayne's recommendation, welcomed by both Clerides and Denktash, the distinguished retired Yugoslav Ambassador Vladimir Velebit was approached, and he accepted the chairmanship. A seminar group of about twenty persons was then assembled from the United States, the United Kingdom, Greece, Turkey, and Hungary (a former economic adviser to the government of Cyprus).

The Americans at the table included scholars and several individuals who had been intensively involved in the effort to defuse the 1967 Cyprus crisis: Cyrus Vance, special representative of President Johnson in the final, climactic 1967 negotiations; Lucius D. Battle, Assistant Secretary of State for Near Eastern and South Asian Affairs in 1967, and myself (Ambassador to Greece in 1967, and Assistant Secretary of State for Near Eastern and South Asian Affairs during the 1964 Cyprus crisis). Parker T. Hart, Ambassador to Turkey in 1967, was also expected but at the last moment was prevented from attending by illness. The British side was ably represented by Sir Michael Stewart, who had been Ambassador to Greece in 1967.

Greek members of the seminar were Evangelos Averoff-Tossizza, a former Foreign Minister (later to be Defense Minister in the Caramanlis government which in 1974 replaced the military junta that had ruled Greece since April 1967) and Dimitri S. Bitsios, formerly Greek Permanent Representative to the United Nations and later (from 1974) Foreign Minister in the Caramanlis government.

Turkey was to be represented by Nihat Erim, formerly and subsequently Foreign Minister. As he had to cancel just before the seminar because of a parliamentary crisis in Turkey, he recommended and the seminar chairman invited Professor Aydin Yalçin, who had headed the majority party's parliamentary party in 1967 and who had, therefore, been intermediary between the Turkish administration and parliament during the crisis negotiations that year.

In addition, an international group of scholars, particularly individuals who were working either on Greek—Turkish relations or on the accommodation of international disputes, took part in the seminar. Such was the group, encompassing diverse and substantial talents and experience, that provided a sounding board for Denktash and Clerides.

The seminar ran for five days and covered a good deal of terrain. The sessions were organized according to the specific topics and categories that had been discussed between Clerides and Denktash. For example, in successive sessions the panel took up questions of taxation, local self-government, powers of the central government, and the areas to be decentralized in authority. In each instance Clerides and Denktash would first state their respective positions and then invite comments around the table. The thrust of the discussion, most of the time, was to suggest ways to broaden the options or identify fresh perspectives. Participants would say, "But have you thought of this?" "Of that?" In some cases, the panelists would comment that a particular position taken by one or the other of the negotiators seemed unreasonable. Occasionally comparatively weighty opinion developed around the table that a certain position of one side or the other ought to be modified if there was to be any hope of getting agreement, but there was no attempt to press either negotiator to change his stand.

Throughout the seminar personal relationships among the participants were very good. Most had worked together in previous years, and there was a shared conviction that the best hope for Cyprus lay in an agreement between Clerides and Denktash. Unless the two of them agreed, neither the formal institutions of the two communities on Cyprus nor the respectively supportive authorities in Greece and Turkey could be brought to agreement. Therefore all the other participants had a desire not to take one side or another, but to help the negotiators accommodate their differences.

Because of the personal relationships, a social milieu developed outside the sessions that encouraged people to talk in small groups even more informally than at the table. Many ideas or half ideas were generated and candidly explored in those conversations with the result that from day to day new proposals came forward.

Like many official negotiations, the Rome seminar sometimes went smoothly but also had its rough moments. At one point Clerides threatened to leave the meeting on the grounds that his position was being misrepresented by Denktash and that there was no further hope. That was patched up. At times each of the Cypriots let his irritation and sometimes his anger show through. But as we moved from point to point in discussing their negotiations, it was possible for the outsiders to comment and make suggestions, sometimes on very narrow points, but in the end presumably with some helpful effect.

Indeed, by the end of the week the negotiators appeared to be taking nearly all the most substantive comments into account. In their concluding comments, both Clerides and Denktash said they thought that the exercise had been worthwhile, citing some technical advances they had achieved. Additionally, describing themselves as having been jaded by talking to each other for four or five years, they averred that they had gained fresh perspectives and fresh interest out of these broader discussions.

Whether they were then ready to modify their positions is another question, because both obviously were working under pressures from home. There were, however, specific instances in which, after discussion, the two of them said, "All right, we have been stuck on this particular point but now we can agree on it." In other words, the seminar did have one of the functions we had hoped it might have, in that the discussions helped in getting unstuck some of the points that had until then seemed insurmountable.

The seminar served another function. It seemed evident that at times Clerides and Denktash as individuals could agree on particular points but were unable to carry their communities with them. As negotiators representing not themselves but their communities, each had to score a certain number of points for his side. When they were ready to compromise they needed a full rationale for the compromise. My impression is that at several stages of the Rome meeting the seminar participants helped Clerides and Denktash develop a rationale that would make it easier for each of them to explain compromises to his community back home.

In retrospect, there is reason to believe that momentum toward a substantial accord was established in Rome. There were subsequent indications that in the ensuing months the intercommunal talks between Clerides and Denktash reached virtual agreement. Some, indeed, would infer that knowledge of that prospect might have helped trigger the coup mounted from Athens in July 1974. In any event, agreements by the negotiators for the two communities, to become effective, would have had to win the agreement of Archbishop Makarios, President of the Republic of Cyprus, and of the governments in Athens and Ankara. That was not achieved before the July coup changed the whole situation.

One of the understandings reached at the seminar was that, depending on how the intercommunal talks might proceed after the negotiators returned to Cyprus, Denktash and Clerides would keep in mind the possibility of asking Bayne to reassemble the panel, or part of it, at a later stage. The prospect of some follow-up seemed to the panelists an important part of the process. In fact, when Bayne subsequently was in touch with Clerides and Denktash there was some discussion of a second go-around. The events of July destroyed initiatives on that front as well, when the whole diplomatic negotiating track came to an end with the coup against President Makarios and the ensuing Turkish military landings on Cyprus.

What lessons are to be learned from this unofficial exploration of the impasse in Cyprus constitutional negotiations that existed in 1973? Plainly, the circumstances encouraged this novel approach: the negotiators had worked hard but were stymied. They both had substantial international experience and knew personally many of those who had dealt with the Cyprus issue in Greece, Turkey, the United Kingdom and the United States. They were attracted to the idea that some of these, in whom they had reasonable confidence, might be brought together as a panel to counsel with them, under institutional auspices and a chairman they trusted. Their confidence was bolstered, I believe, by the patient care with which preparations were made, in the course of more than a year. But the key element was the private, informal quality of the discussions. In formal proceedings prudent negotiators and intermediaries tend to offer ideas or react to others' suggestions within the ambit of their official instructions. In the setting provided in Rome both the negotiators and the panelists could explore ideas, however novel or outside the existing framework, to their logical conclusion. Ideas came to have lives of their own, rather than being the creatures of sponsoring powers. The result was to open up considerably greater flexibility in exchanges and in the exploration of alternative possibilities than might be expected at formal conferences. And it was out of these exchanges that came the occasional advances that the negotiators had previously been unable to achieve on their own.

At the same time, underlying national attitudes were signaled by panelists despite their nonrepresentative capacities. Averoff later reported that after listening to the Americans at the table in Rome he had returned to Athens and advised the Greek regime that the United States would not defend Cyprus against Turkey in the event of another crisis. In the summer of 1974 he was proved a reliable prophet.

It is possible to imagine other conflict situations in which the techniques developed in connection with the Rome seminar might be applied. The first test would be whether the actual negotiators would be prepared to expose their hands outside an official context, and could get authority from their principals to do so. This would seem to depend on their believing they had reached the end of their face-to-face negotiating capabilities but still had an overriding need to compromise their differences. It would also depend on their trust of the sponsor and on the existence and willing participation of respected, preferably prestigious, individuals knowledgeable in the subject and if possible with prior personal relationships so that their counsel could be received as disinterested, friendly, and helpful.

Would great powers employ these devices in major disputes among themselves? That seems unlikely except in instances such as between England (but not France?) and the United States, where there are underlying common bonds. Rarely if ever have Middle East problems since World War II seemed promising for this sort of approach. When one looks at India and Pakistan, however, there seem to have been moments when such an effort might have been fruitful. This is true even though, for the most part, the attitudes of those two countries toward external participation in the negotiation of their differences have been asymmetrical, with India as the larger and more powerful nation preferring bilateral resolution of their disputes while Pakistan has characteristically sought to multinationalize negotiations. At specific times and on particular problems, e.g., on conditions for resumption of trade after 1971, a process like the Rome meeting on Cyprus might possibly have been arranged with fruitful prospects. Some international disputes in the African region might similarly be susceptible to this sort of approach.

In the future there may well be other international conflicts (as, in fact, Cyprus was an international conflict despite the intra-island character of the constitutional negotiations) in which the approach used in Rome could profitably be applied. It is far from having the potential of becoming a blanket approach, however. Progress in this sort of enterprise would always be dependent on the circumstances of the specific case. There is no substitute for carefully hand-crafting any effort of this sort.

TEN

THE PROBLEM-SOLVING WORKSHOP IN CONFLICT RESOLUTION

HERBERT C. KELMAN

HERBERT C. KELMAN is Richard Clarke Cabot Professor of Social Ethics at
Harvard University. In the following essay he compares, contrasts, and evaluates
the "controlled communication" exercises of John Burton and his associates at
the Centre for the Analysis of Conflict at University College London and the problem-solving workshops organized by Leonard Doob, William Foltz, and their associates at Yale University. Kelman himself has been a participant in Burton's exercises and has conducted research on the problem-solving workshop. Although
the goals, rationale, and operations of the approaches differ, both are attempts to
create conditions conducive to a problem-solving orientation. Kelman analyzes
the positive aspects of these meetings, while not failing to point out also the limitations in this form of exercise.——Eds.

T HE IDEA THAT face-to-face communication among parties in conflict, in a context other than diplomatic negotiations, may contribute to conflict management and resolution is certainly not new. The American Friends Service
Committee, in particular, has pioneered in such endeavors. In the
last few years we have seen some exciting new experiments in this
type of international communication, based on concepts and techniques from the behavioral sciences. Notable among these are the
exercises in "controlled communication" of John Burton and his
associates at the Centre for the Analysis of Conflict at University College, London,[1] and the Fermeda workshop, organized by

---

This abridged chapter is reprinted from Richard L. Merritt, ed., *Communication in International Politics* (Urbana: University of Illinois Press, 1972), with the permission of the author and publisher.

[1] See John W. Burton, *Conflict and Communication: The Use of Controlled Communication in International Relations* (London: Macmillan, 1969).

Leonard Doob and his associates at Yale University.[2] Both approaches are designed to bring together representatives of nations or national (ethnic) communities involved in an active conflict, for face-to-face communication in a relatively isolated setting, free from governmental and diplomatic protocol. Discussions, following a relatively unstructured agenda, take place under the guidance of social scientists who are knowledgeable both about group process and about conflict theory. The talks are designed to produce changes in the participants' perceptions and attitudes and thus to facilitate creative problem-solving.

This chapter summarizes the Burton and Doob approaches and then compares, evaluates, and attempts to integrate them. The generic phrase "problem-solving workshop" is used to refer to both approaches,[3] since it emphasizes the fact that these approaches utilize "workshop" techniques, but that their orientation is toward problem-solving rather than sensitivity training or personal growth as such.

The workshop approach . . . is often greeted with skepticism: indeed, I share some of that skepticism myself. Before turning to the work of Burton and Doob, therefore, let me clarify some assumptions that I bring to this analysis—and with which, I believe, Burton and Doob generally concur.

1. I do not assume that most international conflicts are simply products of misunderstanding and misperception that can be cleared up through improved communication.[4] Real conflicts of interest or competing definitions of national interest are often at the center of such disputes. In such cases improved understanding may demonstrate more clearly that the goals of the conflicting parties are indeed incompatible. Communication may still be useful, in that it may reveal more precisely to each party what the costs of

---

[2] See Leonard W. Dobb, ed., *Resolving Conflict in Africa: The Fermeda Workshop* (New Haven, Conn.: Yale University Press, 1970).

[3] Richard E. Walton, "A Problem-Solving Workshop on Border Conflicts in Eastern Africa," *Journal of Applied Behavioral Science* (October/December 1970), 4:453–89.

[4] I have discussed some of these issues in the introductory and concluding chapters of Herbert C. Kelman, ed., *International Behavior: A Social-Psychological Analysis* (New York: Holt, 1965); and in "The Role of the Individual in International Relations: Some Conceptual and Methodological Considerations," *Journal of International Affairs* (1970), 24:1–17.

pursuing various alternative policies are likely to be. Nevertheless, more accurate perception would clearly not alter the realities of the underlying conflict.

Moreover, even where there is misperception, face-to-face communication can directly affect only the perceptions and attitudes of the participating individuals. International conflicts, however, involve not only individual misperceptions, but institutionalized ones—that is, misperceptions that are built into and perpetuated through the decision-making apparatus. Vested interests and organizational commitments become attached to a given perception of a conflict situation at various levels in the decision-making bureaucracy, making it difficult for changed perceptions to penetrate.

Clearly, then, problem-solving workshops are not meant as panaceas or as total solutions. They are merely inputs into a more complex resolution process. They are not alternatives to diplomatic and political negotiations, but rather supplementary or preparatory to them. . . .

2. The problem-solving workshops discussed here are not to be equated with T groups or sensitivity training as usually defined. They do use some of the techniques and approaches derived from T-group experience. The Fermeda workshop utilized fairly standard T groups during its first phase, although in retrospect its organizers are inclined to view this decision as a mistake. In any event, the main task of these workshops is not to increase personal sensitivity, or even interpersonal trust and understanding of the other side; nor is there any assumption that international conflict can be redefined and resolved at an interpersonal level. Workshops are designed to promote trust and openness in communication. However, these are seen not as ends in themselves, but as means toward the development of an atmosphere in which creative problem-solving becomes possible. Unlike the standard T group, the problem-solving workshop is oriented toward carrying out a concrete task and achieving a usable product.

The Burton Exercises
In Controlled Communication

John Burton's book and other papers on controlled communication draw on experiences gained in two workshops,[5] one involving an international conflict and the other an intercommunal conflict. I was on the panel of social scientists in the second exercise, and I base my impressions of the approach on that experience. It differed in several ways from the first exercise and from further ones that Burton and his associates are currently planning—both because of different circumstances and because the technique itself is still evolving—but it illustrates Burton's general orientation.

The exercise dealt with the conflict between the Greek and Turkish communities in Cyprus. It was held in the fall of 1966, in a university setting in London. It lasted a week. The participants included two representatives of the Greek community and two of the Turkish community. They were selected by the top decision-makers in their respective communities, but they participated essentially as private citizens rather than as official representatives. The exercise was presented to them basically as an academic project, which would meet the interests of the sponsoring organization in the analysis of concrete conflict situations. At the same time, the organizers indicated that the communication between the two parties might also contribute to resolution of their conflict. The exercise's potential relevance to conflict resolution was clearly understood on all sides, but the organizers made no promises—nor did the parties, in agreeing to participate, commit themselves to anything other than a contribution to an academic enterprise.

In addition to the four Cypriots, a panel of six social scientists (one of whom served as chairman) participated in the discussion. Meetings were held each morning and afternoon during the week (and continued informally during lunch and tea). The discussions were relatively unstructured and designed to encourage participants to share their definitions of the conflict, their perceptions of

[5] Burton, *Conflict and Communication.*

their own and others' goals and actions, and their assessments of the costs and benefits of alternative conflict resolutions. The chairman and the panel tried to move the discussion away from mutual accusations and legalistic attempts to assign blame and toward a behavioral analysis of the conflict's causes, escalation, and perpetuation, as well as toward efforts to explore possible solutions.

The discussions can be roughly divided into three phases. In the first, the conflicting parties presented their respective views of the conflict; the social scientists generally intervened only to ask questions of detail, which sometimes helped sharpen and clarify an issue or lay the groundwork for subsequent analysis. During the second phase, the social scientists presented various models of conflict. The discussion following each focused first on the origins and processes of conflict in general, and then on the specific conflict at hand. Applicability of the various models to the Cyprus situation was explored, largely by the parties themselves. The social scientists intervened to inform and elaborate, and to propose tentative interpretations of the conflict in terms of the models presented. . . .

During the third phase, the parties considered various approaches to resolving the conflict. The social scientists contributed to this phase in two ways: by bringing in relevant experiences from the resolution of other international or intercommunal conflicts, especially through the development of patterns of functional cooperation; and by systematically attempting to explain why solutions that seemed very reasonable to one party caused anxiety and rejection in the other. The social scientists did not themselves propose solutions, nor did they convey the expectation that an agreed-upon solution was to be found. The assumption was that solutions would eventually have to be achieved through formal channels of negotiation, but that new insights about the conflict and new ideas for its resolution emerging from the workshop would be communicated to the relevant decision-makers and might thus influence the negotiation process.

The outcome of the workshop is difficult to assess. The parties seem to have communicated to each other some new and potentially important facts about their respective goals and intentions. Some new insights about the origins and escalation of the conflict have apparently been developed. Certainly by the end of the sessions, the parties were able to communicate with each other more freely and within a shared frame of reference. Moreover, there is no doubt that the new information and insights acquired by the participants were transmitted to the top leaders of their own groups, because of the relationship of the participants to the decision-making process. We can only speculate, however, about the extent to which and the way in which these entered into subsequent negotiations. At the time of the exercise, the two parties had not been in official communication with each other for some time. Shortly after the exercise, communication between them was resumed. It is quite likely that the exercise played some role in this development, though we cannot be certain. At the very least, it may have provided a mechanism for the two sides to test each other out in a noncommittal fashion and an opportunity to learn whether resumption of negotiations would be fruitful.

The Fermeda Workshop

The Fermeda workshop was named after a hotel in the mountains of South Tyrol, where the Yale team of Leonard W. Doob, William J. Foltz, and Robert B. Stevens organized a workshop focusing on the border disputes in the Horn of Africa between Somalia and its two neighbors, Ethiopia and Kenya. I did not witness this workshop firsthand. My information is based on various written accounts and on personal communications with several of the participants,[6] particularly with Leonard Doob and Richard Walton. In this connection, I also benefited from a working conference sponsored by the United Nations Institute for Training and Research in May

[6] Leonard W. Dobb, William J. Foltz, and Robert B. Stevens, "The Fermeda Workshop: A Different Approach to Border Conflicts in Eastern Africa," *Journal of Psychology* (November 1969), 73:249–66; Doob, *Resolving Conflict in Africa;* Walton, "Problem-Solving Workshop."

1970, in which experiences from both the Fermeda workshop and the controlled communication exercises were presented, discussed, and evaluated in detail.[7]

The African participants in the Fermeda workshop included six Somalis, six Ethiopians, and six Kenyans. The Ethiopian and Kenyan participants all held academic posts; the participants from Somalia—which had no university—were professionals or civil servants working in areas unrelated to foreign policy. Plans for the workshop were cleared with the three governments, but the participants were selected by the organizers and came as private individuals, rather than as official representatives. Participants from the same country did not constitute a team and, as far as is known, did not even communicate with each other in anticipation of the workshop. They were told that the workshop would follow the format of sensitivity-training groups, and that some innovative solutions to the border problems were hoped for. They knew this was a highly exploratory effort, which might or might not yield significant results. In addition to the African participants and the three Yale organizers, the workshop included four American specialists in sensitivity training and related techniques, who came in the roles of "trainers" or "process consultants."

The workshop lasted two weeks, with a two-day break in the middle. From the beginning, the participants were broken up into two T groups, each including three Somalis, three Kenyans, three Ethiopians, two trainers, and one or two of the organizers. During the first few days, the groups, which met intensively, followed standard T-group procedures, aimed at developing self-awareness and open communication among the participants. The trainers did not structure or lead the discussions, but functioned as observers and interpreters of group process. During this period, there were also several meetings of the total group, in which theoretical notions about leadership styles and about cooperative and competitive strategies were presented by the trainers and illustrated through simulation exercises. These sessions were designed both to improve the working processes within the T groups and to provide

[7] See Social Psychological Techniques and the Peaceful Settlement of International Disputes," *UNITAR Research Reports* (1970), no. 1.

concepts that could be drawn upon in later discussions of the border disputes.

During these first few days, the meetings did not deal at all with the substantive issues relating to the border disputes. They focused on individual and group development instead. During the second phase, the workshop turned specifically to the border disputes. First, participants met in their three separate national groups; each group was asked to list its own grievances and the grievances of the other two national groups, as they perceived them, and to present these lists to the total group. The procedure did not work too well, since two of the groups failed to engage in the requested role reversal. In general, the total group seemed to make little progress at this point, and the participants' planning committee (which had since been formed) decided to revert to the original T groups to work out concrete solutions. The general assembly was used during this phase for presentation and practice of brainstorming techniques and for reports of the activities of the individual T groups.

Within each of the two T groups, proposals were developed that all group members, regardless of their national affiliations, were willing to endorse. These proposals were then brought to the general assembly with the aim of achieving a joint solution. However, this particulaar effort did not succeed, apparently because the trust developed in the T groups did not carry over to the larger group. National differences came to the fore; participants who had agreed to a solution hammered out in their individual T group sometimes reverted to rigid defenses of their national position; in some cases, participants from one T group accused fellow nationals from the other group of betraying their national cause by subscribing to a detrimental proposal. The workshop closed without being able to meet the staff's original goal of developing a joint proposal supported by the total group.

Though the workshop did not arrive at a joint proposal, it did have some positive outcomes. Within the T groups, trust and an openness of communication developed. These yielded, in each group, a proposal for resolving the conflict that was generally supported by all group members. In response to a questionnaire, the participants indicated (on the whole) that they had acquired new knowledge about the cultures and problems of the other countries, that they had gained a better understanding of the other countries' views of the disputes, and that they were somewhat more open now to alternative solutions. Participants did not feel that the workshop yielded many innovative ideas for solving the border disputes. About a year after the workshop, Doob carried out follow-up interviews with thirteen of the eighteen African participants to gain some impressions of the impact the workshop had on them and on their respective countries.[8] On the whole, their reactions to the experience (and in some cases to the workshop techniques) were positive; they felt close to the other participants, regardless of nationality, and eager to remain in touch with them, and they showed an understanding of the intense emotional meanings that their respective positions had for each of the parties. On the other hand, their own attitudes on the best ways to resolve the conflict were not appreciably affected. News of the workshop reached important officials in each of the three countries, although most of the participants did not make extensive efforts to communicate their experiences.

The Two Approaches Compared

In comparing the two approaches—and particularly in noting the differences between them—we must keep in mind that neither one represents a "closed system," a set of established and tightly defined procedures. Both are seen by their inventors as exploratory, as requiring further refinement, and as open to change, extension, and recombination. In this spirit, differences between the two approaches do not necessarily reflect incompatible views, but rather different starting-points and experiences. There is every reason to suppose that the two approaches can borrow from each other and be combined in various ways, and to treat them as two variants of a more general model, each applicable to a special set of circum-

[8] Leonard W. Dobb, "The Impact of the Fermeda Workshop on the Conflicts in the Horn of Africa," *International Journal of Group Tensions* (1971), 1:91–101.

stances. The two approaches have several important features in common:

1. *Setting.* In both approaches, workshops are held in settings isolated from political and diplomatic environments. The Fermeda workshop was held in a physically isolated setting; the London exercise was held in an academic setting, removed from the pressures and publicity that typically surround official negotiations. The isolation is partly to reduce distraction and permit participants to concentrate intensively on the task. Most important, it allows participants to explore issues while free of constant preoccupation with the public statements they must issue and the impressions they will be making on their various constituencies.

2. *Sponsorship.* Both types of workshops are sponsored by academic organizations, independent of governmental or intergovernmental agencies. The governments concerned were informed and consulted and, in fact, gave their approval of the workshops, but the workshops had no official status whatsoever. The sponsors' legitimacy depended entirely on their status as scholars and people of good will, whose interest in the exercise derived from their research concerns and their desire to make a constructive contribution to the resolution of a violent conflict.

3. *Participants.* Although the two approaches differed significantly in the criteria for selecting participants, both sets of participants had two characteristics in common. On the one hand, they were prestigious members of their respective communities, who at least potentially (in the London workshop quite clearly and, indeed, by the nature of their selection) had access to their top decision-makers. On the other hand, they participated in the sessions as private citizens who spoke only for themselves. Even the participants in the London workshop, who were almost certainly briefed by their respective administrations, did not come as official, instructed delegates.

4. *Interpersonal atmosphere.* In both workshops, the discussions and the environments were designed to create an informal atmosphere in which participants would be free to express their views openly and to get to know and respect each other as individuals. The atmosphere fostered mutual trust, a sense of shared val-

ues, and commitment to a common task, cutting across national or ethnic divisions.

5. *Discussion format.* Central to both workshops was the opportunity for direct, face-to-face communication among the conflicting parties. The agenda for discussion was relatively unstructured. The initiative for introducing issues—or for following up on inputs from the third parties—was largely left to the participants themselves. Third parties refrained from imposing their definitions of the situation and their interpretations of actions and events on the participants; rather, they encouraged participants to speak for themselves—to describe their own motives and perceptions, express their own hopes and fears. In particular, both workshops were committed to the idea that solutions must emerge from the group discussions, rather than be imposed from the outside.

6. *Role of third parties.* Both workshops were under the general guidance of third parties, defined in terms of their professional skills and knowledge as theoretical or applied behavioral scientists rather than in terms of some official capacity as mediators. Though they participated in the proceedings, their primary task was to provide tools that the participants could utilize in their discussions and analyses, to offer relevant information and suggest interpretations, and to facilitate the group process in other ways. . . .

These common features of the two approaches are essentially designed to achieve two ends. First and foremost, they are designed to give participants the freedom, opportunity, and impetus to move away from a rigid reiteration of official positions and from efforts to justify their own sides and score points against the other side and, instead, to absorb new information, explore new ideas, revise their perceptions, reassess their attitudes, and engage in a process of creative problem-solving. The isolated setting, the academic sponsorship, the participants' nonrepresentative roles, the informal atmosphere, the development of trust, the encouragement of self-expression and of an analytical orientation, and the inputs and attitudes of the social scientists all are geared to facilitating these processes.

Second, some common features of both approaches are designed to enhance the probability that the new information and ideas, the changed perceptions and attitudes, and the innovative proposals for solutions generated by the workshop will be fed into the policy process. The selection of potentially influential participants, the coordination with their governments, and a format that allows the definition of the issues and the development of solutions to emerge out of group discussions, rather than being externally imposed (thus discouraging analyses and solutions that go considerably beyond what the decision-makers are prepared to entertain), are geared to achieving this end. Both approaches, it seems to me, are more effectively designed to produce changes in participants than to feed such changes into the policy process—although the balance between these two ends is one respect in which the two approaches differ from each other.

Let me turn to some of the differences between the two approaches. In terms of the six categories used to describe common features of the two approaches several distinctions can be drawn:

1. The Fermeda workshop, held in a physically isolated setting, placed greater emphasis on the creation of a "cultural island" and on the psychological insulation of the workshop participants.
2. The London workshop was sponsored by a research center concerned with international relations theory, diplomacy, and the analysis of conflict, representing a research project within the center's ongoing program; the Fermeda workshop was sponsored by social scientists interested in African studies and staffed by specialists in group process, representing an experimental application of the human-relations training laboratory to conflict resolution.
3. Participants in the London exercise were considerably closer to foreign policy decision-making and came as a team; those in the Fermeda workshop were more removed from the foreign policy process and came as individuals, thus manifesting greater diversity and division within each national contingent.
4. The Fermeda workshop placed more deliberate emphasis on creating an interpersonal atmosphere marked by emotional involvement, group solidarity, and mutual trust, and in forging cross-national bonds within the working group.
5. To facilitate discussion of the substantive issues of the conflict, the London workshop made greater use of theoretical models of conflict and of illustrative cases, while the Fermeda workshop focused more exten-

sively on the ongoing group process and interpersonal behavior; in discussion of the substantive issues themselves, the Fermeda workshop made more deliberate efforts than the London workshop to hammer out an agreed-upon proposal for resolving the conflict.

6. In the London workshop the social scientists made more theoretical inputs, both in their own presentations and in their interventions, and they were generally more active in the course of the discussion itself; in the Fermeda workshop, they provided more feedback on the basis of their observations of group process and were more active in programming the workshop activities—in setting the tasks to which the participants were to devote themselves.

These differences in detail reflect certain underlying differences between the two approaches, both in their conception of the enterprise as such and in their definition of the workshop task. They differ in their views of the workshop's relationship to the larger process of conflict resolution, and in their views of precisely what ought to be happening within the workshop itself. My formulation of these differences may be overly sharp, but it should be helpful in pointing up the unique contributions of each approach.

How do the two approaches differ, first, in their conceptions of the enterprise? As I have indicated before, both are concerned with creating an atmosphere in which change—in the form of revised perceptions and attitudes and innovative solutions—can take place, in the hope that this change can be fed into the political processes of conflict resolution. However, the two approaches differ, it seems to me, in their conceptions of precisely where the workshop fits into these political processes and what it is intended to accomplish.

In Burton's conception, the workshop is much more closely linked to national and international political processes. The concept of controlled communication flows out of a theoretical orientation toward international relations, containing such propositions as these: that "international conflict is a spill-over from internal or communal strife"; that "the starting point in analysis and resolution of conflict is at the systems level of highest transactions"; that "conflict occurs as a result of ineffective communication, and that its resolution, therefore, must involve processes by which com-

munication can be made to be effective"; and that "since the resolution of conflict depends upon effective communication, it can
come only from the parties themselves. Processes are required that
alter perceptions, and promote the points of view of the parties,
and not of third parties."[9] In Burton's view, then, procedures like
those of controlled communication represent crucial steps in the
conflict resolution process.

In keeping with this conception, Burton's workshops are closely
coordinated with the relevant decision-makers. The participants
must be individuals who are fully aware of the positions of these
decision-makers. Though they need not be officials themselves
(and do not come to the workshop in any official capacity), they
are nominated by the top decision-makers and are in communication with them both before and after the workshop. . . .

The Fermeda workshop was further removed from the political
process. Though the organizers communicated with the governments concerned, their purpose was to inform the governments
and get their approval, rather than to coordinate directly with decision-making bodies. Though the participants were potentially influential members of their societies, they were selected by the organizers and could not be viewed as even unofficial representatives
of their respective governments. Both Burton and Doob took pains
to hold the workshop itself in a setting isolated from the pressures
of political and diplomatic environments, but Doob placed greater
emphasis on separating the total enterprise from the political process.

In Doob's conception, as I understand it, a workshop can contribute to conflict resolution by creating certain products that can
then be fed into the political process. In other words, the workshop
itself is not directly linked to national decision-making or diplomatic efforts at conflict resolution, but its products may well be relevant to these activities. The workshop's potential products are of
two kinds: they may take the form of attitude changes in influential
individuals, which would be reflected over time in the inputs these
individuals make into their national policy debates; and they may

---

[9] Burton, *Conflict and Communication*, pp. 17, 19, 49, 55, 157.

be documents, setting forth possible solutions that would not have emerged as readily from the usual political procedures.

The difference between Burton's and Doob's conceptions of the enterprise thus has some clear implications for what the workshop is intended to accomplish. For Doob, it is a more self-contained enterprise, standing or falling on the immediate products that emerge from it. There is, therefore, more emphasis on the personal learning of the participants—on whether they come away from the workshop with demonstrably greater knowledge and insight. There is also more emphasis on producing an agreed-upon solution, in the form of a document that can serve as an input to the policy debate. For Burton, too, it is important to produce changes in the participants and to promote problem-solving; however, these effects are viewed as steps in the conflict resolution process more than as ends in themselves. There is less emphasis on the personal learning of the participants, except insofar as it influences the new information and insights that they can feed into the policy process. Similarly, there is less emphasis on the production of agreed-upon documents within the workshop itself. The presumption is that the actual working out of solutions must happen elsewhere; the workshop will have made its contribution if it has brought some new possibilities for solutions to the attention of the relevant decision-makers. . . .

What are the means by which the workshop brings about the desired changes, and what roles do the participants and the social scientists have to enact if these changes are to take place?

Both approaches are designed to create the conditions for effective problem-solving. To this end, participants must learn to communicate with each other in new ways, to revise perceptions distorted by a long history of conflict, and—in Burton's words—to see "the conflict as a problem to be solved and not as a contest to be won." In relation to each other, they must move from the roles of antagonists engaged in a zero-sum game, in which neither party dares to yield a point, to the role of collaborators searching for a positive-sum solution to a common problem. The social scientists' role is to facilitate this movement. The two approaches diverge in emphasis in their views of how this movement comes about.

In Burton's approach, the primary mediating process is the behavioral analysis of conflict. The workshop is designed to draw the participants into this process of conflict analysis along with the panel of social scientists. Anthony de Reuck, a member of the Centre for the Analysis of Conflict, has distinguished three roles that participants may play in a workshop: combatant representative, conflict analyst, and cooperative representative. . . .[10] The role of conflict analyst, fostered by the definition of the situation, gradually guides participants into that of cooperative representative. It also remains as an alternative, when the cooperative process becomes too difficult or threatening: participants can retreat into the more intellectual role of general conflict-analyst.

The role of conflict analyst is readily available insofar as the workshop is presented—as was the case in the London workshop—as a research project. The research context, more generally, can facilitate entry into communication and broaden the content of what is communicated. Thus, when research serves as the context of the encounter, it becomes possible to bring together conflicting parties who until now refused to communicate, because to do so would have meant to yield a political point or to take unacceptable risks. The research context permits communication with minimum commitment and minimum risk. Similarly, within the situation, the research context allows participants to discuss issues and entertain ideas that they would have to avoid if they were speaking "for the record." . . .

In short, the research context can surmount some of the barriers to communication that characterize the relationship of conflicting parties—provided, of course, that the sponsors of the workshop are genuinely interested in conflict research and not just using it as a device to bring the parties together. At the same time, the research context makes the role of conflict analyst particularly natu-

[10] Anthony de Reuck, "Controlled Communication: Rationale and Dynamics," paper prepared for UNITAR Workshop on Social Psychological Aspects of Peaceful Settlement, New Paltz, New York, May 15–17, 1970.

ral. After all, conflict analysis is the substance of the research in which the participants have agreed to help out. They are acting as informants, providing data for the social science panel, and gradually entering into the process of analysis itself. Thus the research context creates not only a general readiness to engage in communication, but a natural occasion for the specific process that Burton considers to be a crucial step in conflict resolution. Furthermore, insofar as both parties are working with the social science panel in a research effort, they can more readily come to regard each other as collaborators in a common enterprise.

In line with Burton's definition of the workshop task, the primary role of the social scientists is "to inject into discussion new information, not about the dispute in question, but about conflict, its origins and processes drawn from theoretical analyses and empirical studies." [11] Later in the workshop, when solutions are under discussion, the social scientists also contribute information designed to extend the range of integrative mechanisms and possibilities for functional cooperation that the participants can consider. The social science panel, and particularly the discussion chairman, are by no means oblivious to the group process. They try to encourage movement away from the role of combatant representative and toward the role of conflict analyst and increasingly toward that of cooperative representative. But the key professional input of the social scientists is at the level of theory and empirical findings.

In the Fermeda model, the primary mediating process is sensitization of participants to their own interpersonal behavior and to group process. The workshop essentially offers training in the skills of effective communication through the use of the "laboratory approach to learning." The training is designed to enhance participants' awareness of ways in which their own emotional commitments and the nature of group interaction may hinder effective communication and problem-solving, and their ability to overcome these obstacles. The trainers convey the process of analyzing the ongoing interaction through demonstration, exposition, and the use of special exercises, and they draw the participants into active

---

[11] Burton, *Conflict and Communication,* p. 157.

involvement in this process. . . . To adapt de Reuck's terminology, in the Fermeda model the participants move from the role of combatant representative to that of cooperative representative through adopting the role of process analyst—a role calling for self-conscious attention to what is happening in the group and what each participant is contributing to that process, and thus mediating change from self-defeating to more constructive modes of interaction.

Adoption of the process-analyst role is facilitated by definition of the workshop as essentially a learning experience—a training laboratory. In this context, participants are more prepared to go along with procedures (such as the T group) that have no obvious connection to the substantive issues with which they are concerned, and to accept exercises (such as simulation and brainstorming) that might otherwise strike them as overly artificial. (Even so, some of the participants in Fermeda apparently resented procedures that had no clear and immediate relationship to the objective that had brought them to the workshop.) Furthermore, the context of a training laboratory—like the context of a research project in the London exercise—permits communication with relatively little commitment and risk. In this playful, protective, and insulated environment, the individual is moved to pursue and express ideas that would be unacceptable in other settings, and he feels free to do so without worrying that he will be held accountable for it. . . .

Other important features of the training laboratory situation can help to push the problem-solving process forward. The development of a sense of solidarity, of an openness of communication, and of warm personal bonds within the learning group not only contributes to the learning process; it also constitutes an important element of the problem-solving that this learning process is designed to facilitate. A cohesive group can more readily approach the conflict to be resolved as a joint task for the conflicting parties, to be tackled in a collaborative spirit. Similarly, the deliberate utilization of the here and now as a source of insights through observation and analysis of ongoing interaction, facilitates both the learning process and the conflict resolution itself. . . .

In line with the Fermeda workshop's definition of its task, the primary role of the social scientists is to encourage the development of sensitivity to group process and effective communication patterns. As the group turns to direct efforts at problem-solving, the social scientists' role is to facilitate the process—to help the group identify snags when the process seems to break down and to develop strategies that would keep it moving. In both the training and in the problem-solving phases (which need not be temporally separated), they help the group observe and analyze the interaction in which members are currently engaged. As in Burton's exercises, the social scientists may inject relevant theoretical considerations or empirical information, but their major inputs in the Fermeda model consist of observations and interpretations of the ongoing group process.

The differences between Burton's and Doob's approaches are mostly differences in emphasis. Despite their different origins, both approaches are built on a surprisingly similar set of insights about the use of "clinical" procedures to promote change and collaborative problem-solving among conflicting parties, and about the potential contributions of these procedures to conflict resolution at the political level. Both are concerned with producing change and with its feedback to national and international decision-making; to facilitate change, both use inputs from conflict theory and from group-process analysis. They differ essentially in their ways of maximizing the unique strengths of the workshop approach and of minimizing its limitations.

In the following sections, I consider some of these strengths and limitations of the workshop approach. In each case, I shall try to show how insights from both Burton's and Doob's experiences might be combined to utilize the workshop approach most effectively. . . .

Unique Strengths of the Workshop Approach

In the most general terms, the unique strength of the workshop approach is that it allows certain processes of communication that are almost impossible to achieve in the settings (particularly the more public and formal ones) where conflicting parties usually interact. The workshop facilitates such interactions, first, by providing a novel *context* for communication and, second, by using a unique set of *techniques* and third-party inputs to guide the communication process.

In many conflict situations, the very fact that communication is taking place may be seen, by one or both sides, as a concession—because it suggests that the other side may have a valid claim, or even because it constitutes recognition of the other side's existence as a legitimate entity. Communication may also be avoided because it represents unacceptable risks: the decision-makers may be afraid that their willingness to talk would be taken as a sign of weakness, or that talks would reduce the pressure on the opponent, or that they would inevitably lead to compromises that would weaken the regime's domestic and international standing, or that they would end in failure with a resulting loss in credibility and prestige. Conflicting parties may, therefore, refuse to communicate at all, or at least to engage in meaningful communication. Once such a pattern has been established, public commitments and private fears make it difficult for the parties to break out of it—even when they have come to feel that something might be gained from communication. In this type of situation the workshop may be particularly helpful by providing a context in which parties can enter into discussion with minimum commitment and risk. If the outcome of the workshop seems promising, decision-makers can continue discussions through more formal channels; if it yields nothing useful, they can ignore it without feeling discredited; if, for some reason, it blows up, they can easily disown it, since it was merely an academic exercise to which they had no formal commitment.

These considerations suggest one criterion for determining whether mounting of a workshop is indicated. When there is some desire for communication among the conflicting parties but the official channels for communication are unavailable, or their use entails unacceptable risks at this point, a workshop may provide the needed alternative mechanism. It may allow decision-makers to transmit and receive information otherwise unobtainable, and to see whether officially acknowledged initiation or resumption of communication is likely to have more positive than negative consequences. In the limiting case, a workshop may serve as dress rehearsal for more formal negotiations.

For the individual participants, the workshop also offers an opportunity to communicate with minimum commitment and risk. This fact has a bearing not only on their willingness to participate, but also on the type of communication they are prepared to engage in. . . . The usual norms against deviating from the position of one's own side, so pervasive in a conflict situation, are relaxed in the workshop context. More than that, an opposing set of norms, calling for uninhibited exploration of all possibilities, is generated in this setting. . . .

To provide a novel context, it seems to me, the workshop must be held under the auspices of some institution independent of the political process which can bring an overarching set of norms to bear on the proceedings. In other words, there needs to be some institutionalized basis for the norms governing the workshop, if the participants are to regard them (while they are in the situation) as binding and as superseding their national norms. . . .

For both the London and the Fermeda workshops, the institutional base was the university. They provided the novel normative context of a research project in one case and that of a training laboratory in the other. The research project seems to me to present a very useful context, particularly when the participants are relatively senior and high in status, and when the workshop requires the cooperation of decision-making agencies. Both the decision-makers who are asked to approve or support the enterprise and the participants themselves can usually understand and accept a research-linked workshop without difficulty, and they can readily justify their cooperation with such an effort. It is quite evident why students of conflict would want to meet with representatives of conflicting parties in a face-to-face encounter, and why the parties themselves would be prepared to support such a scholarly enterprise and to regard it as a source of potentially useful findings. Another virtue of the research context is that it offers the workshop participants the roles of expert informant and research collaborator—roles that are inherently rewarding and in keeping with their status. Finally, the research context allows for a continuing relationship between the sponsors and the conflicting parties and a resumption of the workshop if the need and opportunity arise: the natural life of the research project coincides with the natural life of the conflict.

The training laboratory context strikes me as less powerful on all of these counts. Doob and his associates themselves seem to have concluded that the rationale and value of workshops within this context are not always manifest to governments and participants, and that the role of trainee is resented by some participants as insulting and out of keeping with their status. The training-laboratory context is also less amenable to a continuing relationship, since repeated workshops presumably offer diminishing returns from a training point of view. Finally, this context is more vulnerable to failure: a workshop that produces little learning and problem-solving can be assimilated in a research context, since (regardless of outcome) it provides grist for the research mill, but may be quite demoralizing to both participants and staff in a training context. . . .

The context of the workshop, as we have seen, helps overcome some of the barriers to communication that are so prevalent in conflict situations. The relative lack of commitment gives participants the *freedom* to talk more openly and honestly, and the norms of the setting create an *expectation* that they would do so. The fact that the parties have come together for a task defined, essentially, by a third party, makes it possible and necessary for them to abandon, to some degree, their competitive stance toward each other and to adopt a more trusting and collaborative one. To capitalize on this favorable context for communication, the workshop approach utilizes a set of techniques and interventions to guide the communication process. Some of these are more pronounced in Burton's approach; others, in Doob's.

Interactions between conflicting parties are usually highly repetitive and stereotyped. Alternative versions of the historical record are recited, old accusations and justifications are rehearsed, and fine legalistic points about rights and wrongs are debated. The workshop approach is designed to cut through this type of argumentation and to set a more constructive communication process into motion. The social scientists contribute to this end by setting the stage for a different communication process, by keeping the process moving and preventing a reversion to less-productive exchanges, and by injecting ideas, observations, and information on which new learning and insight can be built. . . .

The purpose of initiating and facilitating new patterns of communication in the workshop is to provide opportunities for the emergence of ideas, observations, and information on which new learning and insight can be built. It is such new learnings and insights that make it possible, and sometimes necessary, for participants to reassess their attitudes and reformulate the issues in ways more conducive to problem-solving. Some of the new information is injected directly into the discussion by the social science panel. Much of the information is specifically introduced by participants, or emerges from their discussions, or is generated by their interactions, but the social scientists contribute to the process by helping to elicit the information, by encouraging the participants to focus on it, and by suggesting some of its implications.

One can distinguish at least three sources of new information in the workshop situation out of which potentially new learnings and insights may emerge:

1. In the course of the discussions, participants may acquire new information about the perceptions and intentions of the other side. The relatively private and relaxed setting may induce them to express sentiments that have not previously been acknowledged in public statements. Such information is bound to be useful, by adding depth to one's understanding of the other side's position, but there is also some danger in overemphasizing the significance of this information: the public positions of a government may be better indicators and predictors of policy than the private sentiments of individuals, even if these individuals are high officials (particularly since public pronouncements set constraints on future action). . . .

2. The workshop can introduce the participants to a new conceptual framework for the analysis of conflict, a set of theoretical

propositions, and a body of empirical findings, all of which may be applicable to their own situations. In the London workshop, such information was provided fairly systematically by the panel of social scientists, who then drew the participants into discussion of the theoretical models and their implications for various conflicts. The participants thus acquired some new insights into the nature of conflict, as well as a common language and frame of reference for analyzing specific conflict situations. The learning process may be aided, as in the Fermeda workshop, by the introduction of games and simulations when such procedures might help illustrate and give experimental meaning to a theoretical proposition. In any event, the application of the new concepts and analytical tools to their own situations must be left largely to the participants themselves. The social scientists can encourage the participants to make such efforts; they can ask leading questions, engage in gentle probings, and suggest tentative hypotheses to explain the nature and course of the conflict. But, in the final analysis, the application must be made *by the participants* if it is to have major impact on the resolution process. The timing of interpretations is also crucial, even if they are presented in tentative fashion. . . .

3. As the participants interact with each other and with the third parties in the course of the workshop, they may be illustrating— here and now—some of the underlying dynamics of the conflict between the communities they represent. Their behavior in the group may reflect the nature of the relationship between their communities and the self-perpetuating pattern of interaction that they have adopted. For example, in the course of the London workshop, I developed (but was unable to explore) the hypothesis that some of the interactions of the Greek-Cypriot and Turkish-Cypriot participants, with each other and with the social science panel, could be understood in terms of their statuses as members of the majority and minority populations respectively. The exploration of such hypotheses, based on ongoing interactions, can be a source of profound insight, since the participants can see the conflict in operation. They can observe its concrete manifestations in the very situation in which they are still actively involved and almost at the very moment that the interaction occurs. . . .

In sum, I have described three major types of new information and insight that the workshop can provide and that can facilitate attitude change and problem-solving: direct information about the perceptions and sentiments of the other side, theoretical concepts for the conflict analysis with potential applicability to the conflict under discussion, and analysis of ongoing interactions that might reflect the relationships between the conflicting parties. The first was common to both the London and the Fermeda experiences, the second was more prominent in London, and the third in Fermeda.

The combination of Burton's systematic use of theoretical inputs with Doob's greater emphasis on analysis of group process and on emotional learning would, in my view, maximize the workshop's potential for producing change. Process analysis can promote change, not only by facilitating movement in the group, but also by utilizing the ongoing interactions as a source of new insights. However, problem-solving workshops in conflict resolution ought not to be equated with sensitivity training in the usual sense of that term. Though they encourage interpersonal trust and personal learning among the participants in order to achieve their goals, their purpose is not to promote personal growth or strong in-group feelings. Their purpose is to facilitate creative problem-solving in a specific conflict situation. It is essential that this task-orientation and problem-solving emphasis be reflected in the organization of the workshop and all of its components. In line with this view, I would agree with the tentative conclusion of Doob and his associates that it would be inadvisable, in future workshops, to separate "training" from work on the substantive issues.[12] The substantive issue ought to be the focus of attention throughout, with group process observations as well as special learning devices (simulations, role reversals, or brainstorming) brought in whenever they become relevant.

[12] See Doob, *Resolving Conflict in Africa*, p. 122.

Limitations of the Workshop Approach

The ultimate goal of a problem-solving workshop is to feed the changes and solutions it has generated into the policy process. As I have already pointed out, however, it is more effectively designed to *produce* changes in its participants and to generate innovative solutions than it is to *transfer* these products to the policy process. Much of the workshop's strength derives from its separation from the policy process. It is held under independent auspices, in a setting removed from decision-making agencies, with participants acting as relatively uncommitted individuals, and according to ground rules that encourage the transcendence of official positions. All of these features, by removing some of the usual barriers to change, make its occurrence more probable, but by the same token make its transfer more difficult.

The problem of transfer actually involves two interrelated questions. First, if an individual changes in the workshop setting—that is, if he reassesses his attitudes and accepts a new approach to resolving the conflict—what is the likelihood that he will maintain these new attitudes and formulations once he returns to his home setting? Second, assuming he does—or to the extent that he does—maintain these changes, what is the likelihood that he will be able to bring his new attitudes and formulations effectively to bear on the policy process?

The first question is common to all types of workshops, ranging from those primarily oriented toward individual change to those oriented toward organizational problem-solving. It refers to what has been called the "reentry" problem. The workshop takes the individual into a different world, frees him from the usual pressures and constraints that bind him to a limited perspective, and thus allows him to reexamine his assumptions and to develop new ways of looking at things. But once he leaves this more open and protective environment and returns to the real world, there is a great danger of backsliding. The old pressures will come into play and the dominant frame of reference will begin to reassert itself. Moreover, the individual may find that the new ideas he expresses are met with hostility and that the proposals he puts forth are systematically shot down. Of course, the severity of the reentry problem varies, as a function of many factors. But I think it can be fairly said, that, given an influence attempt that removes an individual or a small group of individuals from their usual environments, any feature that enhances the probability for change almost invariably compounds the problem of reentry.

Workshops involving conflicting nations or communities may well present serious reentry problems, because here the issue of group loyalty is particularly salient. An individual who returns with a less militant view of the conflict may find himself treated as one who has been coopted by the other side, who has betrayed his own group, or who has inadequately defended its position. These pressures may make it difficult for him to express and ultimately to maintain his new attitudes.

The ease of maintaining changes produced in the workshop depends partly on the nature of the setting and the experiences that it provided for the participants. The more different the setting and experiences are from those in which the participants habitually find themselves, the greater the likelihood that the workshop will present novel inputs, break up old thought-patterns, and produce change. These same conditions make the probability of transfer less likely, however. New attitudes may be closely associated with the unique stimuli of the workshop setting and fail to generalize to the home environment's radically different stimuli. Furthermore, a setting so different that it removes all reminders of home fails to prepare the individual for the reactions his new attitudes are likely to elicit upon his return. By keeping reminders of the home setting to a minimum, the workshop may reduce resistance to change, but at the same time fail to build immunity against the pressures to which the new attitudes will later be exposed. . . .

The ease of maintaining changes produced in the workshop depends not only on the conditions of the workshop itself, but also on the nature of the setting and experiences to which the participants return. If they come back to fairly conservative settings that are committed (ideologically or organizationally) to the official group position, then the changes they underwent are less likely to maintain themselves. Thus, for example, changes are more likely to be maintained among participants who return to an academic setting, since diversity in views on national issues is more readily accepted there. On the other hand, participants returning to government agencies, which are committed to a particular way of formulating the conflict, may find their new attitudes and formulations are ignored or rejected. As they continue to work under these pressures and within the built-in framework of assumptions, they are more likely to revert to the official position on the conflict.

The question of participants' organizational background leads us directly to the second problem involved in the transfer of changes generated by a workshop: what is the likelihood that participants will be able to bring their new attitudes and formulations (assuming these have been maintained) to bear on the policy process? Since the workshop is, by its nature, removed from the policy process, the problem of feeding its products back into that process must inevitably arise. The ease of achieving such feedback depends largely on the participants' characteristics and their relationships to the policy process.

In general, it stands to reason that if the decision-makers are involved in the plans for the workshop, if the workshop organizers consult with them both before and after, and if the participants themselves are close to the center of decision-making and are at least informally acting as representatives of the decision-makers, then the opportunity for feedback will be greater. There is probably less *change* in this case than in a workshop where the participants act purely as private citizens. The closer the participants are to decision-making agencies, the more likely they are to be constrained by official positions and decision-makers' expectations, and the less likely they are to be open to change. Whatever changes *do* occur, however—whatever new learnings and insights the participants acquire—will come to the attention of the decision-makers much more readily in this case. Thus it would again appear that there is a reciprocal relationship between change and transfer: the closer the participants are to the center of decision-making, the less open they are to change, but the more capable they are to feed whatever changes they do experience into the policy process.

On closer examination it seems to me that the picture is considerably more complicated than the one I have drawn so far. Whether or not participants closest to the locus of decision-making are most likely to inject their changes into the policy process may well depend on the nature of the changes in question, as well as on the precise relationship of the participants to the decision-making units. For example, if change takes the form of some new learning about the intentions of the other side, then the proposition no doubt holds. Say a workshop participant concludes from the discussions that the other side may be willing (despite their previous public pronouncements) to entertain certain new lines of negotiation; he would be in a much more favorable position to carry this information to the decision-makers and to persuade them to act on it if he is close to the decision-making unit and has in fact been sent to the workshop by that unit (presumably to obtain just this kind of information). On the other hand, if the change he experienced is more fundamental—if he comes away from the workshop convinced that the whole policy pursued by his government is inappropriate, and committed to a thorough reformulation of the issues and the possibilities for solution—then his proximity to the locus of decision-making may make little difference. It may not enhance his ability to inject his new insights into the policy process and may, in fact, reduce it, depending on the exact nature of his relationship to the decision-making bureaucracy.

In conceptualizing this problem, I start by assuming that the workshop approach can change *individual* perceptions, attitudes, and formulations of problems and solutions. Thus workshop techniques can be most useful when directed at those points in the decision-making process at which individual perceptions and formulations of the conflict become relevant and important. It can be argued that diplomats and foreign-policy officials do *not* represent such points in the process. They are relatively unlikely to act as individuals, bringing their own attitudes and perceptions to bear on their official role performance. They tend to act within a highly institutionalized conceptual framework; the assumptions of that framework are built into the routine operations of the decision-making apparatus and constantly reinforced by the interactions of its various units. Perceptions and attitudes certainly enter into the role performance of diplomats and foreign-policy officials, but they are most likely to be the shared and frozen perceptions and attitudes that pervade the decision-making bodies. Diplomats and officials are usually not in a position to reexamine them or to call for their reexamination. Thus, it is not too likely that (acting within their roles) these individuals would effectively use changes gained through a workshop experience.

On the other hand, the situation might be quite different for legislators or their staff assistants, or for the leaders or executives of various powerful pressure groups. These are individuals whose task in the foreign-policy process is to formulate and define issues in keeping with the interests (at least as they interpret these) of the constituencies they represent. Though they can generally be counted on to support the administration's foreign policy, they are not necessarily bound by the perspectives of the decision-making unit and are relatively free to promote changes in the direction or emphasis of existing policy. If they revise their perceptions and attitudes, their own inputs into the policy process may well be affected. These inputs, in turn, while not determining policy, may influence it considerably. I would hypothesize that individuals in these kinds of roles might be best able to make effective use of changes resulting from a workshop experience, because it is their business (unlike that of the diplomat or foreign-policy official) to bring their own perceptions and attitudes to bear on the policy process.

Thus my analysis tentatively suggests that the ideal participants in a workshop (even if its goal is to have maximal impact on the policy process) are not necessarily those who are closest to the locus of decision-making. Such individuals may not only be less likely to manifest substantial changes in attitude, when compared to individuals more remote from the locus of decision-making, but they may also be less able to inject the changes they do experience into the policy process. Perhaps the ideal candidates for workshops are individuals who are at some intermediate distance from the decision-making apparatus. They must be influential members of their societies, preferably with an active interest in foreign policy issues, but—if our criterion is their ability to feed the products of the workshop into the policy process—it may be better if their role is to influence and evaluate foreign policy, rather than to make it or carry it out. . . .

Conclusion

The occasions on which a workshop may contribute to conflict resolution vary widely. The relevance of workshops is perhaps most apparent in situations where conflict has reached violent proportions, but communication between the conflicting parties has never been initiated, or has broken down, or has reached an impasse, with each side frozen into a position totally unacceptable to the other side. Typically, in such situations, the decision-making units on each side are boxed in by a set of images of the other side, assumptions about the nature of the conflict, commitments to a national posture, and real or imagined constraints that prevent them from breaking out of their conceptual prisons and exploring new alternatives. New ideas and insights are desperately needed to cut into these self-perpetuating processes, and problem-solving workshops may be uniquely relevant mechanisms for providing these. On such occasions, it seems to me, the most appropriate participants would be (as I suggested before) individuals at an intermediate distance from the foreign-policy apparatus, who are politically powerful and widely respected and whose loyalty to the national cause is beyond question, but who are not themselves completely caught up in the existing policy framework.

Other occasions for workshops may be tied much more specifically and closely to the process of diplomatic negotiations. There are moments in the interaction between conflicting parties when a workshop might be precisely the mechanism needed to facilitate negotiations—to bridge a rather specific gap between the position at which the parties find themselves and the one they know they want to reach. For example, a workshop may provide a context for exploring (with minimum risk) whether there is a basis for resuming broken-down negotiations; or for running a "dress rehearsal" before making a final commitment to formal negotiations;

or for discussing certain new proposals in a relatively noncommittal fashion, away from the limelight in which official negotiations may be simultaneously proceeding; or, finally, for working out certain technical details of an agreement, which can be handled more effectively in a problem-solving format than in a diplomatic one. Participants in workshops of this type would most likely be diplomats, foreign-policy officials or advisers, or technical experts, depending on the specific occasion for which the workshop was convened.

At the other end of the continuum are workshops that are primarily educational. Such workshops may be occasioned by a specific conflict. They may bring together influential members of the two conflicting nations or communities, such as leaders of civic associations, journalists, intellectuals, business or labor leaders—or perhaps future influentials, such as students. The purpose might be modest and entirely long-range: to develop new ways of conceptualizing the conflict among elite segments of the population in the hope that these would eventually contribute to changes in public opinion and thus help create an atmosphere for alternative policies. . . .

A workshop may be a way of establishing communication between parties unwilling or unable to communicate through official channels. However, if one party has refused to communicate, as a matter of policy, because of an unwillingness to recognize the other as a legitimate entity, then it may be equally reluctant to participate in a workshop. Communication, even in the context of an unofficial workshop, may represent too great a concession, particularly if the other party has *favored* a policy of communication. Thus, the organization of a workshop—creating the conditions under which both parties could participate without feeling that they are compromising their positions—is a complex problem in its own right, requiring some experimentation. To overcome some of the barriers to initiating a workshop, it may be useful to think of it in stages. In some situations, it may be necessary to start with separate workshops for the national groups, paving the way for joint meetings. Such preparatory workshops may also confront divisions within the national groups and select the teams to represent them at the joint workshop. It may also be useful, by the same token, to experiment with separate follow-up workshops for each national group, preferably augmented by other participants from the same society.

One final set of issues requiring further conceptual and experimental analysis concerns the role of the social scientists in the problem-solving workshop. I have discussed their possible inputs to the proceedings in some detail. It would be useful to attempt to specify which inputs are most appropriate on which occasions. It is also important to keep in mind that these inputs are never mere scientific statements or process observations, devoid of value presuppositions. The organizers bring to the situation their own definitions of the nature of the conflict, their own assumptions about the possibilities for resolution, and their own preferences for the directions that resolution should take. It would be well to make these explicit for themselves and for the participants.

ELEVEN

TWO FORMS OF UNOFFICIAL CONFLICT INTERVENTION: THE PROBLEM-SOLVING AND THE PROCESS-PROMOTING WORKSHOPS

WILLIAM J. FOLTZ

WILLIAM J. FOLTZ is professor of political science at Yale University. He has with Professor Leonard Doob and other colleagues at Yale, organized several workshops designed to improve the process of problem solving. Here he analyzes the goals and procedures of the approaches and compares their operation in relation to a border dispute in the Horn of Africa and to the dispute between Catholics and Protestants in Northern Ireland. Besides analyzing the particular strengths and limitations of each of these efforts, he endeavors to assess their value as two of a range of techniques available for dealing with conflicts. After this paper was written, Professor Foltz and Professor Doob were preparing for a problem-solving workshop dealing with the Cyprus issue scheduled to begin on July 20, 1974. On July 15 Archbishop Makarios' government was toppled in a coup and five days later—what was to have been the first day of the workshop—Turkish forces invaded Cyprus.——Eds.

THIS PAPER COMPARES two uses of behavioral science techniques for unofficial intervention in social conflicts. To do so it will draw on the experiences of a group of us at Yale University in attempting to ameliorate two serious conflict situations in other peoples' countries. These experiences dealt with the major territorial dispute between Somalia and its two neighbors, Kenya and Ethiopia, and the dispute over multiple social and political issues between Catholics and Protestants in Belfast, Northern Ireland.[1]

[1] These experiences are more fully discussed in Leonard W. Doob, William J. Foltz, and Robert B. Stevens, "The Fermeda Workshop: A Different Approach to Border Conflicts in Eastern Africa," *Journal of Psychology* (1969) 73:249–66; and Leonard W. Doob and

In organizing these two interventions we (Robert B. Stevens, Leonard W. Doob and I in the first case, Doob and I in the second) confronted roughly similar situations. The conflicts in each case were extremely costly to the governments involved, and even more so to the ordinary people who bore the brunt of the confrontations. While each conflict had its origin in the unfortunate legacy of colonial rule, each has come to involve the national identity of substantial groups of people and to raise issues of ethnic pride and national sovereignty. Each conflict is multidimensional and highly laden with emotion. In approaching these interventions we began with only our academic identities and a few personal contacts as entree to the societies involved. In the Somali border case we eventually obtained the helpful sponsorship of the United Nations Institute of Training and Research, and in the Belfast case the project became sponsored by Yale University "in association with" the Queen's University of Belfast Department of Social Studies, but we assumed responsibility for all planning and implementation of both interventions. In each case we, as organizers, recruited American specialists in group-dynamics techniques who had operational responsibility for conducting the workshops. Our bare-bones funding came from Yale and from a variety of private sources unconnected with government. We and the entire team were thus clearly identifiable as foreigners by all participants in the disputes and with no readily apparent stake in the outcome, though, as citizens of a country widely active in international affairs, we could not hope that our national identities would remain unnoticed by members of the social groups directly involved.

In each case we used our own adaptations of certain powerful group dynamics or workshop techniques to bring individuals from groups normally in conflict together under isolated conditions of intense interaction. At a minimum a workshop should provide greater cognitive and emotional understanding both of one's op-

William J. Foltz, "The Belfast Workshop: An Application of Group Techniques to a Destructive Conflict," *Journal of Conflict Resolution* (September 1973), 17:489–512. I wish to thank the Academy for Educational Development, the Honorable W. Averell Harriman, the James Marshall Fund, the Carolyn Foundation, Mr. John McShain, and above all the Stimson Fund of Yale's Concilium on International and Area Studies for financial support of the work discussed here, and Leonard W. Dobb for comments on this paper.

ponents' and one's own situation and values and promote greater openness and competence in communication. In employing such techniques, we assumed that a high level of mutual understanding between conflicting groups or their representatives is necessary for mitigating conflict over the long run and for diminishing the costs of social change. We did not, however, assume that all conflicts are based on "misunderstandings" or "prejudices" which rational men can overcome once their hearts and minds have been opened. Rather, we appreciated that substantial material and important symbolic interests were at stake for which men were rationally willing to risk their own lives and those of others, but we felt that painstaking clarification and communication of issues and commitments stood a better chance of improving the lives of the peoples involved than would their continued obfuscation.

The precise design of the workshops depended first on the nature of the conflict, and second on each workshop's specific task. These tasks can roughly be dichotomized as "problem-solving" and "process-promoting." Problem-solving workshops gradually take on the appearance of a negotiating session, but one characterized by considerably more openness and willingness to examine radical solutions than is usual in most negotiations. The staff must take great precautions in designing and implementing the workshop that they not produce a general "love-in" in which good feeling is allowed to replace frank confrontation of real issues. Rather, the workshop must facilitate a clear understanding and acceptance of differences where they are in fact immutable. What can be expected, however, is that real issues be separated from surrogate ones, potentially negotiable issues from the utterly untractable. A further important instrumental goal is for each side to think through a rank ordering of its preferences, so that mutual opportunities to attain high preference goals at low cost are identified. The workshop may conceivably result in formal agreements between conflicting parties; more likely, results are communicated back to others in the outside world who then may treat them as staff work for more traditional formal negotiations if they wish.

Process-promoting workshops proceed less directly toward a solution to a conflict. They seek to prepare participants to take back to their ordinary roles in the outside world new abilities and knowledge which will help them function more effectively. At a minimum that knowledge should include a more nuanced view of themselves and their opponents, and the abilities should include greater effectiveness in working within organized groups. Some participants, however, are likely to acquire: a) a heightened motivation to work for less conflicting relations (or less costly ways of settling conflicts); b) skills to increase their ability to act on their motivation; c) personal contacts across the line of conflict which can be used when needed; and d) a bond of trust with other participants which can validate communications across the line, whether those communications originate with and are ultimately destined for participants or the participants are merely contact persons. Process-promoting workshops have a laissez-faire premise; participants take from the workshop whatever they want and do with it whatever they want. Such workshops thus embody an element of calculated risk concerning the uses to which new knowledge and skills will be put.

A Problem-Solving Workshop

The workshop dealing with the Somali border issues was designed as a problem-solving workshop on the basis of our interpretation of the structure of conflict and our judgment as to the groups in each society that might be most susceptible to influence from a workshop and able to act on any results it might produce. We began with one uncontested fact: most of the inhabitants of the Ogaden, which international law recognizes as part of Ethiopia, and of the North Eastern Province, recognized as part of Kenya, are ethnically and linguistically Somalis. Being largely nomads, they shift their herds seasonally back and forth across the formal boundaries with the Republic of Somalia. The contradiction between the nomadic way of life and the fixed boundaries of nation states eager to assert their sovereignty has kept that part of Eastern Africa in a state of tension verging on war for nearly a generation and has led the three governments into heavy expenditures for armaments and continued dependence on major outside powers. One conceivable approach would have been at the level of the populations actually in contact, e.g., the Somali nomads and the neighboring ethnic groups in Kenya and Ethiopia, or perhaps the nomads and Kenyan and Ethiopian police and military officials. We quickly rejected such an approach for many reasons, two principal ones, each adequate in itself, being the low probability that we could find intellectually flexible individuals capable of using English (or indeed any other common language) well enough to participate in a workshop, and the virtual certainty that all three governments would see the enterprise as a particularly insidious attempt by outsiders to stir up trouble precisely at their most vulnerable points.

On the other hand, our enquiries, beginning in 1966, suggested that at least some senior government officials were seriously concerned about the stalemated situation and might be receptive to new ideas for a way out. Equally important, in this international conflict the national governments were in a position to effect substantial policy changes should they be convinced of their desirability. Finally, as foreign academics our easiest access was to the educated elites operating at the national level of the three countries. We made the decision not to go after government officials directly responsible for foreign or border control policies, since we wanted individuals not obliged to argue a particular dossier. In recruiting six university teachers each from Kenya and Ethiopia, and six academically trained professionals from Somalia, all from a variety of ethnic backgrounds and with good general knowledge of the disputes, we chose to sacrifice immediate policy responsibility to obtain what we hoped would be greater intellectual flexibility and creativity in designing possible solutions to the conflicts. Since the communities of the educated elite are quite small in the three countries, and since the three governments involved gave at least tacit approval to their citizens' participation in the workshop, we reasoned that any positive results of the workshop could be easily communicated back to officials able to implement policies based on them.

The actual workshop, which took place for two weeks in August

1969 at the Hotel Fermeda in the Italian Tirol, was divided into two sections. During the first week the training team[2] concentrated exclusively on building rapport, trust, and a high level of honest and accurate communication among participants. The techniques used were those generally associated with the National Training Laboratories and were most effectively employed in the two nationally mixed T groups into which we divided the participants. By the end of the third day cohesion was strong enough in each group that the intrusion of a member of the other group was resented as much by the intruder's countrymen as by his national "enemies." Communication became increasingly open and direct and revealed sometimes painfully honest rethinking of one's own position. For instance, as a way, perhaps, of building solidarity across national lines, two bold participants from country A began voicing their doubts about the wisdom of their own government's policies and leadership. Participants from country B reacted with surprise that those from A should think that way, then found themselves reciprocating with biting criticism of the B regime. This in turn surprised not only the A's but the B's themselves who never thought they could voice such doubts in the presence of outsiders. The three organizers from Yale joined the T groups as participants and shared in the sense of group identity and loyalty. The workshop was less successful in its plenary sessions—which came to be called the General Assembly—where stifling parliamentary procedure replaced the easy and open give-and-take of the two T groups. Various exercises designed to teach communications and creativity skills, or to simulate general conflict processes were undertaken in both plenary and T-group meetings.

After a brief break, the workshop turned to confront the substantive problems of the border disputes. Each of the T groups argued through and eventually proposed a detailed solution to the disputes. The national-interest bargaining within the T groups was intense, but so was the willingness to harmonize these interests where possible and reciprocally to trade off low-ranked preferences when at little cost to one's own side the other could attain a

[2] Charles K. Ferguson (UCLA) director, Richard E. Walton (Harvard), William J. Crockett (Saga Foods), and Tom A. Wickes (TRW Inc.).

highly ranked goal. Support for the proposals drafted within each T group seemed general and genuinely international. On the last day of the workshop, each T group presented its proposal to the General Assembly, and all was confusion. Although the two proposals were strikingly similar and differed mainly in nuances and choice of code words, the General Assembly was unable to agree on a joint proposal. As the discussion went on several individuals became increasingly intransigent and indeed began backing off from agreements they had originally made. Two factors seem to have been at work here, the excessive loyalty to the T group and its joint product as opposed to the weaker loyalty to the total group, and the reentry phenomenon which on the last day turned participants' minds from the solidarities built up at Fermeda to the realities they would soon face at home. The last session ended with the organizers being charged with the task of drawing on the two proposals to present, under their own responsibility, an integrated solution to the border disputes. This we did shortly thereafter and incorporated the plan in a modest book discussing the workshop, which also included contributions by the training staff and one participant from each of the three countries.[3]

Informal follow-up research eleven months after the workshop,[4] and continuing communications with various participants and officials of the three countries, reveal that some of the expectations on which the intervention was undertaken have been fulfilled, though the disputes are still far from definitive resolution. Information about the workshop and what transpired there was successfully diffused to relevant authorities of all three governments. In all three countries informal social contacts were the principal initial means of spreading information, though at least one participant was formally debriefed. In Somalia the military coup that occurred shortly after the conclusion of the workshop catapulted two participants into ministerial positions, and one still holds an extremely important office in his government. In addition to personal con-

---

[3] Leonard W. Doob, ed., *Resolving Conflict in Africa: The Fermeda Workshop* (New Haven, Conn.: Yale University Press, 1970).

[4] Leonard W. Doob, "The Impact of the Fermeda Workshop on the Conflicts in the Horn of Africa," *International Journal of Group Tensions* (1971), 1:91–101.

tacts, the book itself appears to have been a major means of disseminating information about the workshop. We know that two of the governments ordered copies for relevant officials and have been told in correspondence that the embassy of one government found the book "very valuable . . . in the assessment of trends in Somalia after the military takeover." Other information suggests that the actions taken by that same government were less alarmist than they might have been. While no government involved has publicly embraced the central elements of the solutions presented in the book, the fact that some sort of solution could conceivably be agreed on by the three countries seems to have made an impression.

Less directly related to the central goals of the workshop are results involving the actions and attitudes of most of the African participants. With a few individual exceptions, the participants from within the same country feel a strong bond of experience and understanding between them, and warm "family" feeling for their more distant colleagues from the other countries. One participant, now an important administrator, reports using his own modification of group techniques for improving communication and creativity within his staff. Another reports that the book helped open up warmer relations between the Foreign Office and scholars, who have subsequently cooperated on a number of training programs. While the workshop's impact, then, has been limited and mediated by the many other changes taking place in the Horn of East Africa since August 1969, it has certainly had an impact on the individuals directly involved, and more important, has successfully communicated useful information to those in a position to affect the resolution or diminution of the conflicts.

A Process-Promoting Workshop

When work on the Belfast project began in the spring of 1971, Northern Ireland was in the third year of its most recent resurgence of overt conflict and the city of Belfast had experienced two years of nearly continuous violence. We (Doob and Foltz) began our discussions in Belfast in June with the Fermeda problem-solving model in our heads, but with the assumption that considerable modification would be necessary. As in East Africa, our entree consisted of our academic identities and a few personal introductions to academic, religious, and political circles. These contacts rapidly spread, and we were widely encouraged to attempt some sort of workshop. It quickly became apparent, however, that the problem-solving format would have doubtful relevance to the rapidly decaying situation. There were no longer any apparent responsible leadership structures occupying equivalent positions on either side of the central social cleavage who might be able to implement ideas generated in a problem-solving workshop. Although we briefly entertained a request from some members of Northern Ireland's Parliament that we recruit participants from their number, that Parliament's dissolution shortly thereafter made such a design irrelevant, even had we been prepared to act on it. Where a clearly authoritative structure existed, e.g., the British Army, there was no balancing structure of equal weight on the other side. Nor did it seem to us either useful or ethical to design a workshop whose possible results would be implemented not by structures which received the loyalty of the participants themselves, but by an outside government whose challenged legitimacy was part of the conflict. We were thus obliged by the situation to consider a more decentralized approach to a workshop and began to consider ways of bringing together local representatives from adjacent Catholic and Protestant working-class communities whose interactions had produced much of the most costly disruptions in the lives of ordinary persons.

A return visit to Belfast in June 1972, confirmed that the process of social disintegration at the community level had continued; indeed, the large-scale movements of population out of the old central working-class residential areas led us to take all of Belfast as the geographical base for the workshop. With the vigorous recruiting assistance of two American (and therefore religiously neutral) social scientists, one then and the other formerly attached to Queen's University, fifty-six local leaders, mostly working class, almost evenly split between Protestants and Catholics, covering virtually the whole political spectrum, two-fifths women, arrived by ferry and bus at Stirling University in Scotland in August 1972.

The workshop plan the training staff[5] and we designed sought to mix National Training Laboratory methods like those used at Fermeda and a Tavistock approach which emphasizes training participants to analyze issues of authority, group behavior, and group boundaries. The design thus aimed to use a ten-day group experience to teach individuals to analyze problems of organization and inter-group relations and to equip them to work effectively in groups back home. Furthermore, such learning would take place in association with individuals occupying comparable positions on "the other side," and opportunities would be made available for elaborating joint or at least parallel projects of interest to the citizens themselves which they later might carry out after their return to Belfast. The purpose, then, was to assist in reversing the trend to local disorganization, in effect to give some local leadership groups greater control over the impact of the surrounding chaos on their communities, and further to establish human communication links between local Protestant and Catholic leaders that might someday come in handy in building understanding and cooperation at the grass roots. To help extend the processes started in the workshop we planned to convene a brief followup session three months after the workshop and to have the two American deputies in Belfast maintain contact with participants afterwards.

The initial workshop sessions, modified somewhat from the standard Tavistock model, led individuals to think through the intercommunal conflict by reconsidering the various social roles and identities they all carried. Very quickly, for instance, a shared Northern Irish identity became salient as a defense against the Americans who had put the participants in this novel and sometimes painful environment. Identities which cut across the communal boundaries asserted themselves, as young confronted old, women confronted men, lower class confronted middle class,

[5] Edward B. Klein (director), Barbara B. Bunker (associate director), Nancy French, Daniel Alevy, and James C. Miller (all of Yale except Bunker who is at the State University of New York at Buffalo).

moderates on both sides confronted extremists. Particularly in the large-group settings this last confrontation was played out, as for the first time political moderates, particularly those accustomed to prominent leadership positions back home, saw that their attempts at controlling the situation encouraged others to adopt extreme modes of behavior and blocked creative discussion which might permit some differences to be resolved. This learning was painful, particularly for those whose usual styles of leadership were shown to be inadequate in front of the whole group.

The second half of the workshop adopted a somewhat more relaxed NTL approach. In addition to some joint role-playing simulations of group processes relevant to the Belfast situation, much of the activity was decentralized and centered in various planning groups the participants formed in order to discuss the possibility of implementing some joint activities back home. These groups concentrated on problems of housing and redevelopment, community centers, youth projects, and trade union and political actions. This latter group underwent perhaps the most interesting evolution. The trade union group decided early on that they could play their role most effectively if they joined the political group and exerted moderating leadership within it. By doing so, however, they virtually paralyzed the group and made it impossible for some of the more politically "activist" members to discuss delicate issues among themselves. After several painfully unproductive sessions, some of the members of "activist" political organizations back home split the unwieldy group, and taking with them a few of the most creative political moderates, spent the final days of the workshop in exceedingly frank and productive discussion.

Reentry into Belfast's communal turmoil posed a much greater problem than did the return to their accustomed professional positions for the Fermeda participants. The workshop staff was therefore particularly concerned to puncture the millenial hopes that occasionally were voiced, and to leave time for decompression and realistic reconsideration before everyone boarded the bus for the trip back to reality. Underneath the songs, toasts, and warm embraces of the last evening's party, we knew—and certainly hoped—that concern, even suspicion lurked.

Reentry was not smooth and easy. Two participants were reported in a Belfast paper as attacking the enterprise, and their attack elicited a flurry of supportive responses from others. Our two deputies from Queen's University for serious and complicated reasons decided not to continue their relationship with the project,[6] thus making it impossible for us to provide continuing support for the planning groups, and obliging us to postpone for a year the follow-up conference we had proposed. The big questions remained to be answered: what if any difference in individual and group behavior had participation in the workshop made, and what relevance might such changes have to the course of the conflict?

Doob and I returned to Belfast in June 1973 to attempt to answer those questions.[7] Of the fifty-six who had participated in the Belfast workshop, we were able to interview forty. We had brief conversations in a group setting with three others. Six could not be reached because they were abroad, in hiding, or sick; one had moved and could not be traced. The six others we could not get to, mostly for short-term security reasons. Of the sixteen not interviewed, we received good information from friends and family on nine, and from this conclude that our interview sample was not significantly biased. Still, interviewing conditions were far from ideal in central Belfast, and we were hardly neutral interviewers, so results are not reported here with the spurious aura of precision that precise numbers might give.

Of one point there can be no doubt: the Stirling workshop made a deep impression on the participants. Recall of what went on there was sharp and detailed. Technical jargon was used frequently and for the most part accurately. Only one individual claimed not to have been affected in any way during or after the workshop, but on the basis of what else he told us we frankly doubt the report. Although personal, intrapsychic change was not

---

[6] These reasons are discussed in G. H. Boehringer, V. Zeruolis, J. Bayley, and K. Boehringer, "Stirling: The Destructive Application of Group Techniques to a Conflict," *Journal of Conflict Resolution* (June 1974) 18:257–75, and Daniel I. Alevy, Barbara B. Bunker, Leonard W. Doob, William J. Foltz, Nancy French, Edward B. Klein, and James C. Miller, "Rationale, Research, and Role Relations in the Stirling Workshop," *ibid.*, pp. 276–284.

[7] Leonard W. Doob and William J. Foltz, "The Impact of a Workshop upon Grass-Roots Leaders in Belfast," *Journal of Conflict Resolution* (1974), 18:237–56.

itself a goal of the workshop, such changes are not uncommon at similar events and may contribute to the more specific goal of increasing organizational effectiveness. About a third of those interviewed reported some notable, positive change which they connected with actions in some part of their personal or public lives. A few of these went further to speak, with great feeling, of major changes the workshop had brought about, and all of these were corroborated by other participants or friends of those interviewed. The others reported either no or not very significant personal change. One individual seemed perhaps to have changed for the worse as a result of the workshop.

More closely related to the workshop's primary goals is change in individuals' effectiveness within groups and organizations. About two-thirds reported their own actions as having increased in effectiveness and a significant few of those were able to point to solid accomplishments which they and others corroborating their report traced directly to their experience at the workshop. Particularly interesting among the changes were those among women who abandoned their culturally induced passive or stealthily manipulative role to speak out and assume leadership positions, and among men who had learned to eschew a bombastic and self-assertive leadership style for a more quiet one that concentrated on the task at hand rather than on self-promotion. "Now I sit back and figure out what the meeting is about before I speak, rather than jumping in with both feet," was a typical report. Two individuals reported decided change, but were not certain whether it helped or hindered them, or even if it did help, whether they enjoyed their new awareness of self and others. Five individuals had ceased all organizational activities in the nine months since the workshop. Considering what had been the organizational specialty of one such person, we count his inactivity a decided plus for the overall goal of the enterprise.

So, the skeptic must ask, what difference does individual change make in the mess in Belfast? In a few cases, we feel, it makes a considerable difference. In one of the worst-hit central Belfast communities, which had been at the mercy of its own extremist gunmen, a tenants' association leader who had previously been unable to confront the extremists has now found it possible to establish a confident basis of communication with them and thereby lead them into actions which do not threaten the tenuous social fabric of the community. In another case, a man influential in a violent organization has been able to shift substantial organizational resources into more peaceful community-building tasks that had never occurred to him before Stirling. Other participants have increased or changed the form of their political party activity, though as yet without any signal success.

For the most part the intercommunal plans discussed in the planning groups at the workshop have not been brought to fruition, and with one exception the groups were not functioning nine months later. The youth project group met repeatedly throughout the fall, but despite some aid and encouragement from a few of the older participants they failed to obtain the church property they needed for their youth center. This failure, combined with strong environmental pressure, including threats to assassinate "line-crossers," led to the group's demise, though both Catholic and Protestant members have remained active within their own local communities. The community center group never managed a joint Protestant-Catholic meeting after the return to Belfast, though individual members have continued irregular but fruitful contact across the line. The redevelopment group held a few meetings, and several members have continued contact and exchange of information. Even where plans had not been implemented, however, a bond of trust seemingly had been established among participants which permitted them to work together easily or, equally important, to serve as guarantors within their own community for a fellow "old boy" wanting to establish contact with others. This strong bond among "old boys" has a negative side, also. Some nonparticipants with whom we spoke clearly resented what they saw as a new clannishness among their friends who had been at Stirling and felt excluded from an important shared experience. At the very least, participants had to face competing pulls: from old organizational loyalties and previous associates, and from new bonds to other participants, particularly those in the planning groups. In those cases where the loyalties came into direct conflict it would seem that the new bonds had to be sacrificed. We cannot yet tell if easier or changed circumstances will permit their resurrection.

The most impressive result we discovered during our interviews was the development of a core of individuals, most of whom had been members of the breakaway "political group" at the workshop. They had remained in contact, had selectively recruited strategically placed participants and nonparticipants to their number, and had maintained an open channel of communication between at least some of the violent groups on both sides. We believe it likely that some lives have been spared because of their existence, and one audacious undertaking for which they had received mutual guarantees from formally opposed violent groups was still alive a year and a half after the workshop. One aspect of this group's functioning directly traceable to the workshop is the central role played by two political moderates who have sacrificed the psychic comfort of being above the violent struggles of the extremists to work with such individuals to help them find less humanly and socially costly ways of attaining some of their principal goals.

Still, the killing and social dislocation in Belfast continues. The principal impact of the workshop has been confined to a few local areas, and with only a few exceptions more widespread connections have been submerged under waves of violence—for the time being at least. Both the reality and limits of success must be kept in mind in assessing the role future workshops can play.

Workshops in Their Place

The problem-solving and the process-promoting workshop thus employ different procedures because they seek to attain different, though complementary, goals. The two workshops described here differed also in the level of society from which participants were chosen. The African participants, though non-officials, were national-level actors with links to national-level decision-makers; the Belfast participants, for the most part, were active only at the local level. This need not always be the case; one could imagine, for instance, a process-promoting workshop bringing together high-ranking individuals in two conflicting ethnic organizations, though their superiors would have to be unusually enlightened, confident, or perhaps foolhardy to face the risk to their own positions that might arise once the participants returned. More essential than the difference of level is the difference in relations between participants and political or communal authority that is assumed by the two types of workshop. The problem-solving workshop assumes that solutions will be reported back to decision-makers and that any solutions will be implemented through and under the control of those authorities. A process-promoting workshop has a more subversive potential in that the process it promotes may operate quite independently of and indeed counter to the existing authorities and their wishes. This subversive potential must unquestionably be carefully weighed as a matter of ethics and principle by any non-official who would organize an intervention, particularly one affecting countries of which he is not a citizen.

These differences should perhaps not be overemphasized. The use of group-dynamics techniques in each workshop produces much that is common and makes workshops as a class quite distinct from other modes of intervention in conflict situations. These common elements are quite evident in the procedures as discussed above, and also appear in some of the results. The reappraisal of the wisdom of one's own government's actions that took place for some participants at Fermeda may have had some effect on their activities after their return home. The feeling of community among those who participated in that workshop seems still strong, and under proper circumstances is perhaps capable of being reasserted for cooperative tasks within and across national boundaries. The Belfast workshop made no attempt to find general solutions for Northern Ireland's miseries, but did reveal a particularly pernicious pattern of interaction between moderates and extremists that should be taken into account by any British or local authorities who would design political solutions capable of surviving the pressures of the conflict.[8] The simple fact that both workshops were undertaken by private citizens and without government auspices is

---

[8] This will be analyzed more fully in forthcoming publications.

an essential shared characteristic. These were "academic exercises," and it is unlikely that they could have taken place if they had been authoritatively and officially proposed. Furthermore, the unofficial setting, without making the workshops completely unreal, no doubt reduced the already considerable psychological and political pressure on the participants and helped free them of some constraints limiting their willingness to explore creative alternatives.

Both workshops described here had only limited success. Had the projects been blessed with more nearly adequate financial resources to permit fuller staff preparation, more flexible timing, and more careful screening of participants, their impact might have been greater. But measured against the magnitude of the task confronting them and the intractibility of the conflicts that would give rise to them, workshops of any variety are unlikely to provide a panacea. Even setting aside the substantial problem of validating long-term results from a workshop,[9] analogous attempts at producing long-term change even in relatively tranquil organizational environments free from threats of violence and fear of an aroused electorate or a coup d'état, have produced only uncertain results.[10] In recognition of these difficulties practitioners of organizational development have emphasized the need for long-term involvement through repeated follow-up sessions to refresh commitment to change, as well as the need for strong and continued commitment from senior authorities to the goals of the intervention.[11]

Implementing such a long-term strategy in situations of social conflict will not be easy, even leaving aside problems of money. (However trivial the sums may be when set against even the material costs of violent social conflict, they appear daunting to most potential sources of funds.) A problem-solving format would presumably lend itself more readily to a long-term design emphasizing repeated sessions, if responsible top leaders on both sides began

[9] See the discussion and bibliography in Kurt W. Back, *Beyond Words* (New York: Russell Sage, 1972), pp. 20, 247–55.

[10] John P. Campbell and Marvin D. Dunnette, "Effectiveness of T-Group Experiences in Managerial Training and Development," *Psychological Bulletin* (August 1968), 70:73–104.

[11] For example, Chris Argyris, *Behind the Front Page: Organizational Self-Renewal in a Metropolitan Newspaper* (San Francisco: Jossey-Bass, 1974).

with a high motivation to find a mutually acceptable way out of an impasse. Such a design would require continued contact between participants and organizers on the one hand and the leaders on the other, and the continued provision of information that leaders on both sides saw as helpful and nonthreatening. Considerable attention, thus, would have to be paid to establishing and maintaining good public relations between the enterprise as a whole and at least top leadership figures. Perhaps most important, the workshop experience would have to be emotionally rewarding and nonthreatening to participants, especially at the beginning. One would have to begin tentatively and sacrifice some of a workshop's potential power to disrupt fixed attitudes and provoke new thought in favor of building a warm and rewarding experience for participants. Even under ideal conditions, however, a long-range design would have to be problematic. To take only the African case, two of the three governments involved have now been overthrown and projects closely associated with them canceled. Four of the eighteen African participants are currently in jail or in semi-voluntary exile. In Belfast, of the thirty-odd who in August 1973 banded together to help organize a follow-up workshop, only fourteen were not eventually deterred by street violence, family concerns, or cold feet from attending such a session the following November. In short, if the social conflict is severe enough to lead officials to support a workshop, they are very likely to be severe enough to hamper ideal long-range design.

An alternative to such an ideal is to concentrate on making the greatest possible impact in the initial workshop of the intervention, even if it diminishes the chances of future sessions by raising a public furor or scaring those in authority. Choice between these strategies cannot be made in the abstract. Like all other aspects of conflict reduction workshops, such a decision requires careful and detailed analysis of the conflict itself, and the opportunities and constraints its structure offers.

Provision for publication of results should play an important and explicit role in overall workshop design. Careful post facto publication, of course, must be distinguished from early publicity for a workshop. The boundary around the workshop itself and its isolation from the pressures of day to day events at home must be maintained. Publicity at the wrong time would pose a major threat to that boundary. In both workshops described here we went to considerable lengths to avoid a curious press, lest publicity generate outside pressures on the participants. Even retrospective publication must respect many confidences and identities which might, if revealed, seriously compromise participants in their ordinary roles back home. But publication, as Fermeda has shown, provides an important method of prolonging and extending the impact of a workshop and may have to substitute for the long-term series of follow-up sessions that in the best of all possible worlds would be a fixture of the intervention's design.

Perhaps the ideal situation in which to employ a workshop design is one in which conflict, while a latent threat, has not broken out in disruptive and costly form. Here the task would be one of protective maintenance, to make repairs of a social order before it gives way at the seams. Alas, two potential difficulties with such a workshop, whether problem-solving or process-promoting, must be raised. First, it would be most unethical to use a protective maintenance workshop as a way of shoring up an unjust social order by "cooling out" those who would challenge it, or by attempting to convince the unhappy parties that theirs is a problem of making a psychological adjustment to an immutable order.[12] Rather, the workshop must reaffirm the legitimacy of conflict over real issues and force all sides to recognize conflict where it exists. Doing so leads immediately to the second difficulty. The "medicine" a workshop employs is homeopathic; one must bring hidden conflict out in the open and work it through in a protected environment in order to resolve the conflict or reduce its costs. Not only leaders, but even ordinary citizens are reluctant to give up the illusion of health to confront the hidden poison that threatens their well-being in the long run. Then, too, if trouble does break out along the lines explored in the workshop, one can be sure that the

---

[12] A salutory warning against such dangers is in David L. Singer, Boris M. Astrachan, Lawrence J. Gould, and Edward B. Klein, "A Group *is not* a Group *is not* a Group: Psychological Work in Groups from an Organizational and Systems Perspective," unpublished ms., Yale University Department of Psychiatry, 1974.

organizers, sponsors, and perhaps the participants will be blamed for starting the epidemic, not congratulated for having tried to inoculate society against it in time. These are of course not reasons for not trying to establish preventive maintenance workshops, but they are reasons to expect that the task will not be easy.

In broad perspective, workshops must be seen as one of a range of tools available to help prevent, resolve, or reduce the costs of major social conflict. Laid out on a spectrum extending from the least official and most removed from direct contact with conflict to the most official and most involved, a list would include such benchmarks as pure conceptual work, both normative (e.g., theory of justice) and analytic (e.g., game theory); laboratory experiments (e.g., the work of Morton Deutsch and students); computerized conflict data analysis (e.g., the CASCON experiment); exercises simulating specific conflicts and negotiations; workshops; Burton's controlled communication; third-party mediation and arbitration; and of course the various forms of traditional, two-party negotiation.[13] In no way need these techniques be competitive; indeed, each early-listed technique may be useful preparation for or component of each later-listed technique. That all such techniques potentially have a role to play in ameliorating a major conflict situation does not mean that their introduction is easy. As Burton has noted and my own experience bears out in part, responsible officials and perhaps especially diplomats may be reluctant to welcome "irregular" or "disorderly" intervention of non-officials, particularly if such activities involve interaction between real conflict participants, rather than randomly chosen experimental subjects, and produce unaccustomed pressures from previously unnoticed quarters.

[13] Much of the relevant literature is reviewed in Jack Sawyer and Harold Guetzkow "Bargaining and Negotiation in International Relations" in Herbert C. Kelman, ed., *International Behavior: A Social-psychological Analysis* (New York: Holt, Rinehart and Winston, 1965); and in Daniel Druckman, *Human Factors in International Negotiations* (Beverly Hills: Sage Professional Papers in International Studies, vol. 2, 1973). See also Morton Deutsch, *The Resolution of Conflict* (New Haven, Conn.: Yale University Press, 1973); Lincoln P. Bloomfield and R. Beattie, "Computers and Policy-making: The CASCON Experiment," *Journal of Conflict Resolution* (1971), 15:33–46; Frank Edmead, *Analysis and Prediction in International Mediation* (New York: United Nations Institute for Training and Research, 1971); and John W. Burton, *Conflict and Communication* (New York: Free Press, 1969).

Workshop techniques come roughly in the middle of this spectrum. They are thus neither safely distant from involvement in the stuff of conflict, nor safely under the control of established authorities. They are highly unofficial, and because they are the most powerfully equipped to produce innovative ideas and actions, they may seem to some both irregular and disorderly. Of the two workshop techniques discussed here, the problem-solving workshop is likely to seem the less threatening to top political leaders; it may appear the less disruptive and its results can be used or ignored as leaders please. Indeed, as an unofficial event, the workshop's whole occurrence can be formally repudiated by top leaders even as they quietly make use of its results. Many of the most costly occurrences of social conflict, however, are not readily amenable to a problem-solving format at the time intervention may be most productive—just as they may not be amenable to traditional negotiation or to mediation. My own guess is that the more open, pluralistic and laissez-faire design which seeks to promote a process in which ordinary citizens take the initiative themselves may become more, not less, important to world order and peaceful social change in the years ahead.

TWELVE

BELLEX—
THE BELLAGIO "MINI-GAME"

LINCOLN P. BLOOMFIELD

LINCOLN P. BLOOMFIELD, formerly in the Department of State and now professor of political science at M.I.T., has been a pioneer in the use of political games. The present essay briefly reviews the history of political gaming and reports on one specific game designed to elicit the type of information and analyses policy-makers require in handling disputes. In a departure from the usual adversary format of games, Bloomfield divided the participants in an international conference of scholars and practitioners arranged by the Academy for Educational Development in Bellagio, Italy, in 1973 in such a way as to allow the players to interact within the perspective of their real-life roles.——Eds.

W HAT FOLLOWS IS A REPORT on BELLEX—a "mini" political game run for a half-day as part of a Conference on Mediation at the Villa Serbelloni, Bellagio, Italy, in July 1973. (To include this experiment in the short but not unnoble tradition of contemporary political gaming, I have retroactively christened it BELLEX, for the Bellagio Exercise.) Before describing and evaluating BELLEX, it might be helpful to sketch briefly the intellectual history of contemporary political gaming in order to put this effort in its proper context.

Political Gaming

Political games have become a fairly common feature of the educational process, particularly in the United States but increasingly elsewhere. In brief, the political game or POLEX (as we rechristened it at M.I.T.) is a form of simulation in which individuals or teams of players adopt the roles of real-life decision-makers, usually in governments, and react to a "scenario" which spells out a hypothetical situation usually set at a future time, with the guidance of a "control group."

Terms about games tend to be confusing. "Simulation" properly used denotes a reduced reproduction of a dynamic system in which the key variables are specified and their interrelations programmed; a true simulation, in modern social science, is based on a formal mathematical model and run on a computer. "Games," on the other hand, usually denote a form of play in which there are rules, stakes, winners, and losers. Needless to say, in real-life international relations, while there assuredly are stakes, the rules are murky and often no one wins or loses; the best outcome may be merely to survive a crisis, on a "non-zero-sum" (or everyone wins) basis.

For this reason I have chosen to call the free-form, role-playing, all-human political "game" an "exercise."

Such games or exercises have a long genealogy. One root reaches back to war games developed in Frederick the Great's Prussia and universally used since by national armed force planners. Another root lies in the field of small-group psychology and dynamics. Role-playing here generally entails laboratory experiments concerning such phenomena as reaction to peer-group pressures. Another use is for therapeutic purposes, as with psychodramas employed to help the emotionally disturbed bring out inner feelings behind the mask, as it were, of someone else.

Drawing on this past the RAND Corporation in the early 1950s experimented with a political-military type of role-playing game aimed at cold war analysis. The present author, whose concern was the lack of adequate anticipation of dangerous crises, borrowed and adapted the technique in the late 1950s upon joining the Massachusetts Institute of Technology. In the years since 1958, when our POLEX-I was held at M.I.T., the so-called RAND/M.I.T. model has enjoyed wide use and adaptation in the United States and abroad. One major use has been for educational purposes, as a very helpful supplement in teaching and training. A second use has been in policy analysis where we hoped to make gaming a fruitful adjunct to research and planning on foreign policy issues. A third use, increasingly sponsored by governments, notably the American government, has been the exploration of alternative policies or pre-testing a chosen strategy. At a minimum games have been used for the stimulation of bureaucrats to encourage brainstorming.

The POLEX has certain features that have developed over time. Many users, such as the U.S. Joint Chiefs of Staff and most classrooms, have retained the rather free-form nature of the early experiments. In the beginning the POLEX was a "free game" in the sense that a group of people was confronted with an imaginative or challenging future problem and permitted to make moves and interact in any ways that seemed plausible to them; the purpose was to "see what would happen." However, one feature of the free game that made it difficult to use or analyze systematically was the tendency of the "control group" to interject into the play extraneous events such as disasters, assassinations, invasions, and the like, to stimulate the players or revive a languishing game situation. The result is often a more exciting game, and for classroom use the free game may still be the best.

The POLEX as we have further refined it at M.I.T. has sought to move away from the purely free game in the direction of a more structured simulation, so as to create better social science. The Game Designer here must be far more explicit than before about the kinds of research questions he has in mind, rather than simply writing an interesting Scenario and handing it to the teams. His plan will feature hypotheses concerning both team behavior and policy options, which he will then expose to the game situation in a systematic and purposeful way.

This attempt at more rigid experimentation has in turn created new problems. One is how to keep the game "in the air" with sufficient spontaneity on the part of the players, while still guiding its evolution in ways consistent with the research design. For if the POLEX has one unique value, it is the inestimable benefit of spontaneous and unconstrained reaction by the players to a situation not yet experienced, but approached with the powerful tools of experience and historical knowledge.

This latter point surfaces a curious and vexing issue about such games. If the players are students, it is relatively easy to switch in the middle of the game to another subject, or stipulate some implausible condition, and it is easy to demand of them a whole variety of intrusive requirements such as lengthy questionnaires, forms to fill out as they act, observers taking notes in their presence, and so forth. But on the negative side high school students or college freshmen will also take the fullest advantage of the "freeness" of a free game and often make moves which are unrealistic and even seem outrageous to the expert (launching thermonuclear war, changing alliances, etc.).

When one employs professional players, such as those used in the various M.I.T. senior POLEX series (and in BELLEX, which I will shortly report on), the result is almost the reverse. The more artificiality that is introduced through manipulation by "control," or by emphasizing the usual data-gathering artifacts of the social scientist, the more danger there is of losing the quality of verisimilitude so desirable if one is seeking to reproduce a real-life decisional setting. What suffers is the important primary purpose of examining alternative decisions, strategies, or outcomes in the most realistic setting possible. But in a senior professional level game the players, if left to their own devices, characteristically will revert to their real-life bureaucratic mode marked by caution, the instinct to temporize, concentration on purely tactical moves, and above all the failure to do adequate policy planning. This is the chief price for game realism. It is not natural for either real or role-playing practitioners to follow a demanding and painful planner's format, and one has to drive them to do so. (Practitioners do not of course usually follow this format, either in their thinking or in their actions. Instead, they tend to follow the mode defined by Charles E. Lindblom as "incrementalism," with judgments made on the basis of marginal adjustments in ongoing policies and procedures, rather than the sweeping "root and branch" examination of issues which the rational "utility-maximizing unitary actor" model would have us use.)

Since my own interest in gaming has been as much in encouraging better policy planning as it has been solution-seeking in substantive fields (along with experimentation with the fascinating tools of gaming itself), my associates and I have tried to correct in senior-level games for this tendency to act with realistic immobility.

One device for spurring the professionally trained diplomatic tactician to more systematic confrontation of his game problem is to prescribe the drafting of a "Strategic Plan" in the first Move Period of a multi-move game. (The Pentagon adopted the same device in adapting our RAND/M.I.T. games to in-house use.)

The idealized intellectual structure which that Strategic Plan embodies starts with Assumptions, and runs through Goals, Objectives, Alternatives, Preferred Strategies, Policies (under a variety of headings), Contingencies (anticipated), and Actions (to be taken in the event of those contingencies). In short, I have sought from game-players that ideal, logical, rational planning format which is precisely the most difficult to follow in real life, and therefore most evaded by entire populations of responsible policy officials.

Admittedly this is an artificial device, and tends to be resisted. The problem is compounded when one seeks to smuggle better techniques of design, experimentation, and measurement into a setting that by definition should remain as realistic as possible. The rule of thumb is that the more professional the players and the game, the more it looks—often depressingly—like real-life decision-making, but the less the game designer dares experiment on the players as guinea pigs.[1]

Other strands of gaming had meanwhile begun on a much more rigorous and structured road. Chief among those was the Inter-Nation Simulation (INS) pioneered by Professor Harold Guetzkow of Northwestern University, in which countries are synthetic, and in which the play of the "game" is closely regulated in terms of arbitrarily assigned units of power, money, etc. Both the INS and the POLEX have high value for teaching, at almost any level, as devices to focus the mind, to bring several senses to bear, and to imprint on the student certain elements of his course work through

---

[1] These methodological and intellectual issues are analyzed in detail in Lincoln P. Bloomfield and Cornelius J. Gearin, "Games Foreign Policy Experts Play: The Political Exercise Comes of Age," *Orbis* (Winter 1973), 16:1008–31.

a powerful experience of personal involvement. Much the same results are obtained at the training level, i.e., at graduate schools, foreign service institutes, war colleges, and so forth.

The INS, however (and its successors such as the World Politics Simulation), has as its aim the examination of theories of international relations in action. The POLEX, as indicated, has, to some of us, had the goal of improving actual policy research, analysis, and planning. The trade-off is perhaps plain. The less professional games, for example the InterNation Simulation or the World Politics Simulation, typically involve students rather than practitioners and can indulge in a range of didactic or theoretically grounded procedures—but at the price of less serious, realistic, or persuasive analyses of policy alternatives and solutions. The game must be chosen for the purpose, and I have tried to make clear some of the costs and benefits.

The BELLEX Mini-Game

On the afternoon of July 10, 1973—the fifth day of the conference—the conferees took part in a "mini-game" aimed at intensifying the conference focus for a few hours through the medium of a brief quasi-simulation.

Unusual Features

The peculiar conditions of the conference set certain unique requirements for BELLEX. The participants were to respond to a scenario depicting a hypothetical international dispute, bilateral in nature, between two moderately important nations, but of strategic interest to other nations.

The BELLEX mini-game entered into the subtradition of the professional level, somewhat-free, all-man political exercise (rather than an all-free, or student level, or part-machine game). At the same time other conference conditions imposed additional requirements that in turn gave the game several characteristics of high potential interest:

a) One was the "mini-" nature of the game.
b) Another was its insertion in the body of a traditional-type conference on a substantive issue.
c) A third was the international nature of the group.
d) A fourth was its attempt to produce different "inputs" into the solution of the game problem by dividing the players into categories of "practitioners" and "scholars."

The bulk of this report constitutes an evaluation of just how well the last experiment worked out. Before doing that, however, some further background may be helpful regarding the first three of these four.

1. Mini-Games

The typical professional level political exercise runs for at least two days and often for many days intermittently over a longer period of time. The earliest professional-level POLEXes at M.I.T. were reduced from three to two days for reasons of practicality, and a few years ago at the request of the State Department a full-scale (i.e., multi-move) one-day game was experimented with. That day (and night) was jam-packed and very exhausting, although administratively feasible. We believed then that at least three move periods were required to expose adequately some of the key branchpoints, so to speak, in the decision tree.

I later ran a one-day, two-to-three move period "demonstration" game that proved quite successful at the Institute for the U.S.A. in Moscow in 1970, and a similar game that year in Vienna for the International Peace Academy (see below). *One*-move games (or mini-games) are very unusual, lacking as they do the essential element of *interactive* challenge and response. (In connection with my CONEX series at M.I.T. in the late 1960s, my colleague John Steinbruner did run a series of one-move, preprogrammed, and computerized games in which students were employed as subjects. His hypothesis drew not from political interaction but from psychological behavior, and thus was more akin to the comparable one-move, often computerized games to be found in experimental psychology.)

BELLEX was essentially a one-move "game"; what gave it a

dynamic quality was the difference expected between the reactions of the two subcultures of "practitioner" and "scholar."

2. Conference-Cum-Game

Two earlier experiences are relevant. In 1970 the Carnegie Endowment for International Peace sponsored a political game on UN peace-keeping. The game itself was conducted in Geneva with participants drawn from the international community. In an entirely innovative procedure, which was suggested by Leo Mates of Yugoslavia, the *results* of the game were presented at an appropriate point in a conventional-type conference on the same general subject (Amelia C. Leiss and I made the presentation to a conference in Canada of UN representatives from the Committee of 33).

While that procedure was followed to reduce the inhibitions of government representatives faced with hypothetical circumstances (see next section), it also showed the high value of combining a substantive conference discussion with a mini-game for emphasis, stimulation, involvement, and mind-loosening.

3. International Participants

A couple of recent experiences confirmed, at least to the present writer, the possibility of successful political games involving multiple nationalities, even officials currently serving their governments.

IPEX-II in Vienna in 1970, sponsored by the International Peace Academy, and held at the Austrian Diplomatic Academy, included players of twenty-eight different nationalities, many of them serving diplomats or military officers. In that game we arranged to exchange roles so that no one either played his own nationality or one in which he would feel uncomfortable. The result was that the players felt relatively free to act out their professional responses to the situation by viewing the problem in someone else's shoes. Considering that the players included Communist officials, African generals, and nonaligned neutralist ambassadors, one could almost believe in the durability of the nineteenth-century fraternal brotherhood of French-speaking professionals who were essentially interchangeable between the diplomatic services of the great powers.

The Toronto peace-keeping game mentioned above suggested another possible solution, namely the innovation of role-playing at one remove, as it were. Serving diplomats and military officials obviously have great difficulty in expressing themselves freely on speculative questions in which their own government's future policies or confidential thinking may emerge. The Geneva-Toronto experiment suggested that serving diplomats can (and will) express themselves more freely on that sensitive a topic to their governments *if* they do it in the form of critiquing someone else role-playing their government!

Needless to say, it required comprehensive preparation of the diplomatic audiences in both Vienna and Toronto games in order that, by the time substantive issues were discussed, they were in a mood of observing social science rather than betraying state secrets. In both instances it seems persuasive that the indispensable key to such success as was achieved lay in advance preparation of players through a staged series of lectures on social science techniques, leading to simulation, leading to political gaming, leading to the particular game.

The Game Plan

1. Scenario-Problem

The BELLEX scenario and game plan were designed to stimulate "practitioners," when confronted with the problem, to ask what they would want most to know in terms of data and social science techniques in the course of proposing solutions to the dispute.

For the other half of the conference population, who were by profession or inclination scholars in the field of conflict research, the requirement was to stimulate them to draw on their own disciplines for techniques, data, or other kinds of answers that would be relevant to the hypothetical problem.

The scenario designed for BELLEX, while very short, was plausible and, despite its brevity, seemed sufficient to drive the exercise quite adequately (see Appendix A). It described a situation of deteriorating Sino-Indian relations in which the United Nations or the International Court of Justice might play a role, but in which also the superpowers plus China, and above all the parties themselves might be influenced toward either intensification of the conflict or its resolution.

Some additional historical background might have been useful to the participants, along with more detailed military, political, economic, etc. information. But many comparable political exercises have shown that if the game is otherwise adequate and the scenario is professionally persuasive, a minimal scenario can do quite as well as a long and complex scenario in motivating and engaging professional players who then will tend to fill in much of the background out of their own experience.

2. Organization

The most notable innovation represented by BELLEX was to divide the conference participants into two teams based not on "country" but on their real-life professional subculture, one "practitioners," the other "scholars." These two groups consisted of eight persons each. The "practitioners" team was asked to keep in mind the following five questions when confronting the hypothetical scenario-problem:

1. What additional essential information or data would I need to have to work effectively on the hypothesized problem?
2. What advice would I want? What kinds of skills? What kinds of knowledge or data?
3. What direct assistance would I find helpful?
4. What institutions, organizations, or other capabilities would I either turn to, or wish I could? With what characteristics?
5. What action steps would I take or recommend?

The "scholars" team was asked to have in mind the following three questions:

1. What body or bodies of theory would be relevant to understanding this situation with a view to ameliorating it? If none, what theoretical material is needed?

2. What social science techniques of analysis are relevant? Which would be helpful to have that do not now exist?
3. What factual data are relevant and in what form? If not available, what are needed?

The group as a whole was expected to address itself, after experiencing this mini-game, to three questions aimed at illuminating the cultural, intellectual, and operational differences between the two groups and, consequently, the contributions (or lack of understanding) that might be expected from one group vis-à-vis the other:

1. What are the essential intellectual requirements in dealing with a typical international dispute, as seen by the practitioner? As seen by the scholar?
2. What differences are there in the perceptions of the two types as to what is needed, and how social science can help supply it (and which one knows best!)?
3. What general conclusions might we draw as to the match—or mismatch—between this kind of problem-solving from the perspective of the practitioner, and the relevant things that social science does or might do?

As indicated, given the constraints of time and place, the simulation was to be a sharply modified version of the standard political game in two particulars. It would have one rather than multiple move periods; and the players would not role-play specific countries or be assigned named positions in any hierarchy of decision-making.

Evaluation

The purposes of this report will, I believe, be best served by concentrating on two aspects:[2] first, the centerpiece of the effort, the "two subculture" experiment; second, the results of incorporating a mini-game in a conference setting such as that at Bellagio. We

[2] See also Appendix B for a more general comment on evaluating the results of political games.

have the benefit of comments made by participants in the Critique session that followed the exercise. At the same time no special effort was made to inquire into their reactions in detail through questionnaires, interviews, and the like, so my impressions must be just that.

The "Two-Culture Experiment"

As an experiment in comparison and contrast between the practitioners and scholars, BELLEX was not entirely successful. The purposes under this heading were two. First, to examine the differences in the responses to the Scenario situation on the part of practitioners and scholars, both of whom are in various ways professionally focused on conflict problems. By organizing them into teams composed of all practitioners and all scholars, instead of a mix of the two, we were entitled to hypothesize that there would be significant differences both in *style* and in the *categories* with which they approached problem-solving, for the simple reason that in their real-life professional work this does in fact take place. Second, more specifically, we hoped to develop detailed information on the *kinds of conclusions* reached by the practitioners as to what advice, knowledge, data, capabilities, etc. they would find relevant and helpful; and what, given the same factual situation, behaviorally oriented scholars would believe they could contribute or should try to generate that would be also relevant and helpful.

Practitioners: First, some comments on the practitioners team. The reaction of the practitioners to the scenario seemed very positive. They accepted its challenge; they role-played in the broad generic role assigned them of practitioners faced with a hard problem; they considered alternatives; they decided responsibility; and they continued to be seized of the hypothetical problem during the critique. Several individuals reported personal enjoyment and satisfaction. In general, this all corresponded to the usual reaction of high quality professionals.

On the other hand the practitioners team was not very successful in following guidelines prescribed for them by the Game Plan (see above). This in turn is a function of a more general phenomenon which occurs in many political games, in which politically and operationally experienced people instinctively revert to the operational problem-solving mode in which much is commonly understood, values are taken for granted, shorthand is used for longer-term assumptions, and the performance is action and solution-oriented rather than analytical or in any sense theoretical.

Instead they "gamed out" the problem, with some but not systematic reference to what it is they needed in the way of additional knowledge and data, and from whom.

The one area in which the problem analysis by the practitioners coincided with game purposes was the matter of perceptions. There, in the words of their chairman, "was where we hoped the scholars would help us very much." In later discussion of this point one of the practitioners team defended this drastic curtailment of the possible game contribution by the scholars by arguing that "the only one we could see . . . in a short period of time . . . was this question of perceptions."

The heart of the matter in BELLEX was the same as in real life: even if practitioners feel the need for additional help, *they do not know enough about even the categories and conceptual frameworks of social scientists to know what questions to ask.* The solution (if I may quote my own remark at the Critique) is to figure out better "how to organize their scholarly perceptions in ways that can be used by the practitioners, so that these perceptions actually do get cranked into the decision process."

Apart from the "two subcultures" problem, the team proceeded fairly smoothly and was able to produce a "package" of results which were substantively interesting and constructive.

Scholars: The scholars team saw its function, in the words of its rapporteur, as providing "help to the practitioners in breaking out of their subconscious theoretical assumptions and models, and considering alternatives that they might not otherwise consider. It was also to look at a wide range of possibly relevant social science concepts and theories such as deterrence theory, perceptual theory, communication theory, negotiated bargaining theory, theories relevant to bureaucratic politics, and . . . trend analysis."

The scholars team had certain difficulty in generating appropriate responses to the scenario and the design guidelines. Some members later described their assigned mission as "an impossible task": theories seemed abstract without "solid grounding in the situation" and "we would come out looking ridiculous before people who knew a lot more [about facts and realities]"; plus the concern for relevancy: "this is very interesting, but it has no direct relation with the conflict which we have to consider, and we should enter into the discussion of the conflict." The upshot was that the group didn't remain faithful to its task, and played policy-maker instead of social scientist.

The chief reasons for this problem appear to be two:

1. The first reason for failure was the noted surprising reluctance of some members of the scholars team who are in real life full-time social scientists and students of conflict theory to "do their thing." One of these later confessed to some embarrassment at seeming so "theoretical" in the face of "real" problems;[3] but that was of course the very heart of the experiment—to deliberately face the substantive problem in a disciplined, disciplinary, and, by definition, theoretical way, at the same time drawing on institutions, resources, data, technique, and the like, all of which are essentially supportive of the theory-building *métier*. The scholars did not really do this, but rather functioned in a kind of halfway house between operational diplomacy and scholarship, with results that were not entirely satisfactory by either criterion.

2. One reason for that difficulty was that in retrospect it is clear that we erred in choosing as chairman of the scholars group an excellent historian who is also famed as both an entrepreneur of scholarship *and* as a noted practitioner of peaceful settlement diplomacy. With hindsight we can see that it was quite natural for a person with this background to chair the scholars team *en fonction d'entrepreneur* and administrative director, rather than as scholar. This powerfully inclined the scholars team to an operational frame of mind with a problem-solving mode comparable to the counterpart practitioner team, but without doing the practitioner's job full

---

[3] Another said: "We are probably doomed to seem irrelevant to our colleagues in the other room."

justice because of the nagging presence and knowledge of their original mandate to perform in their capacity of full-time intellectuals!

In the light of this, it was inevitable that we failed to surface with satisfactory sharpness or insightfulness the differences we sought between the two subcultures, and the match or mismatch between what practitioners felt to be needed and what the scholar knew could or should be provided. Our hypothesis that their styles and intellectual categories would differently reflect their *métiers* was thus not well confirmed, the differences being blurred by the factors reported above.

In my own opinion, however, this does not prove that the experiment was not worth conducting; only that if it is done again, more attention must be given to certain features which we might have underemphasized, for example, adequate briefing concerning the rules of the particular game; monitoring the team activities in a more dictatorial fashion; and shoring up the scholars team to keep it faithful to the game purpose (*and* to its professed real-life specialty!). Finally, it may be that we erred structurally, and would have done better to run the practitioners game first, then turned the social scientists loose to critique and amend from the standpoint of their disciplinary perspectives.

The Mini-Game

BELLEX showed how readily, given adequate preparation, a mini-game can be fitted into the program of a conference dealing with substantive political, strategic, or economic questions.

In pursuing this point we might do well to put aside for the moment the problems encountered by the scholars team, and look at the practitioners as a test of the experiment's validity *qua* mini-game-in-a-conference. The "game" aspects of BELLEX (as contrasted with the special bicultural experiment just analyzed) seemed to present no particular methodological problems, and encourage the belief that the game format can instruct in ways that conventional discussion, panel formats, and the like can not achieve.

Of course two aspects of BELLEX made the problem easier. The players did not in fact role-play, nor was it an adversary situation. We assumed correctly that the *search for tranquillizing policies* in a crisis situation would not prove as threatening as facing the same group with a *conflict* situation. However, perhaps the most important element was that, with some exceptions, the practitioners were *not actively serving officials,* so we did not have the problem discussed earlier of official reticence.

Nevertheless, with some of the devices mentioned earlier, the same results should also be possible with a true adversary game, and with serving officials.

Given the low payoff of most conferences, and considering at the same time the expense and extraordinary effort which a skillfully put-together full-scale professional game requires, one is struck positively by the notion of incorporating a brief mini-game of this sort in other varieties of substantive conferences, representing a highly useful *mis au point,* as it were, of otherwise conventional discussions of international problems.

Several variations on the BELLEX model suggest themselves. One would be a comparable exercise at the *beginning* rather than at the end of a conference, with the primary purpose of breaking the ice. In effect, the conference would then represent a continuing and structured critique session growing out of this initial intense experience. Another possibility is a mini-game midway in a conference after some substantive ground has been plowed, but with enough time left in the conference to exploit the findings of the game.

There are difficulties with the two devices just suggested, mainly in the continued in-role phenomenon which sometimes goes on for weeks; but that is not necessarily bad if one plans for and maximizes it.

On balance, the mini-game is probably best as the climax of a conference, if enough time is left for a good critique session. It is, after all, climactic in an Aristotelian sense and thus often fatiguing for the wholehearted role-player, particularly if it lasts for a day or more.

I would strongly recommend continued experimentation with the in-conference mini-game as one of the few techniques yet devised by the mind of man to shake up and enliven the often soporific pace and tone of conferences on serious policy issues.

APPENDIX A

Scenario

Assume that the following situation has developed:

1. The question of final demarcation of the Sino-Indian border remains unresolved. The CPR continues to maintain claims to 32,500 square miles in India's Northeast Frontier Agency and 15,000 square miles in Ladakh, while India asserts the legitimacy of the 1941 McMahon Line. India has refortified the Chinese Sikkhim border (as she had prior to 1965). Incidents have increased along these and other sectors of the lengthy border.

2. New unrest is reported in Tibet; Tibetan refugees in India demonstrate for restoration of the Dalai Lama's rule.

3. India solidifies its treaty relationships with the Soviet Union and acquires new-generation SAM missiles, which it deploys along a wide band behind the frontier with China. China meanwhile flight-tests an ICBM over a firing range ending in the Indian Ocean at approximately 75°E by 15°S.

4. Diplomatic relations have remained at the chargé level between the two countries, with the Indian mission virtually isolated in Peking.

5. The internal regimes of both countries are as today. Accusations reappear in the Indian press of clandestine Chinese support for the revived Naxelite and related Maoist movements in West Bengal, as well as for separatist activities among Naga tribesmen. A monitored Chinese broadcast refers to India as a "lackey of the social imperialists and revisionists."

6. A major address to a Party Congress in Peking renews Chinese claims over territories governed by both India and the Soviet Union, which it is asserted were "illegally given away under unequal treaties by imperial rulers of pre-revolutionary China."

7. India responds by publicizing photographs depicting the reopening of border posts and military structures abandoned during the 1962 fighting. An oblique reference is made in the Lok Sabha to India's 1962 offer to take the entire border issue to the International Court of Justice *providing* China agreed to the 1962 rather than the 1959 lines as a basis (which China never had agreed to).

8. The situation further deteriorates as rhetoric, threat, and indignation mount on both sides. UN Secretary-General Waldheim tells a news conference that "the otherwise bright prospects for world peace could be gravely set back if this dispute is allowed to escalate." He hints that he might have to bring the matter before the Security Council under Article 99 if the parties "do not do their duty under Article 33." (Most observers, however, see the Council stalemated given Big Five Involvement.) The United States is understood to be urging Moscow to restrain India, while the Soviet Union is believed to have asked Washington to do the same with Peking.

APPENDIX B

A P.S. on Game Evaluation

In the fifteen years since I started to organize and direct professional-level (and other) political games at the Center for International Studies at M.I.T., there has been virtually no opportunity to review the overall record we have built up. Such an analytical review of our accumulated data would be highly desirable in order to make judgments about such crucial questions as the *reliability of scenarios* in the light of events which subsequently transpired in real life, the *validity of team moves* in the same terms, and the *significance of outcomes* against the background of policy developments since then.

The principal reason why there has been no such research is that our C.I.S. games were invariably developed as an adjunct to other ongoing substantive research, on such topics as the United Nations, international military forces, disarmament, and U.S. policy toward local conflicts. It was thus the write-up of the research itself, rather than of the games as such, which preoccupied us. We have of course prepared reports on the games, both in terms of their substantive implications, and most recently in terms of the methodological developments they represented. The recent CONNEX series (1968–70) was in fact designed to attempt to create better social science through improved experimental method, including the examination of specific hypotheses of a highly policy-oriented nature.

There have been some efforts to sum up the state of the art of political gaming. But it seems to me particularly desirable that a more comprehensive evaluation be done before new investments are made and more effort expended to continue along past lines. Many games have had very provocative results. But in the proliferation of simulation and gaming there is an inevitable tendency slavishly to follow past formats, accepting rigidly devices originally designed to be experimental or heuristic in nature.

The central purpose of the research I think needs doing is not to make judgments about the predictive validity of individual scenarios and games. It is rather to ascertain whether and to what extent certain types and classes of games related effectively, in retrospect, to real-life policy problems and actions. This in turn should throw light on the usefulness of games as an adjunct of both research and policy planning.

THIRTEEN

SIMULATING PEACE-MAKING
IN THE MIDDLE EAST
An Exercise in Reality

MICHAEL HARBOTTLE

BRIGADIER MICHAEL HARBOTTLE (Retired), former UN Chief of Staff in Cyprus in 1966 to 1968, has played a leading role in developing the International Peace Academy's training activities in peace-keeping and peace observation. Here he reports on the use of simulation as a learning tool for individual players of varied official and unofficial backgrounds. The 1971 Helsinki game sponsored by the Peace Academy placed the participants in a role-playing situation concerned with the Middle East conflict. While not conducted to resolve the conflict, the simulation was designed to test various approaches and international instruments that might be applied in the area—one among these the establishment of a UN peace-keeping force. Following the October 1973 war in the Middle East such a force was reintroduced into the area and remains there as of early 1977.——Eds.

MOST STUDIES CURRENTLY being made in the field of international mediation and control of violence include the Middle East and the Arab-Israeli problem, but it is rare for one to be developed in such a multinational forum as that provided by the International Peace Academy's 1971 seminar in Helsinki. It is even rarer to have representatives from the countries most immediately concerned participating fully in the discussion and debate.

At an early state in designing the Helsinki Project, the planning group agreed that the Middle East conflict should be comprehensively covered in two of the courses: (1) Mediation and Negotiation

This chapter is reprinted from *IPA Reports* no. 3 (June 1973) by permission of the author and publisher.

and (2) International Control of Violence. To ensure greater impact, it was also agreed that when dealing with the Middle East the two courses should be integrated. From this concept a structure emerged which aimed to achieve total participation through a combined role play and simulation exercise rather than through discussion and debate. In this way it was hoped that not only would some constructive and positive ideas emerge, but that the participants would experience "live" situations through the roles that they would be playing, and that they would further develop their own skills and techniques in the two disciplines of mediation and peace-keeping. The scenario therefore was set in the present and evolved around a full-scale Security Council meeting (mediation) and the Military Staff Committee (MSC) (control of violence). It may be wondered why the MSC was brought into the exercise, realizing as one does that this committee has remained a dormant and inactive body almost since it was established. The reason is simple. The scenario called for a UN planning group to study the requirements for a new peace-keeping force in the Middle East. For reasons that are well known, no such group exists, and at present none is likely to be set up. Therefore it was convenient and reasonable to use the existing committee, which is recognized in the Charter.

In retrospect it is interesting to evaluate the effect that the chosen approach had on the participants. It is not claimed that their previously held views were in any way changed—that was not the purpose of the exercise. It did, however, provide them with the opportunity to project themselves into a live role and to express themselves, either singly or collectively, in terms of the roles they were playing rather than from their national, professional, or personal viewpoint. In this way they lived the part and were able to develop new ideas and initiatives and to present them as realistic contributions to a very real problem. If it did nothing else it made this multinational group of participants think in real terms of the problem. The fact that the problem was considered seriously and rationally indicates the degree of seriousness with which the participants applied themselves to the problem and worked to find some fresh initiatives that might be useful in dealing with it.

Preparation

Clearly it was necessary to lay a foundation on which the participants could base their thinking. If their ideas were to be constructive, the lessons of the past and present needed to be explained.
Therefore, as a preface to the exercise, a panel of experienced
practitioners was formed, comprising former UN diplomats and
field commanders, to help lay that foundation. The members of
the panel included Pier Spinelli, a former roving special representative of the Secretary-General in the Middle East and Africa and
later head of the UN European Office; Arthur Lall, director of the
Helsinki program and India's former Ambassador to the United
Nations, with experience in international mediation in Laos and in
setting up the UN Emergency Force (UNEF) as an original
member of the UN Advisory Committee. On the military side there
were Lt. General A. E. Martola of Finland and Lt. General Odd
Bull of Norway, former UN Commanders in Cyprus and Palestine
respectively. In addition to these two there was Major General
Indar Jit Rikhye who, as Military Adviser to the Secretary-General
from 1958 to 1968 and the Commander of UNEF during its final
months, is the most experienced practitioner of UN peace-keeping.
It was possible through this group of experts to appreciate the
problems that confront a peaceful settlement in the Middle East
and to analyze some of the lessons learned from their experience.
A summary of what resulted is relevant to this document and to
the development of the exercise that followed. It is therefore given
here in a catalogue form as an expression of opinion by men
whose experience covers many years of Middle East mediation,
negotiation, and peace-keeping.

1. In any conflict situation the third-party peace effort must be
fully integrated. The Middle East has been a prime example of this
not happening. A military presence alone, whatever its potential
and success in preventing fighting, only encourages and preserves
the status quo.

2. Whatever a peace force or mission may provide in the way
of economic assistance and guaranteeing freedom of movement
and the continuance of social services, whatever it may do toward

helping to keep open lines of communication between communities or states, it is unlikely to change fundamental attitudes of people toward each other. Despite the efforts of UNEF and the UN Truce Supervision Organization (UNTSO) in this direction, the basic distrust and hatred of Jews for Arabs and Arabs for Jews are unlikely to alter.

3. The lack of UN political representation with UNEF handicapped the effectiveness of UNEF. Its Force Commander had no authority to make political reports, and UNTSO remained the sole source of political representation in the Middle East at that time. A Political Adviser with UNEF could have played a valuable field role. The pattern later set in the case of the UN Force in Cyprus (UNFICYP), where there is a Secretary-General's Special Representative and a small political staff, is one that should be followed in future operations of this kind.

4. UNEF's task might be said to have been completed by 1960: from then on it was "holding the ring" in the vacuum of any political peace-making effort. The mandate given to UNEF could be considered to have been fulfilled when the Egyptian administration had implemented the measures requested by the UN for curbing incursions by the *fedayeen* and others across the armistice line. Although Israel had shunned the preserving efforts of the Mixed Armistice Commission to stabilize the situation along her southern border and had refused to cooperate with it, UNTSO could have taken over from UNEF, after being strengthened in manpower. From 1960 onwards, UNEF could exercise no greater influence on events than that assigned to an observer mission.

5. The difference between the roles of UNEF and UNTSO was one of patrolling and reporting respectively. The quality of information emanating from UNTSO, though slower in coming, was higher in quality because it had a more thorough system of cross-checking than was available to UNEF. Out of necessity, UNEF operated a military "quick-fire" reporting system, since it had to act immediately on reported incidents. Follow-up for this kind of reporting was often provided by UNTSO's observers from whose reports detailed information was forwarded to New York. This then required the closest cooperation between UNEF and UNTSO.

6. On balance, a built-in intelligence system is an undesirable thing in any UN operation, for it automatically creates inhibitions and distrust on the part of the host country or countries. Good liaison and daily contact pay better dividends. In UNEF this liaison was established with the Israeli government in Tel Aviv and with the UAR through the Egyptian Army Command, and resulted in a constant source of valuable information, which was supplemented by observers and patrols. Political intelligence was another matter, but this is no part of a peace force or mission's mandate.

7. A peace-keeping force must have security tenure until the situation improves or alternative UN arrangements can be made to back up peace in the region. The UNEF experience underlines the vulnerability of a peace force if no such guarantee exists. As part of—or in addition to—the Status of Forces Agreement, executed with the host country or countries whenever a peace force is deployed, there has to be an understanding on the part of the host(s) that any request for its withdrawal must be subject to notice and to a decision by the appropriate UN body. Final notice and its acceptance should allow time for renegotiation and for the safe and orderly withdrawal of the force, its equipment, and its property.

These are only a selection of the points raised, and if their content seems to relate specifically to the position of a UN force relative to the opposing parties, this is because the exercise itself was directed at the considerations that would need to be taken into account were a new peace force to be required in the Middle East.

The Scenario

Simulation and role play exercises depend for their success very largely on the reality of the scenario and the extent that the participants can believe in the setting and the roles in which they find themselves. In this case they were required to play the part of one of the member delegations of the Security Council or of other interested states or group of states whose collective viewpoint could influence the Council debate, for example, the nonaligned and Latin American countries. The situation on which their deliberations were to be based was not unrealistic, but related to actual or likely events in the Middle East, though it contained an element of imagination, designed to direct the participants toward certain goals in their thinking and toward a defined course of action. The intention was not to resolve the Middle East problem, but to encourage the participants to practice skills and techniques of peacekeeping and peace-making through simulated action. The goals given to the participants were structured toward this end:

1. Israel wants peace with the most favorable territorial terms, fearing that its pre-June 1967 territory is inherently insecure.
2. The UAR is willing to make peace with Israel on the basis of the pre-June 1967 frontiers.
3. Jordan is willing to back the UAR.
4. Other Arab states are unwilling to accept Israeli statehood.
5. Palestinian guerrillas insist on a federated state for all Palestine including Israel, which they want reduced to its 1948 frontiers.
6. All other UN member states want a peaceful solution on the basis of the Security Council resolution of 22 November 1967 [242], that is, the full withdrawal of Israel to the pre-June 1967 boundaries in exchange for secure peace treaties, freedom of navigation, and full statehood.
7. Whatever the decision of the Security Council might be, the Secretary-General or another person designated by the Council, must be in a position to direct any peace-keeping operation envisaged, in accordance with the mandate of the Council.

The Security Council debate showed that "the delegations" were less strongly entrenched in their positions than in the meetings of the Council at New York. The will for peace was noticeably stronger among Middle Eastern nationals hailing from countries which confront each other across the cease-fire lines there. There were the expected efforts to bring the sides together by the Latin Americans and the nonaligned, as well as by the United States and the Soviet Union behind the scenes. The final outcome was a brief compromise resolution asking the Military Staff Committee to prepare plans for a peace-keeping force to be submitted to the Security Council. However, the Council itself was unable to resolve all the substantive issues—notably, the matter of Palestinian Arabs—

and therefore could not reach the point at which it could actually order the deployment of a peace-keeping force. Thus, the Security Council exercise demonstrated two things: first the value of discussion in bringing about movement toward agreement and, second, the use that the Council could make of its own organs (for example, the Military Staff Committee).

While the draft resolution was being debated, the groups representing the Military Staff Committee were busy working out the guidelines which would govern the composition, organization, and the deployment of a peace-keeping force if one were to be required. . . . It was at once appreciated that the extent and the cost of such an operation would be considerable. . . .

Simulation As a Method of Instruction

Simulation or role exercises depend for their value on the effectiveness of the players themselves, and the extent to which they are able to project themselves into the real-life situations on which the exercises are based. The tempo at which they are run must be geared to the ability and experience of the participants. If the pace is too hot, the participants can become confused and, finding it too much for them, give up trying; or they start taking liberties with the scenario. Reality does often provide a fast and furious pace and equally often the most hardened diplomat can become rattled and indecisive. It is, therefore, realistic and good training to put the participants under pressure in the simulation counterpart. It does, however, serve a better training purpose if the uninitiated or less experienced are given a little time in which to adjust to their roles and to become sensitized to their parts in the exercise situation, before applying real-world pressure.

In the case of the Middle East simulation, the scenario centered around the debates of the Security Council. This called for carefully planned presentations by the Arab and Israeli UN delegates, who had been invited to attend the Council's sittings on the Middle East; a representation by a spokesman for the uncommitted states; and the preparation and presentation of resolutions by one or more delegations. The problem was one of debate, not action, and therefore there was little or no call on the participants to make quick decisions under pressure. The important roles in such a setting were those of the President of the Council and the Secretary-General. In neither case were these roles played with conviction or authority, and the necessary control of Council proceedings was lacking. As a result, a good deal of time was lost, and it was largely thanks to timely interventions by the participant selected to be an adviser on procedure—a man who had firsthand knowledge of UN procedure—that the Council sessions did not become hopelessly irrelevant.

Exercises of this nature depend on:

1. *Very careful preparation*—and time must be allowed for this. No individual can be expected to assume the posture of the United States, the USSR, the Secretary-General, Egypt, Israel, or any other national delegation on an instant and be expected to act or react as they would in fact.

2. *Good chairmanship,* requiring a clear understanding of the role, the authority, and the procedures to be followed and adhered to. Without these background essentials, whatever personality, adroitness, and expertise the chairman might have, his performance will be ineffective.

3. *Sense of responsibility* has to be present in everyone involved if real value is to be gained from an exercise in the practice of techniques. To prevent the exercise from becoming a meaningless charade, each participant needs to assume the guise of the real-life actor and to play him as sincerely and conscientiously as an understudy, except that in this case it is a matter of projecting his own personality and thought within the context of the role and not those of the real-life character working within his prescribed political brief. The simulation of each player must be a serious representation of his role; as he sees it—a personal performance, not an aping (or caricature) of the way in which the participant believes his real-life counterpart would act. Clearly, the participant cannot take a line of policy which in no way relates to the governing policies of the country or state which he is representing, but he is at liberty to express himself and put forward proposals which are in keeping with the general viewpoint and policy of that country regarding the situation in question.

It may yet be felt that this is still nothing more than play-acting—a good game for a wet Sunday afternoon. Of course it is play-acting, but in the process it helps to develop and transmit ideas and approaches to existing conflict problems which have not been presented before and which are worth consideration. But this again is not the chief purpose nor the main value of this form of exercise. Essentially, these are:

1. To practice the participant in debating or acting out the major conflict problems of the day in a setting designed to give the widest opportunity for constructive thinking and expression of views and positions.

2. To enlarge the horizon of the participants to the extent that they can in a sense live the experience of participating in the problem itself.

3. To provide experience in the art of political debate in a multinational forum, and in the presentation of reasoned proposals and resolutions.

4. To provide a firsthand study in argument and negotiation, and an opportunity for a deeper appraisal of the different points of view and attitudes of the parties concerned.

5. To develop a "feel" for the political atmosphere in which negotiation and mediation initiatives at the international level can be mounted, and in which the process of peace-keeping and peace-making has to be carried out.

The form of the simulation used can be either debate or action-oriented. The former is the less dramatic of the two, but both are complementary to one another and can be used together or separately. In essence, they are an educational device designed to require the participant to give a performance of his own making in a role which is often the very opposite of the one he is accustomed to filling. This is in itself a useful exercise.

A primary objective of the Academy's projects is to alert people to the skills required in the practical application of peace-keeping and peace-making. In all good methods of learning, the instructor provides his students with the opportunity of using all their natural senses. Talking about peace-keeping, peace-making, and peace-building only goes so far. To provide the greatest impact, the student or participant must be involved. The simulation exercise and the role play may not be the real thing, but they do activate the skills—analytical, interpersonal, and organizational—that are essential when studying and practicing conflict management.

FOURTEEN

HOW AN INGO CONTRIBUTED TO BROADENING THE SCOPE AND COMPETENCE OF AN IGO

JOHN GOORMAGHTIGH

JOHN GOORMAGHTIGH, a Belgian citizen, has been the director of the European Centre of the Carnegie Endowment for International Peace since 1950. Mr. Goormaghtigh shows how in the proper circumstances an international nongovernmental organization (INGO) can help bring about operational revisions in the structure of an official international governmental organization (IGO). The United Nations High Commissioner for Refugees arranged with the Endowment's European Centre to invite a number of international legal experts to a private meeting held at the Rockefeller Foundation's villa in Bellagio, Italy, in April 1965, to prepare draft proposals for the revision of the terms of competence and structure of his Office. This approach shows how an unofficial group can, by avoiding the roadblocks of bureaucracy, help bring about significant changes in intergovernmental institutions.——Eds.

I N THE COURSE OF the past century, private organizations have frequently contributed to the establishment of intergovernmental organizations, and many of them have assisted these agencies in fulfilling their objectives. Less well known is the more specific role that some nongovernmental organizations have played in helping bring about new international legislation. There are exceptions. The contributions in this area of the Institut de Droit International and the International Law Association are outstanding. Moreover, one could construct a long list of professional associations that by unofficially preparing draft conventions, agreements, or other documents, have facilitated the legislative task of official international agencies.

This article details how one private organization, the Carnegie Endowment for International Peace, helped to bring into being the 1967 Protocol relating to the Status of Refugees (known as the "Bellagio Protocol" because the crucial meeting was held at the Rockefeller Foundation's Villa Serbelloni in Bellagio, Italy), an international instrument that considerably broadened the scope and competence of a United Nations agency, the Office of the High Commissioner for Refugees.[1]

The 1951 Convention
Relating to the Status of Refugees

To deal with the enormous refugee problem left in the wake of World War II, a temporary specialized agency of the United Nations, the International Refugee Organization (IRO), was created. While in operation, the IRO assisted over 1,500,000 refugees and displaced persons in Europe. As a permanent replacement for the IRO, the General Assembly at its Fifth Session in 1950 adopted a statute creating the Office of the United Nations High Commissioner for Refugees (UNHCR).

At the UN Conference on the Status of Refugees and Stateless Persons held in Geneva in 1951, a convention defining the scope of the Office of the High Commissioner was adopted by the group. Consolidating previous instruments established before World War II, each dealing with the status of a specific group of refugees, and the Constitution of the International Refugee Organization, the 1951 Convention maintained existing guarantees of protection and, in addition, contained a general definition of refugees who were entitled to protection as set out in the Convention:

> Any person, who as a result of events occurring before 1 January 1951 and owing to well-founded fear of being persecuted for reasons of race, religion, nationality, membership of a particular social group or political opinion, is outside the country of his nationality

---

[1] For a more detailed account of the development of the 1967 Bellagio Protocol written by Dr. Paul Weis, former head of the Protection Division of the UNHCR, see the *British Yearbook of International Law,* 1967, pp. 39–70.

and is unable or, owing to such fear, is unwilling to avail himself of the protection of that country, or who, not having a nationality and being outside the country of his former habitual residence as a result of such events, is unable, or owing to such fear, is unwilling to return to it.

Obviously, the key words are "as a result of events occurring before 1 January 1951," a dateline that restricted the groups to which the High Commissioner's protection could be extended.

To understand why this dateline was included, some background to the drafting of the Convention is needed. Written at the height of the cold war, the 1951 Convention was clearly intended to extend established principles of protection to those refugees remaining from World War II and to those from Eastern Europe. The Convention's drafters were fully aware the dateline might cause problems in the future and, as their final act, adopted a recommendation that the Convention be liberally interpreted. Although governments did tend to be liberal in their interpretation of "events occurring before 1 January 1951," no amount of stretching could expand the boundaries of the Convention to cover new refugee situations involving hundreds of thousands of people. By the early 1960s it was clear that the real refugee problems were no longer in Europe, but were the result of struggles for independence in Asia and Africa. Because these events occurred subsequent to the 1951 dateline for eligibility, these new groups of refugees were excluded from the High Commissioner's purview.

The Role of the Carnegie Endowment

In addition to providing international protection for refugees within his jurisdiction, the High Commissioner was charged by the General Assembly with promoting acceptance of international agreements for protecting refugees. Within this framework Dr. Felix Schnyder, then High Commissioner, began to explore how the basic documents governing the operation of his office could be adapted to meet the changed circumstances. As early as 1960 a small meeting of experts was convened to examine possible amendments to the 1951 Convention. Their recommendations, submitted informally to some governments, met, on the whole, with a negative response.

If the necessary changes had been proposed by the secretariat of the UNHCR to the executive committee, there is no doubt they would have been turned down and the matter would have remained blocked for several years. Two factors contributed to this stalemate. First, if governments are generally reluctant to accept new and binding commitments restricting their freedom of action in any area, they are particularly loath to do so in connection with refugees. This can be explained partly by the substance of the matter itself—the complicated problems the presence of political refugees on its territory poses for any country—and partly by customary governmental structure. In most national administrations refugee questions (and therefore those relating to the UNHCR) are handled by the ministries of justice or the interior which, being responsible for the maintenance of law and order, tend to be more restrictive than the ministry of foreign affairs. Second, the secretariat of the UNHCR, as is frequently the case in international organizations, acted with extreme caution when it became aware of the opposition of a number of key governments and was, therefore, not prepared to take the initiative. The secretariat was also very hesitant to adopt procedures that had no well-established precedents in international law or in the practice of intergovernmental agencies. A method was needed to short-circuit this bottleneck if the UNHCR was to perform effectively the humanitarian tasks for which it was set up in parts of the third world where tragic refugee situations had arisen.

The European Centre of the Carnegie Endowment, through its intimate connection with the third world on the one hand and the international organizations in Geneva on the other, was well aware of the complexity of this difficult situation. It also realized that if a solution was to be found a new formula would have to be devised to circumvent opposition and inertia. Dr. Schnyder, who had set his mind on achieving a breakthrough, started to explore ways and means of proceeding. In this attempt he enjoyed the full support of the Swiss and Belgian governments. As director of the European

Centre of the Endowment, I was brought into these explorations at an early stage. It was readily agreed that recourse to any form of intergovernmental procedure, e.g., a meeting of government experts, would, in these circumstances, prove fruitless. Not only was there the negative attitude of the governments mentioned above, but there was also the problem of the relations between the socialist countries and the UNHCR to contend with. It was, therefore, suggested that a private, informal meeting of legal experts should be convened to put forward draft proposals for liberalizing the Convention. The main objective would be to lift the 1951 dateline. A government representative proposed that the initiative should be taken by "one of the large and respected foundations." In view of the Carnegie Endowment's involvement, it was understandable that the High Commissioner asked the Endowment to sponsor such a meeting. The official request was made in a letter from the High Commissioner to me.

The Endowment had picked up the ball but much remained to be settled. In order to give the "private" group some official backing, the Swiss government agreed to furnish its moral as well as material support. It was also necessary to make the group's relationship with the High Commissioner's Office perfectly clear. Accordingly, the meeting was described as, "*sponsored by* the Carnegie Endowment for International Peace, *with the support of* the Swiss government and *in consultation with* the High Commissioner's Office" (emphasis added).

Careful attention had to be given to the selection of participants. They had to be well-established in their profession so that their views would be respected, and they should preferably have firsthand experience with refugee problems so that they could grasp the limitations under which national administrations must operate in these matters. Should nationals of states not parties to the 1951 Convention be invited? And if invited would they accept? A few soundings rapidly indicated that they should be invited, and that they would accept. Ultimately, a small group of lawyers was brought together in Bellagio, Italy, from April 21 to 28, 1965, to examine means for broadening the terms of reference of the High Commissioner's Office.

Meeting privately at the Rockefeller Foundation's Villa Ser-

belloni at Bellagio, thirteen legal experts from around the world—
some of them officials, some of them private citizens—convened
for a "Colloquium on Legal Aspects of Refugee Problems with
particular reference to the 1951 Convention and the Statute of the
Office of the United Nations High Commissioner for Refugees."
The title of the Colloquium and its terms of reference were deliberately kept vague, for although those responsible for the meeting
agreed on the minimum goal—the lifting of the 1951 dateline—
opinions differed on whether to be more ambitious and on how
the objectives should be attained.

The experts were: Milan Bartos (Yugoslavia, professor at the
University of Belgrade, member of the International Law Commission); Mohammed Bedjaoui (Algeria, Minister of Justice, member
of the International Law Commission); E. K. Dadzie (Ghana,
Ghanaian ambassador to Rumania); Edvard Hambro (Norway,
member of the Norwegian Parliament); Louis Henkin (United
States, professor at Columbia University); Sir Samuel Hoare
(United Kingdom); Z. K. Matthews (South Africa, World Council of
Churches); Riccardo Monaco (Italy, head of the legal department
of the Ministry of Foreign Affairs); Philippe Monod (France, min-
istre plénipotentiaire); K. Krishna Rao (India, legal adviser and
director, Ministry of External Affairs); Oscar Schürch (Switzerland,
directeur de la division de police du Département fédéral de justice
et police); Francisco Urrutia (Colombia, UNHCR regional representative for the Americas); and Endre Ustor (Hungary, legal adviser, Ministry for Foreign Affairs, member of the International Law
Commission since 1967).[2] Dr. Schnyder's attendance at the opening session indicated the importance he attached to the work of
the group; for the rest of the meeting the Office was represented
by Dr. Paul Weis, then head of the protection division, and by his
deputy, Mr. I. Jackson. I was in the chair throughout the Colloquium which, in spite of its small and informal character, had
some very tense moments! The Endowment was also represented
by Jean Siotis, professor at the Graduate Institute of International
Studies in Geneva.

The Office of the High Commissioner submitted a background

---

[2] Affiliations listed for participants at the time of the meeting are for identification purposes
only; Colloquium members attended as individuals and did not represent their institutions.

paper to the Colloquium outlining the restrictions of the 1951 Convention and possible means to overcome them. The paper suggested that a legally binding document might be necessary, since in some countries a mere recommendation could carry insufficient weight to remove the dateline. The document's form, the paper noted, could either be a revision of the 1951 Convention or an entirely new instrument.

In its report to the High Commissioner, the Colloquium, stressing the urgent need for extending benefits to then unprotected refugees, agreed that a legally binding instrument was necessary. Given the urgency of the situation, the Colloquium advised that preparing and adopting a new convention would be too time-consuming, and that removal of the dateline could be accomplished more effectively by means of a protocol to the existing Convention. This original and imaginative proposal, for which due credit must be given to Professor Bartos, saved the day, for it is obvious that either of the two solutions put forward by the secretariat—formally revising the Convention or drafting a new instrument—would merely have led back to the deadlocked intergovernmental machinery that the Colloquium was attempting to bypass. It is equally obvious that a simple recommendation or resolution would not have been sufficient to attain the minimum objective that had been set.

Members of the Colloquium disagreed on aspects of the protocol—the compulsory jurisdiction of the International Court of Justice and the possible suspension of certain obligations under the convention in exceptional circumstances—and suggested these matters go to governments for their views. They did agree on the terms of the preamble and substantive provisions of the draft protocol, and also prepared texts of articles relating to the two issues for which they wanted to solicit governmental reactions. The Colloquium further recommended that accession to the protocol should not be limited to those states that were parties to the 1951 Convention.

Copies of the Colloquium's report and requests for comments went to the executive committee of the High Commissioner's program and to governments of states that were members of the executive committee and/or parties to the 1951 Convention. In general the responses were positive to extending the scope of the 1951 Convention by means of a protocol.

In October 1966 the High Commissioner submitted to the sixteenth session of the executive committee a paper entitled "Proposed Measures to Extend the Personal Scope of the Convention relating to the Status of Refugees of 28 July 1951" to which he attached a summary of replies from governments and the text of the draft protocol, based on the Bellagio Colloquium's draft, which was slightly altered to comply with governmental suggestions. Adoption of this protocol, dealing with the most pressing problem—removal of the dateline—the paper noted, in no way prevented a broader revision of the 1951 Convention at a later date.

After requesting some minor modifications, the executive committee asked the High Commissioner to submit the text of the draft protocol to the General Assembly through the Economic and Social Council in order that governments might accede to the draft protocol within the shortest possible time. The High Commissioner did so in an addendum to his annual report for 1966. At its resumed forty-first session in November 1966, the Economic and Social Council unanimously "took note with approval" of the text of the draft protocol and transmitted it, as an addendum to the High Commissioner's annual report to the Third Committee (Social, Humanitarian, and Cultural) of the General Assembly, where action was necessary before consideration by the full Assembly.

After debate and adoption the Third Committee of the General Assembly sent along the text of the draft protocol to the Plenary Session of the Assembly where, after debate, it passed on December 15, 1966, by a vote of 91 to 0, with 15 abstentions. Authorized copies of the protocol were sent to governments by the Secretary-General on March 10, 1967. It entered into force on October 4, 1967, after ratification and deposit of the instrument by the sixth party.

In all fifty-nine governments have at present acceded to the Bellagio Protocol, including the United States, which is not a party to the 1951 Convention. The instrument has made possible large-scale operations throughout the world that the 1951 dateline would have prohibited. Among the numerous refugee situations in many parts of the globe in which the High Commissioner has given aid are the Sudan, the territories in Portuguese Africa, and the areas affected by the civil war in Pakistan. Moving into a new area, the Office of the High Commissioner announced in September 1974 a $12 million program of aid for resettlement of war refugees throughout Indochina, including North Vietnam.

This was a case—there are many others—in which the procedures of an international organization prevented it from adapting its structure and field of competence to meet the needs of a drastically changed world situation. Formal United Nations procedures are notoriously unsuited to bringing about operational revisions. In this instance, however, it was fortunately possible to modify the Convention substantially, thereby extending the protection and assistance of the UNHCR to hundreds of thousands of refugees previously deprived. Such a result was achieved by an imaginative recourse to unorthodox techniques, by patient diplomacy, and by confident cooperation between a UN agency and a nongovernmental organization. To the best of our knowledge, this was the first time that an important international instrument was brought into existence in such a fashion. The positive role played by the Carnegie Endowment in this affair was due to availability and flexibility, to recognized competence and impartiality, as well as the confidence governments and organizations placed in it, and to its intimate knowledge of the issues involved. The Colloquium, it should be noted, was merely part of a long process that started with the first exploratory conversations initiated by the High Commissioner and only ended when the Bellagio Protocol had been successfully steered through the General Assembly.

AFTERWORD

SO DIVERSE ARE the instances of unofficial diplomacy reported or summarized in this volume that it is difficult to draw sweeping conclusions. Nevertheless, certain clear observations seem justified. One thing that should be clear is that the greatest chance of having a positive impact and success belongs to those initiatives that have tacit and sometimes official approval. The instinctive distrust officials seem to have for "outsiders" may in part be explainable by their fears that their authority will be undercut, by their professional and institutional snobbery (as Ashmore and Baggs characterized U.S. State Department reactions to their initiatives), and by past experiences or future fears about working with overeager men and women of good will. And in the end it must be remembered that officials are accountable for their decisions and actions; outsiders are by definition not responsible though they may not be irresponsible.

In the early meetings between East and West at the Pugwash and Dartmouth conferences series, the danger was very real for misunderstanding about what were personal and what were representative of official points of view. Over the years the possibilities have lessened for misinterpretations resulting from structural differences in the political systems represented by participants in unofficial meetings; in part, because participants from the West have learned to be very clear on whose views they are expressing, while the other side has grown more accustomed to the fact that such differences exist. In early encounters misunderstandings did result, and the officials who were "burned" and whose lives were made more complicated as a result of outside actions surely were cautious in their subsequent dealings with non-officials.

Having seen the dangers from the perspective of officials, we should quickly add that when it suits their purposes and when they deem unofficial enterprises responsible, governments have been willing to "use" private channels. Officials have used private individuals as intermediaries and availed themselves of the opportunity presented by unofficial meetings to take informal policy soundings. Many prominent private citizens are very close to officials. There are places in some countries such as the Council on Foreign Relations in New York and Chatham House in London where they meet regularly. Participants in the Dartmouth Conference series possess recognized competence in a particular field; while, apart from the Congressional members, they are unofficial, they have relatively easy access to high officials, and many of them have served in the government or expect some day to do so.

When the initiative for private efforts comes from the outside, unofficial diplomats (without established credentials), may have trouble gaining access to key decision-makers. The Quakers, the Commission of the Churches on International Affairs, and the International Committee of the Red Cross all have special histories of involvement in private efforts. They recognize that the suspicions of officials are a major hurdle to overcome and therefore emphasize their own impartiality and independence from governments. To gain acceptance requires a delicate blend of skills and a clear statement of intent.

What kinds of effects can unofficial diplomats hope to achieve?

None of the private enterprises described here was aimed at competing with national governments or international organizations or usurping the decision-making functions of authorities. In the case of the International Committee of the Red Cross, whose activities in support of human rights in conflict situations may work to change government policies, the approach has been one of cooperation rather than confrontation. In armed conflict, the ICRC at times tries to be "friendly legal adviser" and on occasion has presented itself as an adjunct to public authority rather than a competitor.[1]

Such groups as the Quakers and the World Council of Churches, with limited monetary resources, eschew confrontation with governments in favor of support and auxiliary functions designed to pave the way for official action. The problem-solving approaches of Doob and Foltz and of Burton are aimed at changing the per-

---

[1] David P. Forsythe, "The Red Cross as transnational movement: conserving and changing the nation-state system," *International Organization* (Fall 1976), 30:613.

ceptions of individual participants—responsible officials or those with access to them—with the hope that some new ideas and shared perspectives will find their way back into policy-making processes of national states. The use of simulation as described by Bloomfield and Harbottle is designed to sensitize diplomats and non-officials to different national and cultural points of view by exposing them to roles unlike their own experiences. The intent is to increase the individual's accuracy of perception and analysis of his counterparts in other nations.

In the case of the seminars described by Talbot and Goormaghtigh, each was designed to serve official needs and in both ventures there was close cooperation between official and unofficial parties.

Preparing the way for official policy changes or for improved interstate relations may be a slow-building, evolutionary process of which unofficial efforts may be only part. When in New York in May 1976 for a meeting between United Nations Associations from the United States and the Soviet Union, Georgy Arbatov, the USSR's leading expert on the United States, spoke of the interconnected nature of issues facing the two nations and what would be required to overcome the imprint left by more than a generation of cold war:

> To be successful in arms control and disarmament, we have to build up a mutual trust, step by step, to build a framework and infrastructure of new relationships between the Soviet Union and the United States which will include a constant political dialogue, many contacts on different levels, economic cooperation, cooperation in science and technology, cultural exchanges, and all sorts of things through which we can enlighten our societies in the spirit of peaceful coexistence and cooperation.[2]

In multilateral relations, as well, issues are interconnected, and contacts on many different levels—official, unofficial, and combinations of the two—may be needed to create an environment of accommodation.

[2] "Talking detente with Georgy Arbatov," *The Inter Dependent*, July/August 1976, p. 6.

It seems safe to predict on the basis of developments since the second world war that transnational participation will grow. Much has been written about the impressive growth of transnational organizations of all kinds and the ways their operations now and in the future will affect the conduct of interstate dealings. As we have seen, the support services that nongovernmental groups perform for international institutions have, to a great extent, received the approval and indeed the encouragement of national and international officials. Similarly, most of the instances of unofficial diplomacy described in this volume were for the most part supportive of, or preparatory to, official activities. To say they were supportive or preparatory, however, does not imply they are inconsequential.

Some observers suggest that transnational organizations may in time begin to compete with state authorities for the loyalty of their citizens. They believe that if attachments to international professional or special interest associations should become greater than to national governments, there might be erosion of nationalism and of the decision-making capabilities in the developed states.[3] However, in the past transnational ties broke down in face of war. It is at least questionable whether economic, ideological, professional, and intellectual ties will hold up in a future war or even in future crises of intense nationalism.

On the interpersonal level, transnational life may play a role in diminishing the differences in national cultures which in turn may affect the conduct of interstate relations. Personal contacts across borders seem to hold the potential for influencing the knowledge, motives, and attitudes of those involved; thus, under favorable conditions, an individual might be predisposed toward accommodative foreign policy stands. Yet research on the relationships between the effects of such contacts and the future peace of the world is scarce and the results ambiguous; indeed, the outcomes

[3] Miriam Camps, *The Management of Interdependence* (New York: Council on Foreign Relations, 1974), pp. 12–13. Not all agree that nongovernmental entities are potential competitors of nations. Werner Levi, for example, has concluded that the other role they play as nationals leaves them subject to the political supervision of states, and when the two conflict there is no question as to which dominates. See *International Politics: Foundations of the System* (Minneapolis: University of Minnesota Press, 1974), pp. 82–84.

may not always be positive.[4] There is a tendency on the part of scholars and others, as well, to emphasize rational thought and to ignore the deep-seated impact of sentiment and emotion.

At the moment the effects of transnational activities appear largely indirect and long term. Cross-cultural contacts alone cannot lessen the impact of conflicts of interest between nations; but what they may do is heighten the awareness of officials and non-officials alike to the need to reexamine many inherited premises. While it was long assumed that each nation could undergo relatively autonomous development within the framework of the world political system, it is now increasingly clear that no country, regardless of the nature of its domestic politics, can remain unaffected by such economic and social developments as global cycles of recession and expansion and changes in the environment. So far nations have shown little willingness to give up short-term advantages for long-term benefits. Nongovernmental groups have played a key role in raising the salience of such issues on the international political agenda, in offering expert advice on these issues, and in demonstrating to national and international authorities that there is public support for long-term and global approaches. While nations remain the most powerful actors in international affairs, they are often stymied in their efforts to propose new policy options for a myriad of domestic and international reasons.

Nations still have not developed substantially the ability to settle disputes by peaceful means. As long as that remains true, private citizens who have a concern for peace will intervene if they can, and they may help what is now still an international society become increasingly a transnational society.

[4] Donald Warwick, "Transnational Participation and International Peace," in Robert O. Keohane and Joseph S. Nye, Jr., eds., *Transnational Relations and World Politics* (Cambridge: Harvard University Press, 1972), p. 324.

INDEX